Family Therapy

Family Therapy

A Constructive Framework

Roger Lowe

SAGE Publications
London • Thousand Oaks • New Delhi

SAGE Publications Ltd
1 Oliver's Yard
55 City Road
London EC1Y 1SP

SAGE Publications Inc.
2455 Teller Road
Thousand Oaks, California 91320

SAGE Publications India Pvt Ltd
B-42, Panchsheel Enclave
Post Box 4109
New Delhi 110 017

British Library Cataloguing in Publication data

A catalogue record for this book is available
from the British Library

ISBN 0 7619 4302 1
ISBN 0 7619 4303 X (pbk)

Library of Congress Control Number: 2003115354

Typeset by C&M Digitals (P) Ltd., Chennai, India
Printed and bound in Great Britain by Athenaeum Press, Gateshead

To my own family of origin – my mother, Sadie, my late father, Leslie, and my brother, Grahame – with love

Praise for the Book

'A first! The constructive therapies such as the solution focused and narrative approaches have become more and more popular, none more so than in services to childern and their parents, whether in health, social services, the voluntary sector or education. At the same time the need has grown for a book that will examine specifically the application of these approaches to direct work with families. Roger Lowe achieves the almost impossible task of bringing together various theories, techniques and case examples in clear and accessible ways. Readers of all disciplines, from front-line hard-pressed practitioners to students on therapy and social work courses, will be grateful for the simple and, above all, *useful* way he tackles the burning questions that arise in working with the family group. Highly recommended!'

Harvey Ratner, Brief Therapy Practice, London

Contents

Acknowledgements

Though the writing of this book has been a solitary project, I would like to mention several groups of people who have contributed in different ways to its final shape. Firstly, I thank the students on Master of Counselling courses at Queensland University of Technology whose 'frequently asked questions' over a number of years helped point out the gaps in the constructive therapy/family therapy literature that this book tries to fill. They also provided the model for my imaginary reader. Secondly, I would like to thank my colleagues in the Queensland Association for Family Therapy: Chris Hunt, Michael Locke and Paul Simmons, with whom I have collaborated in teaching family therapy courses in the last two years. Their much broader grounding in systemic family therapy has helped to complement my own more specialized approach. More importantly, our stimulating collaboration has helped me to question many of my previous assumptions, to rethink my own positions, and to develop a greater appreciation of what the tradition of family therapy has to offer. Thanks to you, the book is more 'both/and' than it would have been.

Finally I would like to thank Alison Poyner and her colleagues at Sage, who have contributed at all stages of the process in a consistently professional, attentive, and supportive way.

Introduction

This book brings together two areas of psychotherapy that should converge neatly – but usually do not. The first is the practice of *constructive therapies*, my umbrella term for the brief, collaborative and competency-based approaches that are increasingly popular among helping professionals. For many, including myself, the appeal of these approaches lies partly in their refreshingly positive, optimistic and frankly challenging philosophy, and partly in the possibilities they offer for brief but effective work. The best known and most influential models within this general orientation are probably solution-focused therapy and narrative therapy. The second area is the practice of *family therapy*, involving the fascinating dilemmas of working with relationships. For many helping professionals in the fields of counselling, social work, psychology, education and health, family-based work is a major occupation and challenge. Many practitioners have an interest in constructive therapies. Many practitioners have an interest in working with families. This book is written for those who have an interest in both.

Constructive therapies would seem to be an appealing choice for working with families. However, though there is an abundant literature on constructive therapies and an abundant literature on family therapy, there is a surprising dearth of work that specifically links the two and provides a framework for *constructive family therapy*. My experience of trying to fill in the gaps and make the connections – for myself as much as for my students – produced the impetus for this book. I have tried to write the kind of book that I wish had been available when I most needed it.

How is it that these two areas of psychotherapy have not converged as smoothly as they might? Perhaps one factor is that though, historically, many of the ideas in constructive therapies had their origins in the field of systemic family therapy, the two groups have tended to diverge in recent years and to talk in different languages. The relationship between constructive therapists and family therapists remains distinctly ambivalent, with the two groups tending to develop their own networks, conferences, training programmes and publishing outlets. In constructive therapy circles, family therapy is likely to be viewed simply as one particular context for practice. Other practice contexts would include individual therapy, couple therapy, groupwork, organizational consulting, counselling supervision, etc.

This means that training in constructive therapy typically emphasizes generic processes and skills which it is assumed can be generalized across *all* practice contexts. Less attention is paid to covering specific issues and dilemmas that arise when working with families or to the additional skills that may be required. This often leaves practitioners who specialize in family work with a sense of frustration: they have a broad sketch of an approach, but so much is missing in the way of colour, detail and depth. It is a suggestive starting point rather than a solid framework.

By contrast, in family therapy circles, constructive therapies are likely to be viewed simply as one group of *models* within the broad tradition of systemic theorizing. Other well known models would include structural therapy, strategic therapy, Milan therapy and intergenerational therapy. Family therapy training tends to be eclectic, covering a range of models, each with its own unique concepts and skills, but without providing comprehensive coverage of any. This is frustrating for those wishing to specialize in a constructive framework, particularly as many of the other approaches presented are inconsistent with this orientation. Here we can see the difficulty for those wishing to straddle the two fields selectively: neither group emphasizes constructive family therapy as a specialized approach and a major focus of their training.

In presenting this book as an attempt to bridge these areas, it is important that I declare my position. This is not an eclectic text that endorses any form of integration. My own primary identification is with constructive therapies rather than family therapy (though, like many, I am involved in both areas and value my professional relationships with both groups). Therefore, I will be viewing family work as a particular context for the practice of a generalized constructive orientation. However, I will be arguing that it is a specialized context that requires the incorporation of additional concepts and skills. In focusing on these, I will be trying to fill in the broad sketch, adding the colour, detail and depth that is missing. However, in order to encourage flexibility and creativity, I will also be suggesting ways in which therapists can selectively borrow from other frameworks, including the rich tradition of family therapy. My aim is to offer a framework that is conceptually consistent but also flexible, so that it can be adapted to the needs of the wide range of professionals who work with families.

Approach of the book

In order to highlight the central themes of the book, I introduce a number of analogies from another of my enthusiasms: travel. It has been suggested that family therapy can be compared with making a voyage through an unknown country, on a strange continent (Rober, 2002). It has also been suggested that constructive therapists should 'travel light' and avoid the excess baggage of much conventional therapeutic expertise (Friedman, 1993). These motifs set up the challenge and the structure of the book: if constructive family therapists are going to travel light, what exactly should they 'pack' for their professional journeys? In order to respond creatively and flexibly to the unknown, what are the most important concepts and skills that they need to have at their disposal? What specialized or additional concepts are especially important for constructive *family* therapy? How light can you travel before your resources become over-stretched?

The structure of the book reflects my attempts to address these questions. Each chapter corresponds to one item of essential luggage, one essential element of the framework. Chapter 1 sets out the theoretical foundations of the approach and highlights the distinguishing features and vision of constructive family therapy. Chapters 2–5 set out the central practice skills of the approach, the three processes of *hosting* family members, *negotiating* concerns and requests, and *evoking* possibilities. The focus is on how to adapt these skills to the context of family therapy. Chapter 6 focuses on the dilemmas of working constructively over time. Moving beyond a distinction between 'brief' and 'long-term' therapy, I examine the ways in which family therapy meetings can progress, evolve or re-form as developments occur. In Chapter 7, I address the use of the therapist's 'inner' conversation as a way of overcoming impasses and obstacles. This complements the usual emphasis on the 'outer' conversation of techniques. In Chapter 8, I introduce some important concepts that allow us to 'borrow' knowledge from other frameworks while retaining a constructive orientation. Specifically, I discuss the distinction between *primary, secondary* and *rejected pictures*, and the identification of constraints. This allows us, for example, to use concepts and skills from other family therapy traditions without becoming lost or slipping into a nondescript eclecticism. Finally, in Chapter 9, I outline some constructive responses to potentially challenging scenarios. This complements the earlier focus on generic processes by considering how therapists might approach specific kinds of situations that might prove challenging to a constructive framework (for example, situations involving the need for medication, the use of psycho-educational material, or where collaboration may not be possible). These selective scenarios can help us to prepare for a range of situations that we might encounter in our travels.

Voice, style and audience

One of the difficulties readers encounter in approaching the constructive therapy literature concerns the often dizzying and disconcerting mixture of styles: abstract theoretical discussion (for example, about the differences between constructivism, social constructionism and postmodernism) can sit side by side with the minutiae of technical discussion (when using scaling questions, should the scale go from 0–10 or 1–10?). There can be a similar experience of alienation when encountering the family therapy literature. Reflecting on the field's 'troubled legacy' of systems theory, and its recent 'affair with postmodernism', Rivett and Street (2003) remark on family therapy's penchant for selecting the most arcane and complicated ideas with which to justify its practice. In trying to achieve a practical focus and a consistency of voice and style, I have attempted to write at a 'middle' level of abstraction, avoiding the extremes of either abstruse theoretical discourse or a manual of techniques. I have tried to imagine an audience of therapists who are certainly interested in theoretical ideas and debates but *who are primarily concerned with the everyday issues of practice.*

I am also writing for an audience of therapists who are interested in combining ideas and skills from a number of constructive therapies, rather than identifying with particular models such as solution-focused therapy or narrative therapy. As I indicate in Chapter 1, the degree of 'family resemblance' between these models is a moot point. I will be taking the position that the specific models can be considered as differing 'styles' of constructive therapy (Omer, 1996). I recognize that, in adopting such a stance, I may invite summary dismissal as a dilettante who doesn't grasp the intricacies of any of the models! Yet this is a risk worth taking. At various times in my professional life I have identified with particular models of constructive therapy. I have had the opportunity to attend workshops and training courses with exemplary practitioners of solution-focused and narrative therapies in Australia, New Zealand, the United States and Great Britain. Their influence will be apparent in the book. However, in recent times I have been more influenced by therapists such as Bill O'Hanlon, Bob Bertolino, Steven Friedman and Michael Hoyt who write in more inclusive ways about constructive therapies. Of course, any individual's attempt to integrate different approaches represents a personal and idiosyncratic choice. That is why I am offering *a* constructive framework, not *the* constructive framework.

Some clarifications

To achieve consistency I use the word 'therapist' to refer to a potentially broad group of helping professionals who may find the material relevant to their needs. Similarly, I refer to users of therapeutic services as 'clients' or 'family members'. The case examples that I draw upon throughout the book are fictional in the sense that they do not represent any actual clients with whom I or other therapists have worked. They are realistic composite cases developed from many sources and experiences (including role-play scenarios used in workshops and classes).

A walk in the world of constructive therapy

I would like to make one more comment about my approach to the book and about the way I hope you will respond to it. In his influential book, *The Reflective Practitioner: How Professionals Think in Action* (1983), Donald Schön pointed to some of the problems that exist in the contemporary training of professionals. Among other things, he suggested that when different models are presented, it is often done in a polemical way that produces an either/or contest with rival models. He argues persuasively that such tendencies act to encourage a narrow, technically oriented practitioner rather than a reflective and engaged practitioner.

Schön offers a number of broad ideas for encouraging reflective practice in the training of professionals. In particular, I have used his concept of *frame analysis* for my overall perspective. By this, I mean that the framework I present is intended for your reflections and for comparative analysis with other frameworks. I am not arguing its merits as a definitive model that you should unhesitatingly adopt. Though I am obviously enthused about the ideas in the book, I hope to offer them in a reflective and collegial manner, rather than in a polemical or proselytizing one.

Adapting some of Schön's evocative descriptions, I hope that the book will allow you the opportunity to 'walk in the world' of constructive family therapy, and to experience this world from the point of view of a particular therapist. As you walk in this world, and share in the therapist's enterprises and methods, you will be able to see how you would frame the practice role, how you would construe specific situations, what particular competencies you would require, and what assumptions and values you would need to embrace, if you chose to inhabit it. My aim is to encourage you to 'try on' this framework and get a feel for it, to see what kind of world you would create for yourself, and, indeed, what kind of person you would become if you decided to make it your own. The rest is up to you.

1 Travelling Light

> Maybe family therapy practice can best be compared with making a voyage through some unknown country, on a strange continent. ... The travellers face a lot of uncertainty and insecurity, because on this journey unexpected things are bound to happen. Just like these travellers, the therapist does not have a lot of tools to fulfil the therapeutic mission. (Rober, 2002: 477)

> If one can trust nothing, then the best way to start travelling is to travel light ... .(Curt, 1994: 211)

Foundations of a constructive framework

To set the scene for this book, I will begin with a travel analogy.

Imagine that you are about to embark on an open-ended professional journey that will involve you in many different contexts and applications of family therapy. You don't know how long you will be away or where your adventures as a family therapist might take you. You cannot predict whom you will encounter, what kinds of relationships you will be working with, or what kinds of issues will be presented. You cannot rely on regular consultation with colleagues, and may have to practise alone for considerable periods. If you could pack only a handful of key, durable and adaptable concepts and skills to sustain you on this journey and fulfil the therapeutic mission, what would you take? What would you select in order to have a solid, reliable and robust framework at your disposal? What would be the therapist's equivalent of a Swiss army knife?

This book represents my attempt to address these questions, and to offer a constructive framework for family therapy that may serve your needs on this imaginary journey. The theme of *travelling light* underlies the approach:

> My guess is that we need to travel light and avoid carrying excess baggage in the form of assumptions that draw us into the whirlpool of hypothesis generation and structural analysis. By freeing ourselves of these assumptions, we increase our readiness to listen to the client's story and to generate with the client new meanings and new understandings that will lead out of a problem-saturated world and into a world in which competence and a sense of personal agency become the dominant discourses. (Friedman, 1993: 252)

The preference for travelling light reflects two complementary themes in constructive therapies: *affirmation* of human resourcefulness and possibilities, combined with *scepticism* about many of the claims and uses of professional knowledge. Reflecting on these themes, it is easy to agree with the spirit of Friedman's suggestion that we discard excess theoretical baggage and free ourselves to listen more generously and appreciatively. But putting this into practice poses some inevitable questions. How much can we afford to discard, and what exactly are we going to take instead? Where do we draw the line between travelling light and being ill-equipped? We can consider a number of questions:

- How do constructive therapists conceptualize family therapy? How do they understand their 'therapeutic mission'? How is this different from other approaches?
- Given the complexity and variety of family relationships, how can we work in ways that are simple *and* sustainable, simple but *not* simplistic?
- How can we select from the confusing variety of concepts and skills that are found in the constructive therapy literature? Which will travel best?
- What about other therapeutic traditions? How much extra knowledge do we need, and where should we look for it?
- Can we utilize knowledge from other traditions while maintaining a constructive orientation?
- How can we work in ways that are theoretically consistent but encourage flexibility and improvisation?

In other words, how can we ensure that we travel light, but journey well?

The travelling light metaphor helps to define both the challenge and the structure of the book. Each chapter corresponds to one item of essential 'luggage', one important component of a constructive framework. This opening chapter provides the foundation by setting out some theoretical contours for our framework. It focuses on some of the 'realities' we will select for the journey, our preferred understandings of constructive therapy, family therapy and therapeutic processes.

Let us take the analogy between travel and therapy a little further. Inexperienced travellers carry too much luggage. They imagine every conceivable eventuality that might occur on their trip and try to pack something to cover it. The unused baggage weighs them down and restricts manoeuvrability. Similarly, inexperienced therapists carry too much in the way of complicated and competing theories and skills. Lacking the discernment that comes with practice, and acting from a sincere desire to help, they often try to do too much too quickly, confusing themselves as much as their clients. With more experience, both travellers and therapists learn to travel light – to separate luggage from baggage – and to put their trust in their most useful, durable and versatile pieces of 'equipment'. The art of travelling light involves learning to do a lot with a little.

Where to begin: families or therapy?

Should a book on family therapy begin with a discussion about families or a discussion about therapy? This is not an idle question, but a moot point that will help to clarify some important priorities. If the book began with a discussion about families, this would have the effect of prioritizing knowledge about families. The implication would be that our approach must be derived specifically from a theoretical understanding of families, and that working with families is fundamentally different from working with individuals or couples. On the other hand, if the book began with a discussion of a therapy framework, this would suggest that the main knowledge base we are working from consists of some generic therapeutic principles that can be adapted to the context of family work (and supplemented, where necessary, with additional specialized knowledge). Knowledge about the therapeutic orientation would be prioritized over knowledge about families.

Constructive therapists favour the second option. Their particular theoretical starting point is not an understanding of how problems occur in families but an understanding of *how change occurs in therapy*, regardless of whether you are working with individuals, couples or families (or, for that matter, with groups or organizations). Therefore, it makes sense to focus first on what is common about constructive therapy across all modalities. Then we can consider what is different about working with families, and what additional forms of knowledge may be needed in developing a framework for constructive *family* therapy.

A constructive orientation

I have borrowed the umbrella term 'constructive' from two main sources. In the therapy field, Michael Hoyt (1994, 1996, 1998) has used this term to cover a range of contemporary approaches including solution-oriented, solution-focused, possibility, narrative, postmodern, co-operative, competency-based and constructivist therapies. Acknowledging their theoretical differences, Hoyt suggests that in practice they share several important features:

... a respectful partnership between therapist and client, an emphasis on strengths and resources, and a hopeful eye toward the future.

Each, in its own way, is *constructive therapy*, the *building of solutions*, with language or 'conversation'... being the map if not the territory. (1994: 2)

Hoyt emphasizes two other characteristics:

Constructive therapies are approaches that begin with the recognition that humans are meaning-makers who construct, not simply uncover, their psychological realities. ... [W]e are actively building a worldview that influences our actions. (1998: 1)

Further, in relation to practice he suggests that constructive therapists are especially interested in 'the enhancement of choice through respectful collaboration and the fuller utilization of clients' competencies and resources' (Hoyt, 1998: 1).

Friedman (cited in Hoyt, 1998: 3) has summarized some distinguishing features of constructive therapy practice. These are presented in Box 1.1.

Box 1.1   Characteristics of constructive therapy practice

The constructive therapist:

- Believes in a socially constructed reality.
- Emphasizes the reflexive nature of therapeutic relationships in which the client and therapist co-construct meanings in dialogue or conversation.
- Moves away from hierarchical distinctions toward a more egalitarian offering of ideas and respect for differences.
- Maintains empathy and respect for the client's predicament and a belief in the power of therapeutic conversation to liberate suppressed, ignored, or previously unacknowledged voices or stories.
- Co-constructs goals and negotiates direction in therapy, placing the client in the driver's seat, as an expert on his or her own predicament and dilemmas.
- Searches for and amplifies client competencies, strengths, and resources and avoids being a detective of pathology or reifying rigid diagnostic distinctions.
- Avoids a vocabulary of deficit and dysfunction, replacing the jargon of pathology (and distance) with the language of the everyday.
- Is oriented toward the future and optimistic about change.
- Is sensitive to the methods and processes used in the therapeutic conversation.

Friedman (cited in Hoyt, 1998: 3)

Parton and O'Byrne (2000) have also used the term in their development of 'constructive social work'. They juxtapose two important senses of 'constructive': a theoretical sense relating to the influence of constructionist ideas, and the everyday sense of contributing in a positive, co-operative and practical manner. Building on these uses, I will identify a constructive therapy framework as one that combines two aspects: a *theoretical* stance informed by constructionist ideas, and a *practice* stance that is optimistic, collaborative and competency-based. Before going further, it is important to note that these two aspects are not intrinsically linked. It is perfectly possible to identify with collaborative and competency-based practice without embracing a constructionist framework. For example, it is not unusual for therapists to adopt some of the methods of solution-focused or narrative therapies but to 'relocate' them within humanistic, cognitive-behavioural or systemic frameworks. It is also possible to base many aspects of collaborative and competency-based practice on the findings of contemporary research into common factors of change (Hubble, Duncan and Miller, 1999). A pragmatic approach might suggest that broad meta-frameworks such as constructionism are of little interest to practitioners who should be encouraged to learn a wide range of methods and to do whatever works for their clients.

My suggestion, however, is that if we wish to travel light, and to do a lot with a little, it is fundamentally important that we have some consistent principles to guide our actions. We will need to be able to think quickly and clearly in response to unexpected, difficult and novel situations, and to reflect on our practice in productive ways. At the very least, we need to have an understanding of the connection between means and ends, between what we are doing and why we are doing it. A broadly based constructionist perspective provides one consistent way of integrating many of the contemporary competency-based practices. This does not mean that we cannot draw upon other traditions, or that we must jettison all of our prior learning. However, by linking constructionist ideas to constructive practice we can establish a preferred philosophy and orientation for our framework.

Constructionist themes and constructive practice

Rather than discussing constructionism[1] in general I will focus specifically on particular themes that have been influential in the therapy field. Gergen (1999) has identified four characteristics of constructionist-based therapies: *a focus on meaning, therapy as co-construction, a focus on relationship,* and *value sensitivity.* I will build the discussion around these interrelated themes and then link them to more specific practice principles. At a broader level, these themes highlight the paradigm shift from a realist perspective to a constructionist perspective. As Shotter (1993) suggests, the tension between realist and constructionist positions relates to the different emphasis they place on 'finding' and 'making' – between an assumption that realities are found and an assumption that realities are made. In making these particular connections, it is important to acknowledge the inevitable influence of personal choice and preference. This is my (current) way of making sense of a complex, contentious and always changing field.

A focus on meaning

This theme reflects a shift in emphasis from the analysis of structures and essences to the process of social meaning-making. Problem-oriented therapies have been traditionally concerned with finding the root cause or the essential nature of the problem. The emphasis is on getting to the 'facts' of the case, based on the assumption that the language used to describe it objectively maps what is 'really there'.

Constructionists, however, assert that language is a form of action that works to *make* the world rather than to map it. The terms that we use to understand our world do not correspond directly to what is 'really there' but are derived within particular cultural traditions of understanding, and inevitably involve forms of reification: the confusion of words with things. For example, within the realist tradition of therapeutic discourse, we might take for granted that words like 'self', 'personality' or 'family system' refer to actually existing entities. From a constructionist perspective, however, these familiar terms do not refer to entities but are, themselves, 'inventities' (O'Hanlon and Wilk, 1987). Recognition that such terms are social and linguistic constructions rather than actually existing entities, essences or structures leads us to examine the way they are used in specific situations and the meanings and consequences that follow. Constructionists take the view that, for any given situation, there are 'multiple realities' in the sense of multiple potential descriptions and explanations. Meaning is not derived directly from 'the facts' of the case but is *negotiated* through social processes.

If we view meaning as being created in the social interactions that occur between people, and as being context-dependent and constantly changing, this suggests a new therapeutic emphasis based on the ongoing *negotiation* and *storying* of experience (Walter and Peller, 2000). This involves a shift away from the language of observation, assessment and intervention to a language of conversation, narrative and consultation. The central metaphor is one of therapy as both conversational resource and resourceful conversation, rather than a form of treatment or psycho-education.

Practice principles

- Human experience is inherently *ambiguous* and *negotiable*. People are 'multi-storied' and 'multi-voiced'. However, particular stories and voices inevitably highlight some experiences and obscure others. Constructive therapists choose to highlight experiences of personal agency, hope and resourcefulness in the belief that as we describe the present and past, we simultaneously fashion the future.
- Therapy can be viewed as an ongoing process of *negotiating narratives* with clients (O'Connell, 1998). Certain types of narratives are more likely to motivate and support clients through difficult circumstances. These are 'narratives about competence, skills and qualities which the client can utilize' (ibid.: 16).
- By contrast, certain kinds of narratives are unlikely to be helpful, and tend to constrain time-effective work. Bertolino and O'Hanlon (2002) define four major kinds of problematic stories:

    1. *Stories of blame.* These occur where individuals are labelled, pathologized or blamed as being the 'cause' of the problem, or as having bad intentions or personality traits. **Example**: A wife says, 'Our marriage is under stress because of John's emotional inadequacy!'
    2. *Stories of invalidation.* These occur where an individual's experiences or perceptions are discounted or undermined by others. This makes it difficult for people to be authorities on their own experience. **Example**: A parent says, 'Don't take Julie's tantrums too seriously. She's simply acting out in the usual teenage way.'
    3. *Stories of non-accountability.* These involve situations where individuals are presented as having no choice or responsibility for their actions, which are seen as determined by 'inevitable' forces. **Example**: A father says, 'When they push me over the edge I simply see red. They know I lose control then, so it's their own damn fault if they provoke me!'
    4. *Stories of impossibility.* These involve an assumption that change is impossible because individuals are incapable or unwilling. **Example**: A husband says, 'If I'm emotionally inadequate it's because I've never had a decent role model. *All* of the men in my family are distant and remote. There's a remoteness gene in the male line! We're simply incapable of acting any other way.'

- By negotiating a shift from the themes of these four stories to themes of competence, agency, accountability and personal qualities, the therapist helps clients to 'literally talk themselves out of their troubles' by describing their lives in different ways. (Miller, 1997: 6)
- Change can occur relatively quickly, as what is selectively focused on becomes real. As people interact and observe each other, 'their

perceptions and definitions of what is real frequently shift, sometimes dramatically' (Berg and de Jong, 1996: 377). Therefore, therapy can be (but is not always) brief.

Therapy as co-construction

From a constructionist perspective, meaning is not communicated from therapist to client but is generated conjointly and is different from the contribution of either party (Walter and Peller, 2000). A stance of co-construction involves a move away from hierarchical distinctions and towards a preference for partnership. In attempting to rebalance the professional consultation, the therapist tries to give up the 'grasp of professional realities' and remains curious and open to the client's language and local experience (Gergen, 1999). This does not mean that the therapist totally relinquishes a leadership role in structuring the conversation (clients would probably not return if this were the case!) but uses a consultative approach and is continually guided by client feedback.

Practice principles

- The goals and direction of therapy are co-constructed, and clients are encouraged to be authorities on their own troubles and dilemmas.
- Therapists typically adopt a 'not knowing' position or a 'beginner's mind' in order to suspend professional assumptions that categorize clients. Instead, the therapist remains 'radically particularistic' (Milner and O'Byrne, 2002), seeing each client and situation as unique.
- A collaborative stance aims to 'pool' the resourcefulness of clients and therapists by encouraging both to step outside the constraints of a hierarchical client/therapist relationship.
- Therapists may need, at times, to depart from a collaborative stance (for example, in order to ensure the safety of clients or to make other value-based decisions), but will return to it where possible as their preferred way of relating.

Focus on relationship

For constructionists, meaning is not the product of an individual mind, but is derived from relationships and involves an ongoing process of negotiation and co-ordination with others. This includes not only immediate social interactions but relationships with broader cultural influences and with significant others who may no longer be present. Regardless of whether therapists are working individually or conjointly, an important question becomes: with whom is meaning made, how is this accomplished, and what are the outcomes (Gergen, 1999)? A person's sense of self is not constant or exclusively internal but is 'distributed' among the various relationships in which the person moves (Ziegler and Hiller, 2001). Therefore, as well as drawing attention to observable interactions between clients, a relationship focus provides a space in which clients can 'discover and expand their many relational voices' (Penn and Frankfurt, 1999: 176).

Practice principles

- Different kinds of 'relationship questions' are used to invite clients to adopt another's perspective, speculate about another's experience, and consider relationship goals, values and priorities.
- Rather than being identified as having problems, clients can be viewed as being in a *relationship with problems* (and the various influences that sustain them). This construction, associated with the externalizing practice of narrative therapy, invites an experience of distance between clients and problems, and a sense of choice about the future of the relationship.
- Clients can be invited to reflect on the relational processes that occur in the therapy sessions themselves. This may involve inviting clients to offer feedback, and to articulate the changes they have experienced and the respective contributions of themselves and the therapist.
- More broadly, other significant voices from present or past relationships can be brought into the conversation either literally (by being invited to attend) or 'virtually' by the therapist asking clients to speculate about their views and perspectives.
- Paradoxically, in order to enhance possibilities for individual agency, it is important to adopt a relationship focus that broadens perceptions and perspectives.

Value sensitivity

This final constructionist theme marks a shift in emphasis from the objective application of professional knowledge to a consideration of the values inherent in particular forms of practice. It is a shift from technical rationality to reflective practice. Therapists adopt a stance of critical and reflective practice in which they consider the potential effects of the *discourses* they choose to utilize. Constructionists often talk of 'dominant discourses': the characteristic ways of talking and writing that prevail in certain fields at particular times. An important question becomes: how do these taken-for-granted ways of talking, writing and theorizing *define* and *position* people in particular ways, and how do they act to legitimize particular kinds of behaviour? For example, what assumptions does a particular way of talking contain about what is normal or desirable in family life, or about gender expectations, or sexuality or the nature of violence? Whose position is strengthened or weakened by what is focused upon and what is ignored? Where does the therapist stand in relation to these value-based processes?

Practice principles

- Constructive therapists are sensitive to value dilemmas but differ in the ways they respond. Some therapists are more avowedly political or committed, while others will make their values and positions transparent only in particular situations.
- Therapists may adopt an 'anthropological' role of cultural curiosity (Madsen, 1999) where they seek to learn about their clients' culture and values, noting differences from their own but without trying to teach or convert.
- Constructive therapists engage in ongoing critical reflection about the methods and processes of their own work.

Finally, as Gergen (1999) reminds us, constructionism is not intended as the final word but is itself a discourse that engages in ongoing dialogue with others. Therefore, a constructionist stance cannot be a triumphalist one that proclaims The True Way to practice. Instead, it encourages a process of *reflexivity* (the suspension of taken-for-granted assumptions) to ensure that all therapeutic traditions can be critically compared and that none (including constructive therapies) will be enthroned as the ultimate dominant discourse.

Three 'styles' of constructive therapy

Sheltering under the constructive umbrella are a number of distinct approaches to therapy. Purists and integrationists differ greatly on the extent of family resemblance that exists, and whether it makes sense to mix and merge. At the extremes of both abstract theorizing and specific techniques there are certainly differences. Yet, at the middle level of practice principles, many of us find an encouraging degree of commonality. I prefer to think of the approaches as being distinctive *conversational styles* rather than totally separate models. This allows for greater freedom of movement between the approaches. We can identify a preferred personal style but also incorporate other styles and switch between them where necessary. Omer (1996) has distinguished three styles of constructive therapy: strategic, narrative and conversational. I will use these distinctions, but will substitute 'solution-oriented' for 'strategic' in order to distinguish this style from the broader tradition of strategic therapies. The styles differ in terms of the characteristic *themes* that the therapist seeks to introduce into the conversation.

Solution-oriented style

This therapeutic style is most typically associated with the brief solution focused model pioneered by Steve de Shazer and his associates in Milwaukee (de Shazer, 1985, 1988, 1991, 1994). As Omer suggests, this style searches for a sense of 'unimpeded action and movement' towards the client's preferred future (1996: 328). In practice, this involves bypassing extensive discussion of problems and moving in an 'unimpeded' way towards *change talk* especially in the form of carefully elicited descriptions of the client's hopes, goals, preferred future, and resources. Increasingly, de Shazer's original ideas have been developed and extended by his colleagues and other therapists in a number of different directions, and adapted to a wide range of contexts (for example, Berg and Steiner, 2003; De Jong and Berg, 2002; Lipchik, 2002; O'Connell, 1998; Walter and Peller, 2000; Ziegler and Hiller, 2001). Because of the diversity of ideas and pratices now linked to this style, I have preferred the broader term *solution-oriented*.

The main themes of the inquiry might typically evolve like this:

What do clients want to be different?
How will these changes make a difference to their lives and relationships?
What will tell them (and others) that these changes are occurring?
Have any of these changes occurred already, and how was this achieved?
Building on these developments, what might happen next?

Questions based on these areas of inquiry immediately invite clients into constructions of desire, future goals, the significance of change, the identification of potential signs, steps and successes, and speculation about future possibilities. An important aspect of this style is the possibility it offers for time-effective work. It is based on the assumption that narratives of competence and change can be negotiated from the *beginning* of therapy, without prior discussion or analysis of problems. One of de Shazer's most radical suggestions was that 'solution talk' and 'problem talk' are fundamentally different kinds of practices of 'language games' that have their own sets of vocabularies and rules and need not be logically connected (de Shazer, 1991). The path of inquiry described above is a generic change process that can be used irrespective of the client's situation. It is more important to initiate this change process than to analyse the problem. Of course, in practice this is unlikely to occur immediately.

However, therapists using a solution-oriented style will attempt to negotiate a relatively early shift to the themes of *preferences and possibilities* (Walter and Peller, 2000). The hallmark of this style is the therapist's attempt, whenever possible, to take the express route rather than the scenic route.

Narrative style

The narrative style has evolved principally from the work of Michael White in Australia and David Epston in New Zealand (White and Epston, 1990). Rather than attempting to bypass discussion of problems, therapists using a narrative style are quite willing to talk about them. However, they do this in a way that studiously avoids blame, invalidation, determinism and impossibility. Using a process of 'relational externalizing' (Bird, 2000) they develop the theme of a relationship between clients and their stated problems, encouraging clients to take a position on this relationship, and assisting them to 'story' their lives in a preferred direction. Therapists may typically engage in the following lines of inquiry:

How would clients prefer to describe the problem? How would they name it?
How is the problem restricting or oppressing their lives and relationships?
Who or what are the problem's allies, and how has it tried it to co-opt clients into supporting it?
How do clients prefer to relate to the problem (for example, defeat it, ignore it, learn to live with it, co-operate with it)?
How have clients managed to limit the influence of the problem and take a stand against it?
What might these steps suggest about the qualities and identity of clients?
Who and what might help to strengthen and extend this new story about their client?

The narrative style works to position clients as being in a certain kind of relationship with a problem, a relationship that is oppressive or restrictive but is capable of being changed. By separating the problem from the person, it provides a way of inviting clients to reflect upon the effects of the problem and then invites a consideration of the client's preferred stance towards problems, the choices that are available, and any steps that have been taken to limit the problem's influence. Finally it helps clients to plot these developments into a preferred narrative or 'counter-plot' of competence and possibilities. An important part of the narrative style involves 'thickening' this story by eliciting more and more details and inviting further reflections and retellings (Payne, 2000; White, 1995). As the name suggests, a narrative style attempts to integrate character, theme and plot. Whereas a solution-oriented style is often focused on actions in a specific context ('How did you do that? What steps did you take?'), a narrative style might extend the focus of curiosity to questions of character and identity ('What might this action say about you as a *person*?' 'What kinds of qualities were needed to allow this step to be taken?' 'Who would have predicted this?' 'What did they know about you?').

In some ways this style appears more conventional in that it focuses on identifying personal problems, causal connections and influences. Crucially, however, the careful use of externalizing language allows this to be done in ways that avoid blaming or pathologizing clients, and keeps the way open for choice and possibilities. Compared to the solution-oriented style, the narrative style is more likely to introduce additional ideas for the client's consideration. In some situations, the therapist will typically invite a consideration of broader socio-cultural factors and discourses that might support specific personal problems. For example, an important 'ally' of anorexia might turn out to be gender-based discourses about ideal body-shapes. Likewise, depression may be supported by attitudes or expectations of perfectionism. The influence of these powerful discourses can be made visible through the use of externalizing language. In this sense, the narrative style casts a wider net than the solution-oriented style and is more concerned with the social context surrounding problems. It takes a more leisurely and scenic route towards the storying of competence and change.

Conversational style

While the solution-oriented style invites a sense of unimpeded movement towards the future, and the narrative style invites a sense of continuity of character and plot, the conversational style invites a sense of ambiguity and multiple viewpoints. The conversational style is less directional and more open-ended than the other styles. It is associated with the work of influential therapists such as Harlene Anderson (1997), Harry Goolishian (Anderson and Goolishian, 1988), Lynn Hoffman (2002) and Tom Andersen (1991, 1995, 2001) all of whom, Omer suggests, 'love *ambiguation*' (1996: 320). In a sense, this style involves a suspension of direction in order to expand the range of perspectives or voices for viewing the problematic situation. Andersen (2001) develops an analogy with physiotherapy, suggesting that by helping clients to widen the repertoire of their expressions, we enable them to 'stretch' and loosen up their movements, so that new options may be found. The expansion of voices and perspectives might happen metaphorically or literally.

In the metaphorical sense, clients might be asked to speculate about the experiences of others involved in the problematic situation, or to speculate about what significant others from their own present or past might say or suggest. Therapists might offer some new perspectives or wonder aloud which important voices are missing and need to be brought into the room – or perhaps which voices are present but unacknowledged. The conversational style, used in these ways, may help clients access other voices that can balance those which are currently the loudest ('In addition to the angry voice that condemns your father, is there another voice somewhere that might say something different about him?').

The addition of multiple voices may also occur literally, via the use of the reflecting team process developed originally by Tom Andersen (Friedman, 1995). Using this format, a group of observers (usually colleagues of the therapist) act as a reflecting team and watch the session from behind a one-way screen. At a designated point the therapist and clients switch positions with the team and then observe, as team members offer reflections on what they have heard. The team members develop a conversation among themselves, offering different perspectives and personal reflections on what they have seen and heard. The reflections are based in curiosity and offered in speculative and non-expert ways (I wonder if … could it be that … when that happened I couldn't help wondering if … I felt myself change as I listened to the family talk …). The aim is not to arrive at consensus but to increase the range of voices and views, the potential repertoire of expressions about the situation. The next phase of the process involves the team once again switching positions with the therapist and clients. The therapist then invites the clients to reflect on the team's discussion. The process can be repeated, involving a creative series of reflections on reflections, each adding a layer to the texture of the conversation. The reflecting team process is discussed further in Chapter 7.

The conversational style complements the more directional solution-oriented and narrative styles, in the sense that it expands or opens out the conversation to additional perspectives, continually inviting the 'not-yet-said' rather than focusing attention on particular kinds of constructions and seeking to pursue them.

Widening the lens, sharpening the focus

In considering ways of using all three styles, a useful starting point may be Friedman's (1997) suggestion that a therapeutic conversation involves two alternating processes: widening the lens and sharpening the focus. Constructive therapists will often wish to sharpen the focus on the storying of change, competence and the preferred future. At other times, however, it will be necessary to pull back and take in a broader perspective, to gather more grist for the constructive mill in terms of additional information, or extra perspectives – the 'not-yet-said'. Once this has occurred, a new sense of direction may emerge and the focus can be sharpened once again. In alternating these processes, my preferred approach is to begin by using a solution-oriented style, attempting to sharpen the focus as soon as possible on the preferences and possibilities. In some situations, this style alone may be sufficient. In other situations, either at the client's instigation or the therapist's, it may be important to depart temporarily from the express route and widen the lens by switching to the more 'scenic' narrative or conversational styles. For example, constructive therapists will sometimes switch from a solution-oriented to a narrative style in situations where clients have defined or organized their *identity* around the problem and where concerns are life-encompassing – for example in cases of schizophrenia, severe depression, obsessive/compulsive behaviour and eating disorders. In such situations, clients may require an 'identity overhaul' (O'Hanlon, 1994) involving externalization of the complex discourses at work. In many situations, it may be important to incorporate all three styles. However, the solution-oriented style is the 'home' or 'default' style of the constructive framework I will be assembling. It is where you begin and where you hope you can return as often as possible. *We take the express route where possible, and the scenic route where necessary.* When using the term 'constructive therapist' I will be implicitly assuming this stylistic preference.

Constructing 'family therapy'

Having assembled the foundations for a general constructive framework, we can now turn to the major focus of this book: adapting the framework to the specific context of family therapy. We can address the question of what is different about working with families. What are some of the potential hazards and opportunities, and what additional concepts and skills might we need to 'pack'? This will involve a discussion of some of the points of difference between constructive therapies and the broader systemic tradition in family therapy.

Perhaps the starting point, however, should be the more fundamental question of what we mean by 'family therapy'. Achieving consensus on family therapy is about as difficult as achieving consensus on 'the family' itself. This once prompted de Shazer to resort to a deliberately ironic and tautological definition: 'Family therapy is what family therapists do when they say they are doing family therapy' (1991:13). For some therapists, it literally involves a commitment to working with families. In this view, the *modality* of working with families (involving the presence of at least two generations of clients in the session) is more important than the particular therapeutic orientation used. For others, however, family therapy is primarily a commitment to a specific *theoretical orientation*. This is often described as 'systemic practice', involving a focus on relationships, process, context and meaning. One can work 'systemically' with individuals, couples, various formations of family members, organizations or other groupings. The theoretical orientation takes precedence over the constitution of the client group. Also, even when different therapists are working with families, they may disagree on the main purpose for doing so. Some may view family therapy as a forum for addressing relationship concerns involving all family members. Others, however, might use it for the purpose of indirectly influencing a particular individual's 'symptoms'. How would a constructive therapist approach these questions?

It is important to reiterate that constructive therapists do not make a *theoretical* distinction between working at the individual, couple or family level (or, for that matter, the group, organizational or community level). The same change principles are applied in each context. Therefore, the choice to work with family groupings is not compelled by theory, but is largely pragmatic. Therapists may make personal choices based on their own interests, skills and work context, but these are not inherently linked to a constructive framework. While a relationship focus is an important theme in constructive therapies, this does not translate into an assumption that conjoint therapy is always to be preferred. In fact, constructive therapists maintain that effective couple or family therapy can be conducted with an individual (so long as the focus remains on relationship issues and the absent voices are brought into the conversation).

The decision to work with families, therefore, is negotiable on a case-by-case, session-by-session basis. In many situations, conjoint therapy might prove more effective than individual therapy (for example, if family members have the opportunity to hear, appreciate and share new developments) but in others it may be counterproductive (for example, if family members persistently engage in conflict or seek to undermine the therapy process). Many constructive therapists prefer to work with whoever comes through the door, rather than seeking to convene particular groupings.

Furthermore, when a decision to work conjointly is made, constructive therapists do not necessarily attempt to convene the whole family but are more likely to work with those who are most involved in the presenting issue and who want to work on change. Rather than working with the 'family system', constructive therapists prefer to work with the 'preference-determined system' (Walter and Peller, 2000) comprising the therapist plus those who share in the particular goals and purpose of the meeting. The key distinction is that ongoing involvement is based on a shared sense of purpose, and is defined from within. Therefore, the 'system' may also include non-family members such as other helping professionals, housemates, friends or neighbours who may be involved in the particular issue at hand. It is also accepted that membership is fluid, and may change from meeting to meeting. Therapists would not necessarily feel that progress had been compromised because a key family member dropped out of therapy. Nor would they subscribe to a 'more the merrier' perspective, assuming that keeping a whole family in therapy is necessarily the best option.

A pragmatic definition

However, in choosing examples for this book, I have chosen to prioritize particular uses and applications. For this pragmatic reason, I will define 'constructive family therapy' as the adaptation of a constructive framework to situations involving (i) conjoint sessions with diverse groups of family members, (ii) the presence of at least two generations of family members, and (iii) a focus on relationship concerns rather than an individual's problems. Theoretically, the approach could accommodate a much wider range of situations, including individual sessions, separate sessions with parents or siblings, and combinations of family members and others. However, my experience as a trainer suggests that practitioners are mainly wanting skills to assist with conjoint family sessions involving parents and children, and focusing on relationship issues. Therefore, most of the examples will be of this kind.

Hazards and opportunities

The relevant question is not theoretical but severely practical: what is different about working with families, and what are the potential hazards and opportunities in a particular situation? On the one hand, constructive therapists view the prospective involvement of family members in a positive light, as potentially contributing a multitude of additional resources to the therapy process. While no one is blamed for problems, everyone can contribute to solutions. On the other hand, constructive therapists also prefer to work with those who are motivated and committed to working collaboratively. How might the practice of constructive therapy be potentially undermined *or* enhanced through working with families? Here are some typical possibilities, presented as a series of 'what ifs?'.

Potential hazards

- What if a family has many serious problems and goals that may appear mutually exclusive – where do you start?
- What if each family member remains adamant that someone else needs to change?
- What if family members engage in open hostility and arguments during the process, turning every question into an opportunity to blame or attack others?

- What if someone doesn't want to be there and sets about undermining the session?
- What if someone is unable or unwilling to say what they are wanting?
- What if an individual has a particular personal difficulty that is connected with the relationship problems?
- What if you have trouble forging a connection with people of different generations, or are perceived as taking sides?
- What if family members have different age-related cognitive and language abilities? How do you work out the appropriate language and pace to use?
- What if there is chaos and confusion in the meeting – how do you keep track of what each person thinks is important, and maintain a rapport with them?

On the other hand …

Potential opportunities

- What if parents hear a young person articulate what is bothering him in ways that are different or new?
- What if a young person hears her parents speak of the admiration they have for her abilities, the faith they have in her future, and the changes they have noticed in recent times?
- What if people surprise each other (and perhaps themselves) by their ability and willingness to stay in the same room and work through some serious concerns?
- What if people have a new experience of speaking and listening without interruption or attack?
- What if family members discover that they share some important mutual hopes and concerns for their relationships?
- What if people have the experience of hearing an external voice valuing and validating all of their perspectives and also their resources and achievements?
- What if people collectively discover (or recover) the strengths of their relationships?

Many of us would agree with Lipchik (2002) that working with families can be the most difficult *and* the most rewarding form of therapy (sometimes, I suggest, in the same session!). While there are obvious hazards, there is also the opportunity for solutions that are worked out in the present to be shared, appreciated and 'passed on' in future relationships. The shared experience of therapy has the potential to assist families to emerge more resilient through adversity and more resourceful in collaboratively meeting future challenges (Walsh, 2003). In a practical sense, the main focus of this book is on how to minimize the hazards and maximize the opportunities of family therapy. To the extent that you feel confident about being able to maximize the potential of family work, you will be able to make a more considered choice about who to invite in any given situation.

Constructive and systemic perspectives: degrees of difference

> O body swayed to music, O brightening glance,
> How can we know the dancer from the dance?
>
> (W.B. Yeats, *Among School Children*)

It is informative to compare a constructive framework with the broader systemic tradition in family therapy. It is important to make the qualification that I am talking about degrees of difference rather than extremes. Many constructive therapists have been trained in systemic family therapy, and many systemic family therapists have a constructive orientation. This means that, especially in practice (as opposed to declared theoretical stances), a considerable degree of overlap typically exists. Both perspectives emphasize relationships and context, meanings and process in their understanding of human difficulties. The systemic family therapy tradition, however, has theorized family processes in much more elaborate ways, producing a large vocabulary of concepts that have been used to map family dynamics.[2] These include:

- levels of analysis: a systemic perspective invites us to analyse behaviour and experience at different organizational levels, for example individual, couple, family, extended family, neighbourhood, social, cultural and spiritual;
- stages of the family life cycle, focusing on internal and external pressures for change, and key developmental transitions;
- family structures: triangulation, sub-systems, coalitions, enmeshment and disengagement;
- family myths, scripts, rules, and secrets;
- family patterns of circularity and homeostasis;
- functionalist concepts which depict symptoms as serving a function for the family;
- intergenerational influences and patterns of attachment.

A key aspect of a systemic perspective is its holistic emphasis on the 'family system'. In systemic discourse, a family is conceptualized as an integrated, dynamic and organic entity or system that is made up of organized, dynamic sub-systems (Street and Downey, 1996). To understand its processes and transformations, we need to analyse the recurring patterns of interaction that occur both within and between these various levels. In other words, a family is more than a collection of individual members and their experiences, in the same way that an orchestra is more than a collection of players, and a dance is more than a collection of dancers. The system consists of the dancers and the dance, the individual parts *plus* the way they function together (Nichols and Schwartz, 2004). In therapy contexts, this holistic emphasis often translates into a working assumption that an individual problem (such as a child's misbehaviour at school) is a 'symptom' of a problem at the level of the family system (for example, marital discord detoured onto the child) and requires intervention at that level.

This is probably the major area of tension between constructive therapists and family therapists. Wishing to travel light and avoid being drawn into the 'whirlpool of hypothesis generation and structural analysis' (Friedman, 1993: 252), constructive therapists prefer to eschew many aspects of family system discourse and the proliferation of terms it has engendered. This is partly based on an abiding concern with the reification of deficit-oriented terms and the potential for these 'inventities' to be used in ways that are implicitly normative and pathologizing. Systemic concepts are evocative images or metaphors that can be illuminating for clients in some contexts, but have sometimes been used in ways that emphasize themes of problems, normative judgments and impossibility. For example, families can be positioned as being inappropriately organized, as failing to negotiate key developmental transitions, as incapable of breaking free from homeostatic patterns, or as unconsciously requiring problems to be maintained; while individuals can be viewed as failing to separate from intergenerational patterns of attachment and behaviour. If used indiscriminately, these forms of discourse can have the effect of simply shifting pathology from individuals to families. Systemic discourse tends to be problem oriented in the sense of focusing attention on patterned regularities that constrain change, rather than on differences that enable change. Furthermore, the very proliferation of professional family-deficit terms has the potential to lead back in some familiar directions: towards the privileging of professional knowledge and the language of technical rationality (observation, assessment and intervention, etc.).

Seeing families as quasi-biological organisms or entities also has the potential to discount possibilities for the personal agency of its individual members. Constructive therapists remain wary of concepts suggesting that unique qualities or powers reside in a system, other than the combined preferences and behaviour of the people who constitute it. There can be a tendency (particularly in earlier forms of family therapy) to present the family system as possessing an almost mystical quality that transcends the qualities of its members. However, a more contemporary view suggests that, though the whole may be qualitatively different from the sum of its parts, it is not greater than those parts in the sense of superiority or profundity (Rivett and Street, 2003). Nor does it possess any greater 'power' than those parts. Efran, Lukens and Lukens (1990) make the point that if any one dancer in a *corps de ballet* refuses to enact his or her assigned role, the choreography of the dance changes. In this sense, any individual has the 'power' to change the dance.

To constructive therapists, therefore, much of the family systems discourse has the potential to complicate and mystify therapy unnecessarily. Whereas constructive therapists tend to view the family simply as a particular context for practice, there is a sense in which systemic therapists go further and view the 'family system' as a *client* (with a view to changing 'its' problematic properties). In their approach to conjoint work, perhaps we could say that constructive therapists are more likely to focus on the dancers, whereas systemic therapists are more likely to focus on the dance. Constructive therapists are likely to focus their attention on the hopes and experiences of *family members*, whereas systemic therapists are more likely to speculate about the invisible workings of the *family system*.

Rather than viewing families as systems, constructive therapists are more likely to invoke a metaphor of the family as a site or space for intersecting personal stories. For example, Parry and Doan (1994) see the contemporary family as 'a crossroads in which its different members go forth to and return from different worlds where different languages are spoken, different stories are told, and different selves are employed' (1994: 26). Using this metaphor, family members inhabit a number of actual and virtual worlds. They leave the family daily and return 'bearing new and strange narratives' (ibid.) – the children from their peers and schooling; the parents from their jobs, co-worker interactions, and other affiliations. Building on the differences between these kinds of metaphors, many constructive therapists would endorse the view of O'Hanlon and Wilk (1987) that 'family therapy' should be understood simply as relationship counselling where the focus is on helping people to get along better – to coordinate their differing stories – and no attempt is made to undertake hypothetical exercises such as restructuring the family organization in order indirectly to influence one person's 'symptom'.

I want to reiterate, however, that I am talking about degrees of difference. I am not wishing to paint constructive therapists and systemic therapies into corners and caricature them. Skilled systemic therapists can and do utilize family system concepts in collaborative and empowering ways. Skilled constructive therapists can and do draw upon systemic concepts in order to re-orient their search for competencies. By highlighting differences, however, we can point to potential difficulties. Taken to extremes, the two groups may err in opposite directions. Systemic therapists may see underlying systemic connections everywhere, while constructive therapists may see them nowhere. If systemic therapists can be accused of over-theorizing family relationships, constructive therapists can be accused of ignoring them.[3]

My aim is not to totally bridge the divide but to invite constructive therapists to expand their repertoire of concepts and skills when approaching family therapy. There is a clear tension between the conceptual richness of systemic family therapy and the minimalist discourse of constructive therapy. How light can we travel before our available concepts are stretched too far? Might it be possible to adapt systemic ideas and use them in 'constructive' ways? Can we attend to both the dancers and the dance? These are questions that we will need to return to (Chapters 8 and 9).

Constructive family therapy: a vision

I would like to conclude this opening chapter by offering a 'vision' of constructive family therapy. These descriptions are part of my own essential luggage and convey the spirit and the aspirations of the approach that I will develop. They constitute what I will later call my 'primary pictures' (Chapter 8). By a vision, I mean a collection of favourite ideas, images, expressions, definitions and quotes that we find personally stimulating and that can help to sustain us in difficult times. They are more important than technical or professional definitions. They are akin to the personal mementos that we take on journeys in order to remind ourselves of who we are, and what is really most important to us.

To arrive at a personal vision for your work, I recommend some of the questions used in the process of 'appreciative inquiry' (Cooperrider and Whitney, 1999) where consultants ask questions such as:

- When you are working at your best and feeling most creative, inspired and committed, how would you describe what you do?
- What description of your work does justice to your finest moments?
- What affirmative view gives life to your work, and helps to sustain you?

A vision of therapy

Whatever the specific issue being discussed, I try to maintain a vision of constructive family therapy as being *the co-operative search for the best in people and their relationships* – a search for the aspirations, qualities, skills and commitments that give 'life' to their existence, sustain hope in the face of adversity, and offer possibilities for desired change. This connects with the emerging professional emphasis on *family resilience*, which involves a search for 'strengths under stress' and looks to the potential for both personal and relational transformation in confronting adversity

(Walsh, 2003). I think of my own contribution as the crafting of *unconditional positive questions* (Cooperrider and Whitney, 1999) asked from a position of affirmative curiosity.

Not all therapy is like this, of course. Sometimes it seems like a struggle with no end, sometimes it feels distinctly un-co-operative, sometimes it becomes mired in problems. But this is how I have come to value and understand the best of my work. And the importance of having a preferred vision of therapy is that it motivates you to find ways of enacting it even in the smallest way in the most unfavourable circumstances.

The heliotropic principle

This idea, also taken from the field of appreciative inquiry, is about as simple as an idea could be. A major insight from this field of organizational consultation has been that, in the same way as plants grow toward the light, 'human systems grow toward what they persistently ask questions about' (Cooperrider and Whitney, 1999: 248). This simple proposition helps me to think about 'human systems' in a positive way and to remain clear about my preferred role when working with families. A central part of the constructive therapist's 'mission' is to invite clients to *look elsewhere*. My role is to persistently ask questions – and encourage others to ask questions – about the desired, the good, the better and the possible.

The principles of parsimony and minimalism

Constructive therapists seek to work in ways that are time-effective, not time-limited. If the work is relatively brief, this is because it is focused and effective, *not* because it is the best we can do in the time available. The challenge for constructive therapists is to work in ways that are *parsimonious*: brief but effective, simple but not simplistic. I like to invoke Friedman's suggestion that the principle of parsimony involves an ethical commitment to work in ways that are:

- least disruptive to clients' lives
- least stigmatizing
- least likely to encourage dependent behaviour, and
- least demoralizing (Friedman, 1997: 35)

This helps to crystallize the importance of studiously avoiding the temptation to label and categorize individuals or families, or to be swept up in the four problematic stories of blame, invalidation, non-accountability and impossibility. This, itself, is a challenge in our psychologically oriented culture where there is a tendency to explain life using 'fancier' concepts than those we use to live it (Efran, Lukens and Lukens, 1990: 183), and where, to adapt a phrase from Marx, 'human deficit vocabularies are the opiates of the masses' (Cooperrider and Whitney, 1999: 254).

Instead, the therapist's aim is to act as a catalyst for change: to facilitate and then get out of the way. This connects with the principle of *minimalism* which suggests that:

> individuals are most skilled at writing their own story and the therapeutic encounter simply seeks to place the pen in their hand. Our belief in minimalism does not imply minimizing the concerns of others. Instead, it continuously asks, 'What is the least or most minimal effort required – in service of protecting the destiny and character of these individuals – that might sponsor change?' (Amundson, Stewart and Valentine, 1993: 120)

These principles encourage us to maintain a *beginner's mind* in the face of the complicated issues and more specialized forms of knowledge that we will inevitably encounter in our travels.

The heroic clients and the disappearing therapist

If I were asked to write a definitive case study that would exemplify the client–therapist relationship in constructive family therapy, I think I would call it 'The Case of the Heroic Clients and the Disappearing Therapist'.

The metaphor of the Heroic Client (Duncan and Miller, 2000) has been developed to invert the traditional emphasis on great therapists and to switch attention to the importance of the client's personal resources in producing therapeutic outcomes. Duncan and Miller cite research on common factors of therapeutic change to argue that client factors (individual qualities, skills and social resources) appear to be the most important in successful therapy, perhaps contributing up to 40 per cent towards positive outcomes. This is *not* an assumption that clients have all the resources they need to solve their problems or that they have unlimited potential for change. It is a recognition that clients are the prime agents or engineers of change, and should be given most of the credit.

The image of the Disappearing Therapist comes from some client feedback given to a solution-focused therapist. A client remarked: 'When you are asking the right questions you disappear – it's only when you are asking irrelevant ones that I notice you!' (George, Iveson and Ratner, 1999: 36). To a constructive therapist, this is an enormous compliment! If my questions are relevant, I am happy to go unnoticed. If I can assist clients to *appear* in new ways in their own lives, I am more than happy to *disappear* from their lives. This doesn't mean that therapists should attempt to hide their personalities and retreat into an anonymous and impersonal role of asking questions. This would greatly detract from the possibilities for the relationship. It is more a question of attitude or outlook. Perhaps we could use another travel analogy. The best tour guides are often the least obtrusive. They don't need a constant repertoire of jokes or stories to sustain your attention, highlight their knowledge or shape your experience. Instead, they are able to find a way to draw you into the experience of what they are showing you and allow you to connect with it in your own way. Like an unobtrusive tour guide, constructive therapists stand beside people and help them to look elsewhere. You act as a conduit to the future, as you personally disappear from view.

Expertise without The Expert

Contrary to some popular impressions, embracing a constructive framework does not require us to renounce all forms of professional expertise. Instead, it encourages therapists to carefully conceptualize and prioritize their use of expertise. Constructive therapists prefer to define their primary expertise as *the crafting of questions that evoke client expertise*. The therapist's expertise complements the expertise of clients. Clients have expertise in the form of unique knowledge about their lives: their experiences, desires, skills and memories. Therapists have expertise in crafting questions that assist people to access this knowledge and put it to use. The therapist's expertise is related to process whereas the client's expertise is related to content. Ideally, these forms of therapist and client expertise interact in a reciprocal way, each stimulating or 'calling forth' the other.

However, there are other forms of expertise that can be used to supplement our primary approach. One consists of the sheer accumulation of the therapist's professional experiences: their own ideas, learnings and hunches gained from working with other clients and talking with other therapists. There are also specialized forms of knowledge about current research findings, potential psycho-educational material and basic information about access to resources, support networks and referrals. Therapists are like walking libraries of other people's voices and experiences, and these can be pulled off the shelf and selectively offered to clients. The key word is 'offered'. These forms of expertise are offered in the nature of a tentative gift rather than a professional pronouncement. Hence, it becomes expertise without The Expert. Constructive therapists are not against expertise *per se*, but against non-reflective, taken-for-granted impositions of expertise. This kind of 'expertosis' often becomes the helping professional's 'default setting', one that we are tempted to fall back on under pressure (Turnell and Edwards, 1999).

A final form of therapist expertise consists of self-awareness – the ability to monitor your 'inner' conversation and reactions, to be sensitive to bias, and to be aware of temptations to intrude, judge, solve the problem, resolve your own anxieties, or shepherd the client in a particular direction. Until recently, this important area of reflective practice has been relatively neglected in the constructive therapy literature (Lipchik, 2002; Rober, 1999). I will return to it again in Chapter 7.

Two sets of skills

Here is my favourite 'nutshell' description of therapeutic skills, taken from the work of James and Melissa Griffith:

> There are two sets of language skills in which expertise is especially needed if a clinician is to conduct therapy productively. The first is skill in *establishing optimal conditions* for the kind of reflection that generates new meaning; the second is skill in *crafting questions* that facilitate therapeutic change. With these skills, a clinician hopes not only for patients and families to find good answers for their current problems, but also that they will learn how to ask fruitful questions that bring answers to future problems without the intervention of a professional. (Griffith and Griffith, 1994: 155, italics added)

When learning constructive therapies, trainees often become preoccupied with the second set of skills and overlook the first. In order to establish optimum conditions for reflection, we need to foster a relationship with clients that encourages an emotional environment of *safe play*, where clients feel safe enough to take risks and play with future possibilities. Only then will they engage with the therapist's techniques. It is salutary to remember that a therapeutic technique does not directly 'do' anything for a person; rather it is *the person who does something with the technique* (Neimeyer, 1995). If we cannot create the optimum conditions for reflection, clients may simply not 'do anything' with our questions, no matter how well they are crafted.

If, however, we can use both sets of skills, we may hope, with the Griffiths, that clients will not only answer, but will also learn to ask, 'fruitful questions' that will bring answers to future problems, without the aid of a professional.

An enduring challenge

I will end this chapter with a question posed by Harlene Anderson that, for me, encapsulates the constructive therapy project:

> How can therapists create the kinds of conversations with their clients that allow both parties to access their creativities and develop possibilities where none seemed to exist before? (cited in Anderson and Levin, 1998: 47)

No matter how and where we travel, this fundamental question provides an enduring challenge. Having assembled some theoretical foundations and a vision for therapy, we can now consider some practical ways of addressing it.

Notes

1. This is a complex area fraught with debate even over basic terms (for example, constructionism, constructivism, postmodernism). For a general introduction, see Gergen (1999). For a specific discussion about issues relating to family therapy, I suggest Rivett and Street (2003).

2. Given the scope and priorities of this book, it is not possible to cover this range of concepts in depth. For an extensive overview, I would recommend a general family therapy text such as Carr (2000), Nichols and Schwartz (2004) or Dallos and Draper (2000). For practical examples of case studies in the different models I would suggest Lawson and Prevatt (1999).

3. Particularly in the briefer approaches to constructive therapy, working with relationships is often confined to a small section of a general book or may be reduced to a topic such as 'working with more than one client' or 'working with multiple clients'. No particular significance is placed on *family* relationships.

2   Hosting Family Members

Good family therapy creates an environment where conversations that should happen at home, but don't, can take place. (Nichols and Schwartz, 2004: 365)

... the first rule of doing therapy briefly is this: To get rapid results, go slow. *Festina lente*: Hasten slowly. (O'Hanlon and Wilk, 1987: 164)

In Chapter 1, I briefly described two key sets of skills: creating optimal conditions for reflection, and crafting therapeutic questions. This chapter examines the first set, which I will call *hosting*. The second set of skills will be divided into two processes called *negotiating* (Chapters 3 and 4) and *evoking* (Chapter 5). These chapters (2–5) set out the most characteristic skills that define our constructive framework. They are the skills you will use most on your travels.

Any form of therapy requires an initial period of relationship building before the 'work phase' commences. This 'getting to know you' phase may include a sequence of activities proceeding through social chit-chat, initial greetings and information giving, to more systematic practices of joining with clients in order to build trust and rapport. At the initial encounter, there is a sense in which it is important for the participants to meet first as people rather than as clients and therapists. A distinguishing feature of constructive therapists is that they are keen to keep it that way – continually to engage people as co-contributors and partners in the therapeutic enterprise, not just at the beginning but for the whole journey. There is a sustained attempt to avoid positioning people in fixed roles as clients and therapists, supplicants and experts. In fact, the most flattering comment a constructive therapist can receive is 'It didn't feel like therapy.' By way of contrast, I once heard a family therapist describe the initial process of joining as being like the anaesthetic before the surgery – a very different metaphor. This chapter examines ways in which therapists working with families can act as therapeutic 'hosts' to foster an environment of safe play and to 'create a space of dialogue and wonder' so that a collective sense of purpose can evolve (Walter and Peller, 2000: 32).

Hastening slowly

In approaching conjoint meetings, constructive therapists may experience a dilemma. On the one hand, they recognize the importance of taking time to engage with family members who have different agendas, priorities and degrees of interest. In order to create a reflective space for inquiry, the 'getting to know you' phase may need to be greatly extended. But, on the other hand, constructive approaches are often identified with change-oriented and time-effective therapy. How can these apparent opposites be reconciled? Does this mean that relationship therapy always takes longer?

Many years ago, at one of the first workshops I ever attended on brief therapy, the presenter made a statement that seemed puzzling and para-doxical, but which I now see as being profound. He said that *brief therapy moves slowly*. What he meant is that brief therapy is not 'quick' therapy. It does not give the impression of being rushed or cluttered – of trying to squeeze in more techniques per minute than any other approach. Indeed, the slower it proceeds, the more effective it is likely to be. It becomes more collaborative as the therapist shows a willingness to adapt to the client's pace and needs, rather than enforcing a scripted agenda. This encourages client motivation and participation so that fewer mistakes are likely to be made, fewer blind alleys and red herrings are likely to be pur-sued, and fewer sessions are likely to be required.

More than anything else, the experience of working conjointly with family members serves to highlight the importance of this adage. One of the most obvious differences between individual and conjoint therapy is that, in the latter, we are 'doing it in public', where everyone can hear what is said about themselves and about others, and has the opportunity to respond. This alone has the potential for greater volatility and unpre-dictability. For therapists coming to family from individual work, it takes considerable practice to be able to attend and respond to the desires and needs of a group of people of different ages, language styles and tem-peraments, and to initiate paths of inquiry which proceed in a direction and at a pace that engages all participants.

Constructive therapists often describe their work as a process of 'collaborative inquiry', but one of the most typical problems encountered by therapists who are new to conjoint work is trying to balance the two con-cepts in this expression. There is often a tendency to focus on the 'inquiry' end of the expression too quickly and too insistently, before a colla-borative environment has been established. We have gone straight to the second set of skills rather than building on the first. Swept along by our own enthusiasm, we may find ourselves pursuing a well-oiled path of inquiry (for example, well-formed goals, scaling questions, or externalizing questions) before clients are ready to 'do anything' with these techniques. If the therapist is the only person in the room who is vitally interested in the questions being asked, the process of inquiry is not collaborative. In relationship therapy, the extra time that is put into fostering optimal conditions for reflection is an important 'investment' in human resources. It is a long-term investment that may facilitate short-term therapy.

The emotional climate of therapy

Increasingly, constructive therapists are preferring to look beyond the teaching of techniques and to describe their orientation as primarily a way of relating with clients and a way of thinking about clients and therapy. Madsen (1999) describes this as a shift from technique to attitude, and emphasizes the importance of our *relational stance* towards our clients. Madsen advocates adopting a relational stance of 'appreciative ally' towards clients and suggests that our concepts and practice should be consistent with this philosophical position. This can have profoundly different effects on the therapeutic relationship from an alternative relational stance such as 'professional expert'. Our relational stance (how we *are* with clients) informs both our conceptual models (how we *think* about clients) and our clinical practice (how we *act* with clients).

Along similar lines it has been suggested that, instead of becoming preoccupied with questioning techniques, we need to pay greater attention to cultivating and monitoring the 'emotional climate' in the room (Lipchik, 2002). In general terms we can think of a conducive emotional climate as one that encourages openness, safety, participation, dialogue and wonder. I have found some similar concepts developed by Griffith and Griffith (1994) to be particularly helpful in conceptualizing how different kinds of relational stance can affect the emotional climate in relationship work. Drawing on some simple ethological principles, they suggest that, in a biological sense, emotions are a *bodily predisposition for action*. They involve the readying of the body's physiological systems for a particular path of action: to do or express something. For example, with fear, the body is predisposed to take flight; with anger, the body prepares to attack; and with shame, the body prepares to hide. These bodily dispositions are associated with shifts in cognition which heighten attention and vigilance towards potential signals of threat. The Griffiths use the term 'emotional postures' to describe the configurations of body and cognitive readiness that help animals and humans anticipate and prepare for action in different situations. In humans, emotional postures appear as interpersonal behaviours.

However, they draw an important distinction between two fundamentally different kinds of emotional postures – those encouraging *mobilization* and those encouraging *tranquillity*. Emotional postures of mobilization relate to contexts of perceived threat and are associated with interpersonal behaviours such as justifying, scorning, shaming, controlling, distancing, protesting and defending – the typical 'fight or flight' scenario (Griffith and Griffith, 1994: 67). By contrast, emotional postures of tranquillity are apparent in contexts where threat is low, attention is more inwardly focused and the body is at rest. These emotional postures are associated with reflective behaviours such as listening, wondering, creating, musing, fantasizing, playing and day-dreaming. Griffith and Griffith make the point that effective work in therapy usually occurs only during emotional postures of tranquility when people are less defensive and more open to receive new information. In relationship therapy this allows people to *respond* to each other rather than simply *react*.

I will simplify these terms by naming them *reactive* and *reflective postures* and have summarized their most relevant features in Box 2.1.

Box 2.1   Reactive and reflective postures

Reactive postures are associated with:

- emotional climate of mobilization
- bodily readiness to protect oneself, to fight or flee
- cognitive readiness to perceive threat, attention focused outwards in an attempt to predict or control
- interpersonal behaviours of justifying, scorning, shaming, controlling, ignoring, distancing, protesting and defending

Reflective postures are associated with:

- emotional climate of tranquillity
- bodily readiness to care for oneself or another
- cognitive readiness to focus inward on oneself or on resonance with others
- interpersonal behaviours of reflecting, listening, wondering, musing, fantasizing, understanding, trusting, affirming, loving

Effective therapy is most likely to occur when both clients and therapists display reflective postures.

The first major task for the constructive therapist, therefore, is to establish and maintain an emotional climate where reflective postures are the norm. This requires the *therapists themselves* to enter the room with reflective postures and to use a relational stance such as appreciative ally to invite reciprocation. Of course, this is an ideal state of affairs that is unlikely to be achieved in a consistent way in any actual conversation. Nevertheless, I find these simple ethological concepts extremely helpful in assisting therapists to monitor both their clients' and their own emotional responsiveness during a meeting, and to become aware of the need to pace the conversation or change direction where necessary. Often, when therapy is stuck or misdirected, the first sign of this is a change in our own emotional postures. For example, we may start to feel impatient or critical and show this in our body language towards clients.

These concepts are also helpful in reminding us of the importance of hastening slowly in conjoint work. In a stressful family situation, the first meeting is likely to see most, if not all, participants, operating initially from reactive postures, predisposed towards fight or flight and primed to react rather than respond. Using solution-focused terminology, (Berg, 1994; De Jong and Berg, 2002; de Shazer, 1988), there may be no 'customer-type' relationships (where clients indicate a willingness to work at change), but either 'complainant-type' relationships (where clients blame others and demand that *they* change), or 'visitor-type' relationships (where clients have been coerced into attending and don't wish to be involved). In such a context, if a process of inquiry is begun too soon, it is likely that people will perceive the actual questions themselves as invitations to display further fight or flight behaviours. For example, a simple question about family members' hopes for the session might elicit responses such as: 'I dunno'; 'Why don't you ask Sue instead, it's her fault'; 'I want Dad to stop persecuting me'; or 'It's not my problem, I don't know why I'm here.' The inquiry process can actually contribute to a mutual exacerbation of these reactive postures. When the relational stance between family members is antagonistic, this emotional climate can quickly spread to affect relationships with the therapist. Therefore it is important that therapists proceed slowly and adopt a relational stance toward *each* family member that encourages reflective postures for the therapeutic relationships in the room.

An imaginary exercise

What kinds of procedures and skills can therapists use to foster a therapeutic context where reflective postures and safe play become the norm? In addressing this question, I would like to suggest another imaginary exercise:

Remember a time in your own childhood, when your family was experiencing some intense conflict or stress. Imagine that, rightly or wrongly, you were considered to be the 'cause' of the problem and that your family found themselves preparing to attend a conjoint therapy session.

Remembering the age you were at the time, and knowing your parents and siblings as you do, how do you think that you would approach the session? If you knew that you were going to be the focus of the session, how would you decide to present and protect yourself? If you knew that your parents were going to talk about your failings, how would you prepare to react? What would be the respective agendas of each family member? Who would most want to be there, and who would least want to be there? If a therapist wanted to encourage a co-operative environment where reflective emotional postures were the norm, what kinds of activities would help? Conversely, what would be the worst mistake a therapist could make in trying to build rapport with your family? How long do you think it would take to create a safe space of inquiry for your family? Could it be achieved in one session, or would it need to develop over time?

This kind of exercise helps to ground abstract principles in personal experience and serves to highlight some of the extra considerations that need to be considered in family therapy sessions.

Beginning before we meet

Our skills in creating a reflective emotional climate are frequently called into action before we actually meet our clients. It is important to remember that our therapeutic conversations begin when the first contact is made and we begin to negotiate realities. For example:

- A mother calls to ask if you will talk to her 12-year-old son who has been diagnosed with Attention Deficit Hyperactivity Disorder. She says, 'There's a lot of stress in the house at the moment and I think this is making things worse for all of us.'
- A general practitioner wishes to refer a family because of a teenage girl's depression. The doctor believes that this is related to her parents' recent decision to have a trial separation.
- A father calls to make an appointment relating to escalating conflict with his two step-children. There are also two younger children in the family. He wants to know exactly what is involved, who to bring to the meeting, and what to do if they refuse to come.
- A woman is keen to undertake couple counselling but her partner steadfastly refuses to attend. In desperation, she asks: 'Is there any point in me coming on my own?'

One way in which relationship therapy differs from individual therapy becomes apparent even at this pre-meeting stage: there is often more discussion and negotiation about the processes and practicalities of therapy. Do we all need to come? Should I come alone the first time, and bring my partner later? What if my son won't come – should the rest of us come anyway? Will we be seen together or one at a time? Do you talk to the children alone? How long will it take, as we have to get home in time for dinner, to go shopping or attend sporting practice? Do you work in the evenings, as we can only come after school or after work or when the babysitter is available?

Whether a therapist deals with such inquiries directly or whether they are delegated to others, it is useful to have some general guidelines in place. In terms of the processes and practicalities of therapy, it is important to inform clients about any practices that they may find threatening or alienating (for example, the use of reflecting teams, one-way screens or video equipment) and to distinguish between what is negotiable and what is not. If some aspects of your practice are not negotiable (you always use reflecting teams, or you always see clients conjointly), it would be helpful to offer callers some alternative referral possibilities. In addition to telephone discussions, it is helpful to post relevant information in the form of letters, brochures and maps.

In terms of discussing the specific content of the case, many family therapists prefer to have minimal, if any, contact with clients or referrers before the first meeting and to start fresh at the meeting. One reason concerns the possibility of establishing an alliance (or even the perception of an alliance) with the referring party, and informally beginning the therapy process before hearing everyone's point of view. Despite your best intentions, it is easy to become caught up in one person's narrative account and their characterizations of the other family members involved. With clients who have had a history of previous referrals there is also the danger of getting caught up in the deficit language of 'file-speak'. Another reason, closely associated with constructive perspectives, relates to the principle that change is ongoing, and that each meeting is potentially a new beginning. Rather than being constrained by an account of the family concerns given several weeks before the meeting, a constructive therapist might prefer to start afresh on the assumption that change could have already occurred, and that the main priority is to focus on where the clients are, and what they are wanting, *now*. In fact, the therapist may take the opportunity to ask 'pre-session change' questions, which specifically explore changes that have taken place since the appointment was made.

However, while remaining alert to the potential hazards of pre-meeting consultations, constructive therapists may be willing to consider potential opportunities, particularly as they are less committed to the necessity of seeing an entire family and may be content to work only with the person who calls. Remembering that callers may be highly ambivalent about the prospect of conjoint meetings, and uninformed about what is involved, it may, in fact, be useful for the therapist to engage them in conversation in order to establish some basis for continuity, to clarify what is involved, and to prepare the ground for a conducive emotional climate. One possible approach is deliberately to channel the conversation away from a focus on content (the actual relationship issues or concerns), and towards practical issues and concerns relating to the meeting itself. It may be helpful to say explicitly to clients that you prefer to wait until the meeting to discuss the details of their situation but would be happy to discuss any questions or concerns they may have about the conduct of the meeting itself and who should attend. Depending on your work context and referral processes, these initial inquiries and negotiations may be handled by a trained recep-tionist who will refer more specialized inquiries to a therapist.

If contact is made with referrers such as doctors, school personnel or particular agencies, it is helpful to think of the referrer as a potential resource person whose contribution may be extremely valuable. They may also be the individuals who are the most concerned and who most want change for the family. While there may be a temptation for referrers to engage in 'file-speak', there is also the potential for new possibilities to emerge as the conversation develops. Building collaborative relationships with referrers is an important part of constructive practice. Depending on the role they play in family members' lives (which may be far more influ-ential than the therapist's), they are often in a position to notice, appreci-ate and encourage change. It is also conceivable that, at some point, they will participate directly in the therapy sessions.

Convening the first meeting

Here I will focus particularly on questions relating to who should attend the first meeting, and how this can be negotiated with potential clients. I will list some general guidelines but also point to dilemmas and suggest possible options. As mentioned in Chapter 1, the decision about who should attend is largely informed by the principle of the 'preference-determined system', which suggests that membership is fluid and involves those who share a particular sense of purpose. This allows us to maintain an emphasis on the ways in which problems and preferences are con-structed in conversation between participants – whoever they may be – and also helps us avoid the energy-depleting situation of working with people (such as siblings or young children) who may not be directly involved in the situation at hand, and who have no wish to participate. For example, consider the situation where a school counsellor suggests family therapy in a relation to a child's truanting. The principle of the preference-determined system may result in a number of possibilities. The therapist may end up working with the whole family, or, if the child refuses to attend, with everyone except him or her. Alternatively, the meeting may consist of one parent and the child, with one or more siblings. Or, it could consist of the school counsellor, some family members and the child, or perhaps include some school friends of the child who are involved in the situation. Conceivably, if no family members are willing to participate, it could involve just the school counsellor and the therapist! The point is that none of these configurations is viewed as more theoretically correct or inherently desirable than any other. Membership is decided by participants on a session-by-session basis, with each conversation seen as a unique event, rather than an incremental contribution to changing a predetermined structure or problem.

The concept of the preference-determined system appears straightforward and many constructive therapists simply choose to work with whoever comes through the door. However, when convening the first meeting, and discussing who should be invited to attend, a number of practical dilemmas can arise. A typical scenario occurs when one person makes an appointment on behalf of others, and often presumes to speak for and about them. One partner phones to make an appointment for both. One parent calls to make a family appointment relating to a particular child's behaviour. Another professional phones to refer a family who they think needs counselling. We are hearing only one voice and one perspective.

In order to pre-empt potential difficulties arising from involuntary, confused or resentful participation, it may be useful to explore some avenues of inquiry with the person requesting the appointment. Has the person discussed the possibility of counselling with the other relevant participants? What was their attitude? Who most wants to come? What are the person's thoughts on who should be invited? For example, if a child is the focus of concerns, would the presence of siblings help ease the pressure or make things worse? What would be the best and safest way to proceed? It is important for clients to know they have a choice. It is not unusual for people to phone for a family appointment because they assume this is obligatory in a family-oriented agency. They are often relieved to know that they can attend alone for the first meeting, and discuss other options later. Conversely, if a parent expects the therapist to see a child alone (as in the previous example where a mother calls in relation to her son's Attention Deficit Hyperactivity Disorder), it can still be useful to suggest a conjoint meeting for at least part of the session. This provides greater scope for discussing any relevant relationship issues, as well as providing a way to ease into any work that is done with the child. Quite often, especially if there are relationship factors exacerbating individual problems, the conjoint work may be the most valuable.

If directly asked by the caller who should attend the first session, one approach is first to offer the general suggestion that anyone who could potentially contribute to helping with the problem is welcome. You can then discuss more specifically with the caller who they think would be most willing to help and who they think needs to be there. The main concern is to avoid implicitly blaming any family member. If it seems clear that the identified client or some other family member will not come voluntarily, and that attempts to coerce attendance may be counterproductive, it may be best to encourage only the caller and other motivated people to come for the first meeting. Such situations are often difficult to resolve. Is it better to see only those who initially wish to come, and miss out on the potentially important contribution of significant others? Or is it preferable to arrange for a reluctant family member to attend, in the hope that if the meeting goes well, that person may become more interested? Also, do we actually know what each person wants to do, if we base this solely on what the caller says? In some cases, the final choice may depend on the individual therapist's preferences and skills. Some therapists might prefer to work with one motivated client rather than face the prospect of a roomful of unwilling participants, whereas others might relish the opportunity to work conjointly, and trust in their ability to conduct the conversation in a way that overcomes initial misgivings.

Therapists may also differ on the advisability of involving children in therapy from the outset. Parents are usually more concerned and motivated, and have more power and influence (though they often feel anything but powerful at the time). Therefore, it is often more productive to work directly with them so that they can change their own behaviour in relation to their children. Many therapists take the view that it is preferable to protect children from the potential stigma of therapy unless the parents are adamant that the problem belongs to a child and wish the therapist to work with the child (Lipchik, 2002). However, if children are not admitted, their voices and viewpoints will go unheeded and unacknowledged and their experience will be filtered entirely through the parents' perceptions. The involvement of the children might yield important new information and experiences for everyone, as well as being beneficial for them as individuals. Wilson (1998) cautions therapists to reflect on their own sense of comfort and confidence when contemplating child-focused work, suggesting that this is often a factor in the decision not to involve children. If this is the case, therapists may be rationalizing their decisions and will never improve their skills, as a self-fulfilling prophecy has been set in motion.

If uncertainties remain, a useful compromise may be to suggest that the whole family attend the first meeting in order for the therapist to gather as many views and ideas as possible. Then we can negotiate who, if anyone, will come to any future meetings. This allows ambivalent members to attend at least once, without feeling pressured to commit to ongoing sessions. In convening such a meeting, it is important to convey the message that no one is being blamed for the presenting concern. We can implicitly (and sometimes explicitly) make it clear that while no one is being blamed for the problem, we think that everyone can potentially contribute to the solution. Everyone has a unique perspective that deserves to be heard, and each person's contribution is a valuable resource. In this sense, and at least for the first meeting, it is a case of the more the merrier.

If the person making contact decides to ask other family members to attend, it can be useful to spend a few minutes discussing ways of inviting them. This can be a difficult task for many clients and sometimes results in unhelpful interactions and unintended negative consequences. Typical examples include: making the appointment first and informing others later ('I've made an appointment with a marriage counsellor and we're going tomorrow'); failing to clarify what the appointment is about ('We're going to see a man who's going to talk to you'); threatening people ('If you don't come to counselling …'); implying that family members are at fault ('The counsellor said he wants to see you all because you're all part of the problem!'); and telling people at the last moment or not telling them at all (a colleague once told me of a situation where parents told their children they were going to McDonalds, and took them to counselling instead!). In the example mentioned earlier, where the father wanted to know whether to bring only his step-children or the younger children too, part of the discussion might turn on the question of how the children will be told about the meeting. Who has been consulted so far? Does his wife agree that counselling could be helpful? Who does she think should attend? Should the two parents agree on a plan for talking to the children about counselling so that it comes from both parents rather than only the step-parent?

These preliminary conversations, whether conducted by the therapist or other contact personnel, can help to smooth the way for a fruitful and productive first meeting. They help to avoid misunderstandings, inform clients about processes and options, and increase the likelihood that those who attend the first meeting can approach the occasion with minimal anxiety and some degree of interest, information and motivation.

The therapeutic 'host'

The metaphor of 'hosting' therapeutic conversations was originally developed by Furman and Ahola (1992) who offered the image of the therapist as a talk-show host, with clients featured as guests. I like to extend the metaphor of hosting to include the ways in which a good dinner party or social host behaves. Good hosts find ways to greet each guest as though they are special. They find ways to set people from different backgrounds at ease, and to facilitate conversations with other guests. They work hard to establish a certain kind of mood, perhaps through a combination of theme, environment and music. They work hard to anticipate and pre-empt foreseeable difficulties and keep an active eye and ear on the emotional temperature of the evening. They do not take centre stage, but work unobtrusively to create and maintain an environment where guests can feel free to enjoy themselves. At times they might intervene discreetly to steer the conversation in particular directions in order to avoid embarrassing or antagonizing their guests.

As might be expected, the daily practice of relationship therapy isn't quite like this – though some therapists have been known to offer coffee or popcorn in their waiting rooms, and to hold parties with families in order to celebrate change. However, the metaphor of hosting offers a useful way of thinking about the process of encouraging a reflective emotional climate, especially when considering the priorities of a first meeting.

Varieties of problem-free talk

To outline the process of hosting the initial meeting with a family, I have expanded the concept of 'problem-free talk' (typically used by solution-focused therapists) to include a number of specific activities. A defining feature of problem-free talk is that it occurs in the 'getting to know you' phase and before the 'getting down to business' phase of the meeting. It includes simple socializing and information-giving, but may move beyond these to forms of conversation which actively search for client resourcefulness. The aim is to invite participants into forms of conversation that, at the very least, help them to feel welcomed, informed and included, and, if possible, may help to encourage a more positive and appreciative perception of themselves and each other. Problem-free talk can also alert the therapist to areas of client resourcefulness that might be called upon at a later point in the conversation.

A degree of problem-free talk might be seen as a useful activity in any therapeutic approach. It might be seen as a way of setting people at ease, rather like the small talk that often occurs at the beginning of a formal meeting. There is also a degree of preliminary information-giving that seems relevant in all approaches. This might involve information about intake procedures, the process of the meeting, confidentiality, access to records, and so on. However, constructive therapists are more likely to examine the potential for problem-free talk to be therapeutic in itself, and to embody the change principles that inform their whole approach. It is a way of asking, 'Who are you outside of your problems?' It provides a way of getting to know people before problems, and also allows family members to experience the therapist first as a person rather than a professional (George, Iveson and Ratner).[1] In an approach that seeks to value and call forth the personal knowledge and abilities of all participants, this is a preferred way of positioning ourselves in relation to our 'guests'.

When used appropriately, problem-free talk has the potential to build a *context of competence* from the beginning. This can provide a balance to any subsequent focus on deficits, and can help the conversation to withstand some of the challenges it may face later. Problem-free talk is, in a sense, a preview of things to come, and remains consistent with the conversational tone and style of the entire meeting. It is not used simply to induce compliance in order to prepare clients for the difficult work ahead. It is not the anaesthetic before the surgery!

In negotiating a phase of problem-free talk with clients, it might be useful to say something like: 'Before we start to talk about the reasons you have come here, I'd like to take some time to get to know you, and for you to get to know me. It can be a bit off-putting coming to a place like this, and I'd like to ease our way into it. Is that okay?' Depending on your methods of working and any time constraints, it can also be useful to indicate a specific time-frame for this phase (for example five or ten minutes, or longer) so that clients know how long it will take, and will not become unduly impatient to move into the next phase.

Here are some varieties of problem-free talk that can be helpful in the hosting process.

Purpose of the meeting

It is often reassuring to present the first meeting as an opportunity for family members to work out if they need to see us and if they want to work with us. It is a chance for people to decide what they would like to talk about, and to get to know the therapists and their ways of working. No obligations are assumed and no sudden decisions will be made. This way of framing the meeting suggests that families do not come with a clear-cut 'need' for therapy, but with the *idea* that therapy might be helpful. The meeting will help them decide if this idea is insightful or, perhaps, misplaced.

Information and clarification

Sometimes, families are simply given referrals or appointments and may know little about your actual agency or your profession (for example the distinction between doctors, psychiatrists, psychologists and counsellors; or about aspects of confidentiality and liaison with other agencies or institutions). Or it may be the case that not all family members have been informed about the nature of the agency and its work. Therefore it can be helpful to allay anxiety and provide clarity by giving basic information about the work of your agency and your own professional background. Clients can then be invited to ask any questions they may have.

The process of the meeting

It is helpful for clients to know how you intend the meeting to proceed, and to have the opportunity to ask questions about this. Sometimes people are unclear about whether they will be seen together and/or separately or about what the therapist will actually do. An important factor with children often concerns the time that will be involved, so specifying a clear time limit can be reassuring. I usually tell people that my job is not to take sides or decide who is right or wrong, but mainly to ask questions in the hope that this will help them work out the answers that will be most helpful to them. If you are using a process that may seem unusual (calling in a reflecting team or taking a break in order to gather your thoughts) these processes should be explained in advance and a rationale given. Hopefully, such information will have been conveyed when the appointment was made and confirmed, but it may not have been fully understood or communicated to all family members.

In situations where some family members seem unclear about why they have been asked to attend, and appear concerned or resentful, it can be helpful to convey explicitly your view of relationship therapy: that you believe no one is to blame for the problem that has brought them, but that everyone might be able to contribute to the solution. Therefore, you are grateful that everyone has agreed to attend this session in order to act as a resource person, and that any further attendance will be welcome, but can be negotiated at the end of the session.

Previous experiences of therapy

It can be useful to ask people if they have had previous experiences of therapy and what they liked and didn't like about these. This will help to clarify family members' expectations for the meeting and to distinguish your approach from others they may have experienced. For example, based on previous experiences, clients might expect to be involved in anything from family sculpting to psychodrama, so clarification is important. If they have had unhelpful experiences with professionals you can seek to reassure them that you will avoid repeating what was not helpful. Conversely, you can undertake to build on what they may have found helpful from other therapists.

Contexts of competence

This is a more extensive and ambitious use of problem-free talk, and involves inviting clients to share aspects of their lives that are functional, successful and enjoyable. We are curious about people's interests, skills and passions, and invite an appreciation of these. As well as contributing to a context of competence, these areas of inquiry may yield conversational resources that may be useful at a later point in our work. Knowledge of competence or interest in areas relating to work, sport, the arts and various hobbies, may provide the opportunity to 'import' metaphors or skills from these areas into the problem context (Lamarre and Gregoire, 1999). It is useful for therapists to note these areas carefully for future reference as, once the conversation shifts to problem-saturated stories, narratives of competence can tend to become swamped. We are, in effect, asking: 'What creative and enjoyable parts of your lives are being obscured by the present situation? In what ways are you more than the sum of your problems?'

The gathering of information about contexts of competence can be informal or structured. One structured way to accomplish this process is through the use of a *resource-oriented genogram*. The tracing of a genogram is one of the most characteristic practices in family therapy. It can be useful as an ice-breaking activity, a way of joining with clients, or as a more formal tool for assessment and intervention. However, as with most assessment tools, the conventional emphasis has been on problems and pathology, with therapists attuned to concepts such as intergenerational patterns and family traditions. For many therapists, genograms are *the* definitive family therapy tool and form an essential part of joining, assessing and helping any family (McGoldrick, Gerson and Shellenberger, 1999). Whole sessions can be devoted to the activity, which can extend over a number of generations. Constructive therapists, however, generally tend to use genograms in a more circumscribed way as a collaborative activity that engages people and records competency-based information about individuals and their perceptions of each other. I tend to use a simple scheme that covers only the number of generations required to include the participants in the meeting. If I am working with parents and children, I will include two generations; if I am working with grandparents, parents and children, I will include three generations.

The gathering of resource-oriented information using a genogram can be conducted in a number of ways. It can be brought out in conventional conversation with the therapist who makes notes or writes on large sheets of paper. Or the therapist can stand at a white board filling out a genogram. Another possibility is to ask one or more family members to stand at the whiteboard and write in the details as they emerge. This is often an interesting way to involve the younger members of the family.

The therapist can gather resource-oriented information about a number of areas:

- Paid or unpaid work: What does a person like most about their work? How did they get into this area? What are they especially good at? Do they see a long career ahead of them? What would colleagues say is the most impressive part of their performance?
- Hobbies, interests, skills outside of work: If I was to drop in on the weekend, what would I find them doing? What sports, crafts, hobbies, etc. do they particularly like? What is it about these that they are particularly drawn to?

- For children at school: What do they like most about their studies? What are they most enthused about? What are they good at? What would teachers or friends say is the most impressive or likeable thing about them? Do they have a sense of what they would like to do when leaving school?
- Contribution to family relationships: What does each person contribute to family or relationship life (for example, humour, practical skills, being a good listener, etc.)?
- Who or what else is important to the family (for example, relatives, friends, going to church, going on picnics together, etc.)?

Usually, a therapist will simply talk to each person in turn. Sometimes, however, it can be useful to ask family members to talk about the resources of another. For example, rather than directly asking a mother to talk about herself, we can ask a teenage son what his mother is good at, what she likes to do in her spare time, and what particular contribution she makes to the family. We could then ask other family members to add to this description. Or we could use a combination of both: asking a person to talk about themselves and then asking others if they would like to add anything. Rober (1998) suggests that when a child is the focus of therapy, it is important to engage both the child and the parents in a positive story about the child (for example, a good-humoured account of something the child has done, is good at or loves to do). Also, by asking parents to comment on a child's competencies we help to position them as experts on their children. Asking family members to comment on each other's resourcefulness has the potential to build a collaborative context of competency, though it also has a potential downside in that people might engage in negative comments. The choice to invite others to comment is usually based on the therapist's reading of the emotional climate at the time, and his or her judgement about the likely consequences.

An example: the Edwards family

The Edwards family consists of Kevin, aged 41, his wife Sandra, aged 38, and their two children, Jessica, aged 15 and Daniel, aged 12. They have made an appointment at the suggestion of the counsellor at Daniel's school. According to the referral information, Daniel has been getting into fights in the playground, and the counsellor suspects that this is related to conflict at home. When Sandra called to discuss an appointment, she agreed that the whole family was under stress, Kevin having been made redundant. Kevin was reacting very badly to this, showing increasing impatience with the children, and placing extra pressure on Sandra who worked part-time, but was, at least for now, the main breadwinner. Her

Figure 2.1   Resource-oriented genogram for the Edwards family

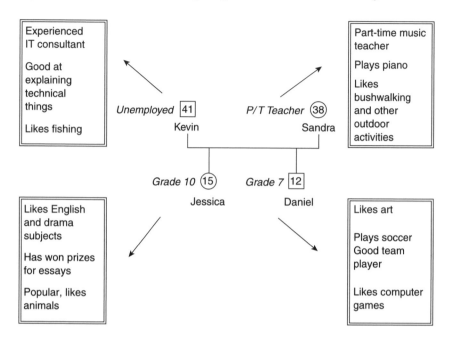

Experienced IT consultant

Good at explaining technical things

Likes fishing

Unemployed 41
Kevin

P/T Teacher (38)
Sandra

Part-time music teacher

Plays piano

Likes bushwalking and other outdoor activities

Grade 10 (15)
Jessica

Grade 7 12
Daniel

Likes English and drama subjects

Has won prizes for essays

Popular, likes animals

Likes art

Plays soccer
Good team player

Likes computer games

health was being adversely affected. Though Sandra knew Kevin would be reluctant to come, she thought it would be best if the whole family attended the first meeting. After some discussion with the therapist, this was agreed.

Figure 2.1 shows an example of a concise resource-oriented genogram that might be developed through conversation with these family members.

In gathering this informal inventory, the therapist's curiosity might be particularly drawn to examples which seem to contradict the story that has been told so far. The fact that Daniel is known to be a good team player in soccer suggests he may have skills in co-operation, and in avoiding the kinds of conflict that has resulted in the referral. Kevin has apparently been displaying impatience with the children, yet who would know more about patience than a keen fisherman? In the process of 'mining' for family resources, these are potential gems. How, when and whether the therapist seeks to utilize them will depend on factors such as client responsiveness to the problem-free talk and the degree of prior knowledge possessed by the therapist. In this case, where aspects of the presenting situation are already known, the therapist might attempt, even at this early stage, to engage Daniel in a discussion about how he has earned the respect of his team in soccer, and how he avoids the temptation to be provoked into fights on the field. The therapist might also be curious about Kevin's interest in fishing, particularly in relation to how he remains quiet and focused for long periods of time. In other situations, where little, if anything, is known at this stage about the reason for the referral, the therapist would take a more general interest in these potential areas, but note them carefully for future reference.

This kind of competency-based exercise often initiates a typical pattern of conversation that is common in constructive therapies, and will be emphasized in the formal 'work' phase of the meeting. When asking about client competencies, the therapist will often encounter negative comments or criticisms of one person by another. The therapist will seek to acknowledge these perspectives (verbally and non-verbally), but not encourage or develop them. Instead, the intent will be to change tack slightly in order to maintain an emphasis on highlighting potential resources. In conjoint work, gentle persistence, often linked with humour or other ways of lightening and shifting the tone, are important conversational tools. For example:

Therapist: I'm keen to find out about some of the interests and hobbies you have, and the things you like to do in your spare time. If I dropped around on the weekend, what would I find you all doing?

Sandra: These days you'd probably find Kevin moping around the house in a foul mood trying to find someone to pick a fight with ... and Daniel trying to stay out of his way by roaming around the streets, while Jessica copes by staying in her room and chatting on the Internet, and I try to avoid having a nervous breakdown.

Therapist: That sounds pretty dreadful for everyone. I don't think I'd want to visit on a weekend like that! What if I came around on a happier weekend, when things were going better for the family, and more the way you'd *really like* them to be? What would I find you all doing then?

How long should this process take? I might spend ten to fifteen minutes on the various kinds of problem-free talk. On the other hand, I have met therapists who routinely spend forty-five minutes on problem-free talk with family members. This can be particularly important in building rapport with children (such as Daniel) who are the identified focus of a family consultation. It is likely that once the work phase of the meeting begins, the children will be 'talked about' by parents rather than talking for themselves. What parents say about children tends to set parameters for what the children feel able to say about themselves. To enable children to develop a voice before their problems become the focus of the meeting, a therapist can deliberately choose to begin a phase of problem-free talk by addressing the children first. In this example, the therapist might choose to speak to Daniel first when gathering the genogram information. This could allow him to have a positive and perhaps novel experience of speaking about his strengths before his parents attempt to shift the conversational goalposts. If younger children, especially, are not engaged early in the process, they may 'switch off' for the entire session. As Rober (1998) has suggested, creating a safe therapeutic culture for children is a neglected area in family therapy training, often requiring careful preparation of the physical environment and specific skills and strategies in the session itself. Aspects of a child-friendly environment might include having small chairs and tables where a child can write or draw pictures, and having a selection of puppets and other age-appropriate toys on display (de Jong and Berg, 2002). The use of competency-based talk is one contribution to creating a safe therapeutic culture. However, it does not have to be literally all talk or even occur in an office. For example, therapists working with children or adolescents often find it helpful to invite their clients to go for a walk in a park or around the block.

Staying responsive and flexible

In the hosting of conjoint meetings, the use of problem-free talk poses some dilemmas. Because this first phase of the meeting appears relatively structured and predictable, it can easily slip into a set routine which is never varied. However, as good hosts, we must continually monitor our guests' responsiveness for signs of irritation, confusion or boredom. While *we* can think of good theoretical reasons why clients should benefit from extensive stretches of problem-free talk, they may not. Clients may be so beset by their difficulties that they want nothing more than to cut quickly to the chase and get down to business; or they may be so hostile toward each other that any attempt at talking about resourcefulness is doomed to backfire. Or, despite our best intentions, they may experience our efforts as annoying, irrelevant or patronizing. Problem-free talk is based on our assumption about what is needed to get things off to a good start. However, if it is imposed in a set way as a technique, it risks undermining some other basic principles of constructive therapies – that the conversation should be collaborative, and that its direction should be shaped by clients' goals. As we have not yet asked clients about their hopes of goals, how can we be sure that problem-free talk really fits with what they are wanting? And if we plough on regardless, we cease to be collaborative. Ironically, we may end up inviting the very emotional postures of fight or flight that the exercise has been designed to avoid.

It is important to remember that the main priority of problem-free talk at this early stage is to contribute to the process of hosting and to the establishment of an emotional climate that will encourage safe play and reflection. Anything else is a bonus. We may need to adapt, abbreviate or totally abandon the process if necessary. In many cases, the actual working conditions of individual therapists will determine what forms and duration of problem-free talk are feasible. For example, unless you have unlimited time and remarkably patient clients, it may be practically impossible to cover everything that has been mentioned above – and still leave enough time to address people's hopes and concerns adequately. For this reason, many relationship therapists make a practice of scheduling a longer time for first meetings than for subsequent meetings (for example, ninety minutes instead of an hour). This again, however, has to be flexibly adapted to working conditions and client responsiveness, especially where younger children are involved. Where children appear distracted or stressed, de Jong and Berg (2002) suggest that a good rule of thumb is 'the shorter the better'.

It is also important to remember that there will be many more opportunities to explore contexts of competence systematically. For example, some therapists like to spend the *last* few minutes of a meeting talking about non-problematic things such as plans for the weekend and other 'extra-therapeutic' activities. This can be a useful way of lowering the temperature of a meeting prior to ending, as well as bringing out potentially useful information about client resources. These themes may also be developed at the beginning of a second meeting when the therapist catches up with what clients have been doing between meetings and may take the opportunity to inquire about non-problematic areas of life. If the first meeting has proved helpful to clients, they may be more willing to participate in these forms of talk at the second, as a more optimistic outlook has been achieved.

When attempting to use problem-free talk, therefore, it is important to remember our priorities and to remain responsive and flexible. If people seem restive or merely going through the motions as they answer questions, or if they turn the question into an opportunity to move into problem talk, it may be necessary either to explain why you are wanting to pursue this process or to cut it short and shift into the next phase of the meeting. Sometimes, in seeking permission to continue with problem-free talk, it may be useful to say something like this:

> The reason I'd like to talk about these positive things before we focus on your concerns is that if we start immediately on why you are here, we often only see one side of people. People usually don't come here to talk about their positive qualities, and therapists only get a picture of negatives. This is very unfair to you. I'm sure that there's much more to you than your problems and I'd like to bring this out before we focus on why you are here. It helps to provide a balance and sometimes it can give us a clue about what kinds of resources the family can draw upon.

Hosting as an ongoing priority

This chapter has emphasized the importance that constructive therapists place on what the Griffiths have described as the first key set of therapeutic skills: establishing optimal conditions for reflection. This involves creating a safe therapeutic space for inquiry, where reflective emotional postures are the norm. In conjoint work, it is especially important to remember the adage that brief therapy moves slowly, and to resist the temptation to pursue therapist-driven paths of inquiry before establishing at least the foundations of a collaborative relational environment. The metaphor of hosting can be used to group together some practical ideas which therapists have found helpful in convening and beginning a first meeting. In particular, I have described various forms of problem-free talk, and discussed some of the options and dilemmas involved in using them.

An interesting way to conclude the chapter is to return to the exercise introduced earlier. Imagine yourself attending a first therapy meeting as a child in your own family of origin. As you reflect upon the key ideas of this chapter, imagine a therapist attempting to use them with your family. Ask yourself how the different forms of problem-free talk might need to be adapted in order to have the desired effect. It has been said that clients teach therapists how to help them. This being so, what would your family members teach a therapist about how (and how not to) host them? If you feel that few, if any, of the practical suggestions in the chapter would be effective with your family, can you think of alternative methods that might achieve the same end?

In our constructive framework, hosting is an ongoing priority rather than an activity that is completed at the beginning of a meeting. It is a foundational process upon which the other major skills are built and on which they often depend. While there may be more structured forms of hosting near the beginning, we need to remind ourselves that the hosting role doesn't end when the first course is served. The emotional climate cannot be assumed to remain stable. Therefore, the therapist's role is not merely to create a safe space for inquiry but to monitor and maintain it throughout the subsequent conversation. The craft of constructive inquiry requires a delicate balance between the two sets of skills: hosting the conversation and crafting questions that facilitate change. In this chapter, the emphasis has necessarily been on the first set of skills. In the next chapter, where the meeting 'gets down to business' and turns to the question of specific client concerns and requests, we need to shift emphasis but maintain the balance: to act as constructive therapists while remaining effective hosts.

Note

1. Solution-Focused Brief Therapy Course Notes, compiled by Evan George, Chris Iveson and Harvey Ratner of the Brief Therapy Practice in London (7–8 Newbury Street, London, EC1A 7HU). These were presented to participants at a two-day course I attended in 2000.

3 Negotiating Concerns and Requests

> So, instead of asking, *'How do we know what is real about the client?'* we have decided the more relevant question is, *'What do our clients want and what new ways of speaking or conversing might help?'* (Walter and Peller, 2000: 32)

It is now time to enlist the second major set of skills: the crafting of therapeutic questions. As mentioned previously I have divided this set of skills into two processes called *negotiating* and *evoking*. In this chapter and the next I focus on the process of negotiating a sense of purpose and direction in conjoint meetings. It is important to acknowledge that though these groups of skills are presented in a 'logical' order – hosting, negotiating and evoking – in actual practice they are typically intertwined in less predictable ways.

Perhaps nothing distinguishes the constructive orientation so clearly as the proposition that family members' concerns do not relate to objectively existing conditions or afflictions, but are representations that are continually *negotiated* through conversation. Rather than assessing presenting problems in an objective sense, the constructive therapist attempts to negotiate descriptions of family members' concerns and requests that acknowledge the difficulties being experienced but maintain an emphasis on possibilities for change. The very choice of the term 'concerns and requests', as opposed to 'problems', 'conditions', 'afflictions', or 'treatment needs' embodies an active preference for a certain way of talking. The constructive agenda is to introduce ways of talking that are both more generous (in the sense of avoiding negative attributions) and more generative (in the sense of evoking possibilities and resourcefulness). As Walter and Peller (2000) put it, the key questions that guide inquiry are not based on attempts to find out what is 'real' about our clients and their relationships, but are focused instead on their *desire for change*: what do our clients want, and what new ways of speaking or conversing might help? This is the underlying theme in the negotiation of concerns and requests. The skills of inquiry that we use do not fall neatly into the category of objective assessment tools but are intended to be 'therapeutic' in themselves as they actively shape the horizon of possibilities.

Hazards and opportunities revisited

In Chapter 1, I posed the question: how can constructive therapists work to minimize the hazards and maximize the opportunities of conjoint relationship therapy? In order to combine the two sets of skills – to encourage reflective postures while simultaneously inquiring into difficult and contested areas – how should therapists position themselves in relation to the multiple realities that confront them? For many, like myself, who trained first in individual therapy and then had to learn to work with couples and families, the initial experience was daunting. There was a sense of confusion about how long to talk to each person, where to direct the focus, and how to keep track of everything that was going on. At the same time, I longed to be able to get to know each family member in depth. When working with families, therapists not only have to address the ongoing dilemma of what to talk about and how, but also the dilemmas of who to talk to, who to talk about, how, and for how long.

In Chapter 2, I mentioned that one of the hazards relates to the prevalence of complainant-type and visitor-type relationships at the beginning of family therapy. In complainant-type relationships, while clients may identify an area of concern, they tend to believe that others are at fault and should change. In visitor-type relationships, clients either cannot identify an area of concern (for example, children who are confused about the purpose of the meeting) or they have been coerced into attending and may be resentful about this and unclear about what to expect. The practical upshot is that, in a first meeting with a family, there are frequently no *customer-type relationships* anywhere in sight. For example, mother and father complain about their teenage son's behaviour, and about each other's role in making it worse. The teenager in question complains about the ways in which he is being unfairly picked on by his parents. Meanwhile, his younger brother and sister are becoming restive, having no idea why they have been asked to come, and what the meeting is about.

In these circumstances, a meeting can very easily turn into what Méndez, Coddou and Maturana have memorably called a conversation for 'characterisations, accusations and recriminations' (1988: 167). Hudson and O'Hanlon (1991) have used the metaphor of 'bad trance' inductions to describe the ways in which couples systematically provoke and react to each other through habitual patterns of negative interaction. In therapy sessions this can have a 'hypnotic' effect on both clients and therapists. In conjoint work an attempt must be made to stay out of trance by interrupting or preferably pre-empting these conversational routines before they take hold. If not, the emotional climate could become so reactive that the therapist might have to relinquish a preference for partnership and more actively manage the conversation. I remember a brief therapist once saying that family work can be like manoeuvring your way through a minefield – you might spend a lot of time, carefully wending your way, only to trip on the very last mine. The point he was making is that family therapists need to be constantly alert to the changing emotional climate in the room. Something can 'blow up' in the last five minutes of a meeting, and become the abiding memory of the whole session, cancelling out much of the good work that was previously done.

Choosing a pattern of engagement

One important consideration is carefully to choose a pattern of engagement with family members that is best suited to the emotional climate in the room. If you observe a number of different relationship therapists at work, you will see a variety of interactional patterns between therapists and clients. Some therapists prefer to shift the conversation quite rapidly around the room, moving the focus from person to person, without spending a lot of time with any individual. Others prefer to spend a considerable amount of time talking to each individual in turn, and only occasionally addressing the clients as a group. Some therapists actively encourage interaction between family members and may invite individuals to comment on other people's responses, or even ask family members to engage in a discussion about their situation while the therapist sits back and observes. These different styles may be linked to some key principles of the therapist's orientation, or may be a personal preference. In attempting to articulate the micro-practices of constructive relationship therapy, I have found it helpful to identify three simple patterns of therapist-client engagement, and to examine the ways in which they can be most effectively used. These are described in Box 3.1.

Box 3.1   Three patterns of engagement

- **Individual engagement**: The therapist develops an extended conversation with one person at a time, while others listen. For example, therapist talks to A, while B, C and D listen.
- **Collective engagement**: The therapist addresses questions and comments to dyads or family groupings, rather than to individuals. For example, therapist addresses A and B, or A, B, C and D collectively.
- **Reciprocal engagement**: The therapist invites one or more listeners to comment on what they have just heard others say. For example, therapist invites B to reflect on what A has just said.

The **individual engagement** pattern is helpful in situations where there is an environment of reactive emotional postures and a tendency to engage in characterizations, accusations and recrimination. An obvious example is a first meeting where people may be competing to put their point of view to the therapist. In such situations, where differing views on what is important and who is responsible are evident, attempts at focusing on relationships or inviting comments from others can be counterproductive. On the other hand, if the therapist can develop an individual engagement pattern with each person (which might occur over a number of conversational turns), there is an opportunity to foster more reflective emotional postures as the ensuing conversation has the opportunity to offer a new experience for both speakers *and* listeners. In a sense, this pattern invites listeners to take up informally the 'reflecting position' associated with reflecting team practice. It invites people to have a different experience of listening.

The **collective engagement** pattern is helpful when attempting to establish a relationship focus for the session, to shift attention away from individual agendas, or to encourage a sense of mutuality. It is also helpful when attempting to highlight shared experiences, competencies or hopes ('You seem to be a family who really values expression of personal opinions. Where did this quality come from?'; or 'When these changes occur, who will be the first to notice?'). When engaging in this pattern the therapist typically looks from one person to another while asking a question, encouraging anyone or everyone to reply. The collective engagement pattern is an important complement to the individual engagement pattern.

The **reciprocal engagement** pattern is particularly helpful in the co-construction of appreciation, competence and change, where members of the listening audience can contribute their observations of important developments. For example, in an individual engagement with Person A, the therapist might have uncovered an episode which appears to defy the usual problem pattern. After discussing this with Person A, the therapist might then turn to Person B (and others in the room) and ask if they were aware that this episode had occurred, and what it might mean. This pattern may also be helpful if Person A finds it difficult to identify or articulate any positive developments. The therapist might ask Person A's permission to inquire of others in the room, and then ask Persons B, C and D if they have noticed any differences in Person A's behaviour. In using the reciprocal engagement pattern, it is helpful if the hosting process has succeeded to a point where reflective emotional postures are in evidence. Otherwise, it can result in Person B attempting to undermine rather than affirm Person A. It is *not* used simply to give Person B the right of reply. If Person A is engaging in accusations or recriminations against Person B, it is usually more helpful to use the individual engagement pattern with Person A, and to influence the tenor of *that* conversation while Person B listens.

Each of these patterns of engagement will be helpful at different times. My own rule of thumb is that when reactive postures are the norm (for example, in the early negotiation of concerns and requests), it is usually better to spend most time in the individual engagement pattern, and to switch to the other patterns when a suitable opportunity presents itself. While there can be no hard and fast rules, and allowing for personal preferences, I find that constructive family therapy often lends itself to a pattern of extended interaction with individuals rather than passing the conversational torch from person to person every few moments in the interests of systemic engagement or perceived evenhandedness. With practice, relationship therapists can learn to remain engaged with both speakers and listeners: *directly* engaging with the speaker, while *indirectly* engaging with the audience of listeners. You may engage with some family members primarily as speakers, while engaging with other family members primarily as listeners. For example, with a teenage client who doesn't want to be there, attempts at direct engagement may be counterproductive, especially if the therapist begins to try too hard. It may be much more helpful to spend time talking to a parent or sibling *about* the teenager while the young person listens (and hopefully hears something different). An important lesson for newcomers to relationship therapy is that perceptions of neutrality or evenhandedness are not synonymous with giving people equal time to speak. A therapeutic relationship with Person B can be indirectly maintained (or even enhanced) through the therapist's conversation with Person A – depending on the content of the conversation.

Multiple engagement

One way to mitigate existing relationship tensions between family members is for therapists to focus their attention on another set of relationships: that between *themselves* and each person in the room. As I have suggested, this can often be achieved through a pattern of engagement in which the therapist develops separate but public conversations with each individual. For the therapist, multiple-engagement means 'striving for a simultaneous "I–Thou" encounter with each of the contrasting perspectives that make up the conversation into which she has been invited' (Real, 1990: 270). Multiply-engaged therapists may talk at length with different individuals but are always respectfully engaged with the multiple realities in the room and the changing patterns of relationships that occur. In talking with each family member, therapists are careful to use language that will support their relationship not only with that individual but with each listener. As Real suggests, the therapist engages other system members 'collaterally'. This is depicted in Figure 3.1.

Figure 3.1 Multiple engagement with family members

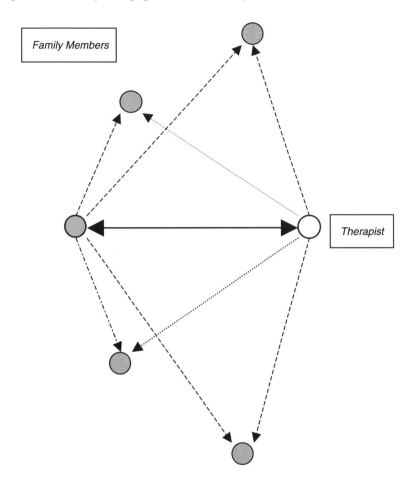

Here we see a typical example of a therapist engaged in conversation with one particular family member (as shown by the thick, black two-way arrow). However, the therapist remains multiply engaged in the sense of remaining attuned to the effects of the conversation on the matrix of contrasting individual perspectives and agendas in the room. These forms of indirect communication emanating from the two speakers are represented by broken lines and one-way arrows. The therapist is conscious of maintaining a simultaneous 'I–thou' encounter with each other person and their reality, and is also mindful of the changing relationships between people as the conversation develops.

This position is characteristic of contemporary forms of family therapy (sometimes called second-order approaches) where the therapist is included in the preference-determined system, and the emphasis is on the

Figure 3.2   Family system engagement

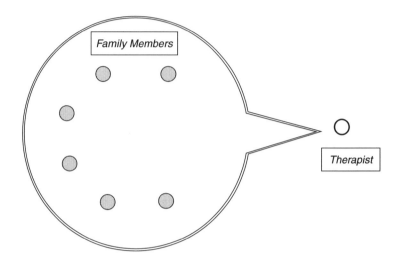

evolution of meaning rather than on specific interventions (Real, 1990). This contrasts with earlier forms (first-order approaches) where the thera- pist was positioned outside the family system as an objective observer who decodes interactions and acts upon the system (Dallos and Draper, 2000), as depicted in Figure 3.2.

Here, the therapist engages with the family as an entity (a family system), and is concerned with relating individual concerns and requests to underlying systemic concepts (for example, recurring interactional patterns or organizational structures). Engaging with individual realities is seen as a means of gaining access to a broader systemic reality.

In practice these two therapist positions are not mutually exclusive, and the therapist may sometimes shift from one to the other (as described in Chapters 8 and 9). However, constructive therapists prefer to position themselves in the preference-determined system, maintaining a stance of multiple engagement with all perspectives.

Finally, by attempting to remain multiply engaged the therapist increases the likelihood of achieving a position of *multipartiality* (Anderson, 1997) in which the therapist takes *all* sides simultaneously. When this is achieved, each person feels that their concerns, hopes and goals are as valid and important as every other person's, and that he or she, along with everyone else, is being supported by the therapist. Like Anderson, I prefer this con- cept to the more negative term 'neutrality' in which the therapist strives to be non-committal and avoid being seen to take anyone's side. It is prefer- able to take everyone's side than no one's side.

Negotiation or assessment?

As their orientation is based on the social negotiation of realities – on making rather than finding – constructive therapists remain distinctly ambivalent about the relevance of 'assessment' to their work. However, rather than eschewing the term or taking an extreme position (constructive therapists *never* assess!), I find it more helpful to draw some distinctions that might help us to clarify our priorities and to engage more productively with colleagues who use the term differently. What aspects of assessment concern us and what aspects can we accommodate?

When used in a general sense to refer to the systematic way in which therapists from different orientations work out how to proceed in a particular case, 'assessment' can be a useful term in helping to explicate and compare approaches. Textbooks routinely use comparisons of 'assessment methods' to clarify the decision-making processes that inform each approach, and to show the way in which different therapists arrive at their formulations. Regardless of orientation, there tends to be a relatively systematic process of inquiry and decision-making that occurs in a first meeting, and this can be helpful for explication. A constructive framework could accommodate this general notion of assessment.

However, there are several other uses and connotations of assessment that constructive therapists find problematic:

- an evaluative or diagnostic use in which a family is implicitly compared with a normative or healthy ideal, so that its deficits can be identified for remedy;
- a connotation that problems are stable and unchanging, and that the assessment process simply maps these without, itself, making a difference;
- a sense of objective expertise being used in a unilateral manner (therapists probe clients, interpret their responses, and arrive at definitive formulations);
- a structured temporal sense suggesting that 'assessment' and 'intervention' are distinct activities and that therapy proceeds by way of clearly defined stages: assessment – formulation – treatment plan – intervention, occurring in a fixed sequence.

It is for these reasons that many constructive therapists prefer to avoid the formal term 'assessment' when referring to their work. Its dominant connotations simply do not represent their experience or their priorities in working with clients. A collaborative and competency-based approach would seem to favour 'negotiation' or 'co-construction' as its guiding terms. This does not mean that a constructive therapist would *never* use assessment methods in the conventional sense, but that this would be done within the priorities of their own orientation (perhaps as a 'secondary picture' as I will describe in Chapter 8). Nor can we simply choose to ignore a term that has such a prominent place in the professional discourse of psychotherapy. For example, even therapists who are sceptical about assessment processes may be professionally required or requested to collect formal assessment information in some form, and to make interpretations and recommendations.

Rather than avoiding or rejecting the term, therefore, it is more helpful to clarify our preferred use of it. If I were to conceptualize 'constructive assessment', I would use the term simply to elucidate the process through which practitioners systematically pursue their therapeutic agenda in the context of a first meeting with clients. What is being 'assessed' – for purposes of explication and comparison – are the therapist's actions and intentions, not those of clients. The major interest would be in articulating the dilemmas and processes of inquiry that are particularly important for constructive therapists, and in providing some useful guidelines for practice. This will be my focus for the rest of this chapter and the next.

Getting down to business

Let us imagine that a process of hosting has been undertaken, and you have managed to engage family members, to some degree, in various forms of problem-free talk. You now feel that a reflective space for inquiry has been provisionally established and that it is time to initiate the next major activity. As is typically the case in constructive therapies, you are intending to ask all clients about their hopes and goals for the meeting. However, depending on factors such as client responsiveness and interactions during the hosting experience, it may be necessary to bridge carefully into this process.

If the therapist senses a lingering tension, hostility or reluctance among family members that the hosting process has been unable to dissipate, a sudden switch to questions about hopes or goals may be experienced as too abrupt. In such a situation I will sometimes bridge from problem-free talk into the work phase by retracing the steps that were involved in arranging the meeting.

> I'd like to start by going over how you got to be here today. Who first had the idea of making an appointment? When was this? How did the others respond to the idea of coming here? How did you decide to choose our agency? How did you finally work out who would come to the meeting?

Because these questions focus on relatively straightforward facts about how the meeting was convened (rather than on why it was convened) they can be a non-threatening way to build a bridge to inquiring about concerns and requests. It can also be helpful to ask clients to take a few moments to think about what they want to say and don't want to say, and also how they want to talk in the meeting. This helps us respect the wishes of clients and avoid the temptation of trying too hard to get everyone involved in an 'equal' way.

Another situation requiring careful bridging occurs where the therapist has considerable prior knowledge about the family situation. Like many therapists, I prefer to know very little about the presenting situation before I meet clients, in order to start afresh and avoid presuppositions. However, if I have had significant contact with family members or other referrers (for example, by telephone or letter), and have been told in some detail about their concerns, it may seem rude, dismissive or disingenuous to pretend this hasn't happened. Therefore, before inquiring about client goals, I sometimes like to acknowledge the efforts that various people have made in helping to convene the meeting, and to share my current understanding of their situation based on what I have been told. Naturally, I am careful to put this in a constructive way. I will then normalize the possibility that things may have developed *since then*, and indicate that I'd like to start anew by asking what they are most wanting to talk about *today*.

If a therapist intends to use a more lengthy process of formal assessment it can be helpful to orient clients to the process by stating that you would like to gather information about *two* equally important areas: the family's concerns relating to the situation that has brought them in *and* the family's strengths, resources and solutions (Bertolino and O'Hanlon, 2002; Selekman, 1997). As most assessment processes tend to be overwhelmingly problem-focused, this conveys a more balanced approach and maintains an orientation towards possibilities. It may also be helpful to demarcate clearly the change of focus from problems to possibilities when this occurs. This could be done simply by announcing a shift of emphasis ('We've talked about a lot of serious things so far. To give me a more balanced picture, can you tell me about things that you think are really positive about the family?'), or perhaps by having a 'stretch break' before focusing on family resources, or perhaps by physically moving to a different part of the room or changing the lighting or seating configuration. The aim is to provide a different context or mood for possibility talk and to move it out from the shadow of problem talk.

Beginning the process of inquiry

How do you typically begin the inquiry process in a first meeting with clients? How does the approach you take relate to your fundamental therapeutic principles? Constructive therapists may differ considerably, depending on their preferred style. As mentioned in Chapter 1, I prefer to begin with a solution-oriented style and focus my interest on two related themes: *what are family members wanting, and how are they hoping that therapy can help?* In relationship therapy, there is an additional focus of curiosity: 'How are you wanting your *relationships* to be different, and what are you hoping will be different *between* you?' These interweaving themes shape the paths of inquiry in the evolving conversation. Often, it is useful to begin with an 'individual engagement' pattern. This can be helpful when family members have seemingly incompatible goals and remain reactive to each other.

Here is a typical example of how a therapist might initiate this process:

> I'd like to begin by asking each of you about your main hopes in coming here. Who'd like to start?

As the conversation develops, and this question is reiterated in various ways, a useful distinction is made between people's *life hopes* (what they are wanting to happen or be different in their lives) and their *therapy goals* (the specific contribution they are wanting therapy to make towards realizing these hopes: 'what are your main hopes in coming *here*?'). By distinguishing life hopes from therapy goals, we can begin to demarcate a specific role for therapy and also a potential end point. In order for constructive therapy to be time-effective, it is important to remember that the time needed to accomplish therapy goals is not the same as the time needed to realize life hopes. For example, it may take a family some years to work through a process of grief or to reshape their lives in the face of traumatic events. These are life hopes. However, this does not mean that families necessarily require ongoing therapy for all of that time. The endpoint of relationship therapy (the achievement of therapy goals) may be conceived as being the point at which family members feel able to utilize their own personal and social resources to address these ongoing issues. Thus, the successful conclusion of therapy does not necessarily signify that a problem has been finally solved, resolved or overcome, or even that anyone is particularly happy. The endpoint is where clients decide that they no longer need *professional* assistance in order to pursue their ongoing life or relationship hopes. The late John Weakland of the Mental Research Institute once said that ordinary life is just 'one damn thing after another' while a therapeutic problem is 'the same damn thing over and over' (O'Hanlon, 1998). Perhaps the endpoint of constructive relationship therapy is where family members no longer feel constrained by repetitive patterns of thought, talk and action, and feel able, once more, to confront the ordinary 'chaos' of human relationships.

Themes and variations: additional questions and considerations

In constructive therapies, the process of inquiry often takes the form of variations on a few central themes. The question, 'What are your main hopes in coming here?' is presented as a useful prototype. However, it is not intended as a formula question, and may be unsuitable in some contexts. For example, it may be experienced as too abrupt, challenging or unexpected. It is more helpful to begin where clients feel comfortable, and to lead gradually into the major themes.

Here are some other ways in which various constructive therapists might choose to begin or follow up an initial process of inquiry:

- What would it be most helpful for us to talk about today?
- What brings you in?
- How will you know that coming here today will be helpful?
- How would you like to use this meeting?
- How are you hoping that this meeting will make a difference?
- How are you hoping that talking with us here might be different from talking at home?
- What will tell you that this meeting has been helpful?
- Imagine leaving here in an hour or so feeling glad that you decided to come, and that it was all worthwhile. What do you suppose would have to happen for you to leave here feeling like that?

These questions are meant to be suggestive rather than prescriptive, and to encourage you to reflect upon the way in which you initiate inquiry. What you will notice about these questions, of course, is that they do not invite a discussion of problems, or the extensive telling of a problem-oriented story. The therapist does not begin by inviting the clients to name problems or problem people, or to start at the beginning and tell the whole story leading up to the meeting.[1] These themes might still emerge if they are high enough on the client's agenda, but the therapist seeks to begin the negotiation process by offering a different way of talking.

The particular kinds of expressions used, the combination of questions, the pace at which they are asked, and even who they are addressed to, will also be affected by considerations such as the therapist's personal style, practice context and particular skills. For example, when working with combinations of adults and children of differing ages, you will need to consider the appropriate level of vocabulary and syntax when crafting questions. It may also be important to pace the questions more slowly, the conventional wisdom being to proceed at the pace of the younger clients who may be left behind if a therapist continues with a rapid battery of questions. Also, rather than inviting anyone to respond ('Who'd like to start?') some therapists may prefer to start by talking to the parents first and then the children (or by seeing the parents alone). This approach helps to demonstrate respect and support for parents (who often feel blamed or undermined in family therapy) and recognizes that parents are usually the prime movers of change with the most power to influence the outcome.

However, as I mentioned in Chapter 2, there are also arguments for including children and actually addressing them first, especially if everyone knows that a particular child is the 'identified problem person'. This can help to engage the young person's attention immediately and provide an opportunity to 'get in first' before others begin a process of talking about them and defining 'their' problems. A young person's responsiveness during the hosting process might offer some clues as to whether they feel safe and involved enough to respond to such a direct approach. It can also be helpful to ask permission to ask questions: 'Is it okay for me to ask you some questions?' 'Is it all right to ask you some difficult questions?' 'If I ask you some questions, will you try to think about them?' 'It's okay if you don't want to answer any questions, but is it all right with you if I ask your mother about the situation?' This is more respectful than simply barging in (in typical adult style) and assuming you have a right to interrogate young people. When in doubt about whom to address, I usually start by talking to the person who made the appointment, which seems a polite and reasonable way to begin.

Conversation as negotiation

In the title and focus of this chapter, an implicit metaphor has been used throughout. I have suggested that the therapist's agenda is to 'negotiate' constructions of presenting concerns that will maintain an orientation toward preferences and possibilities. The metaphor of negotiation is used in two familiar senses: firstly, as a process of reaching agreement or compromise (as in negotiating a sale, a salary package or a deal) and, secondly, as a process of co-ordinating movement so as to clear or pass an obstacle (as in negotiating a curve or other difficult terrain). Therapist and clients work collaboratively to negotiate the difficult 'verbal terrain' of therapeutic problems. In doing so, they attempt to negotiate a way of talking about the purpose of the meeting that is satisfying for all participants. As O'Hanlon and Wilk (1987) suggest, this sense of negotiation also points to the fact that there is no objectively 'real' definition of a therapeutic problem, any more than there is an objectively real value for a house or other item for sale. What is real is the price that is negotiated at a particular time. Similarly, therapeutic realities are negotiated through particular conversations at particular times. O'Hanlon and Wilk argue that, in this sense, the therapeutic problem to be worked on does not exist outside the therapist's office: it is a product of the clients' and therapist's talking together. It is created verbally and addressed verbally.

This does *not* mean that constructive therapists believe that client problems are 'fictional' in the sense of having no basis in observable facts, sensory experience and material conditions. Nor does it mean that any kind of problem can simply be talked out of existence. Contrary to some popular misconceptions, a constructionist position does not assert, for example, that phenomena such as schizophrenia, addiction, chronic fatigue syndrome, post-traumatic stress disorder, etc., are non-existent. Further, it does not assert that therapists should dismiss out of hand the potential value of diagnostic classification systems or other forms of professional knowledge. As narrative therapists Drewery, Winslade and Monk (2000) suggest, it would be both naive and foolhardy to deny the contribution of modern therapeutic practices. The identification of symptoms that accompany the kinds of problems I mentioned above, together with knowledge about appropriate medications and psycho-educational material, can obviously assist families and help to absolve them from blame. While labels may be 'inventities', they can also provide a sense of identity and hope that is preferable to confusion and incomprehension.

However, what remains negotiable in the therapist's office are the individual *meanings* and *experiences* associated with various problem descriptions, and, in particular, the ways in which individuals are positioned in terms of agency, resourcefulness and possibilities. Consider this response:

> A woman once called to ask if we 'worked with addicts' … . In this instance, the therapist responded, 'No, I work with people – some of whom think of themselves as being addicted to something.' (Efran and Fauber, 1995: 300)

While this response is not from a therapy session, it exemplifies the kinds of themes that a constructive therapist might attempt to introduce in conversational negotiations. The response avoids identifying the label of 'addict' with the person in question and, instead, presents it as an *idea* that may or may not prove helpful in the particular situation. The aim is neither to endorse nor refute the concept, but to suggest that its meaning is negotiable on an individual basis rather being a categorical given. People come first and labels come second. The response also draws attention to *context*: people may be 'addicted' to specific things on specific occasions, as opposed to being presented as generalized addicts or addictive personalities. Of course, some clients might *choose* to think of themselves as addicts (and this framing may be an important resource for them), in which case the therapist will again be curious about individual experiences: how, specifically, does the category description make a difference and how is it helpful?

As a constructive therapist, I am actively trying to negotiate a role for my particular skills and enthusiasms. I begin by making a 'linguistic offer' to the clients – an invitation to talk about concerns and requests (such as addiction) in a particular way. In the ensuing negotiation process, clients respond with their own 'counter offers' that may be very different from mine. For example, I may begin the negotiation process with a question about a client's future hopes, and the family member might respond by relating her history of addiction from childhood! Clearly, we are poles apart at this point – I may have introduced a future focus too quickly, and the client feels that I haven't connected with her distress. Therefore she rejects my 'offer' and makes one of her own. I must learn from the experience and adjust my response. As the process of verbal negotiation evolves, however, we will hopefully move closer together so that a conversational 'deal' can be struck, and the various parties are, at least provisionally, speaking the same language. As in most negotiations, you don't get everything you want, but it is important to get enough of what you are wanting to feel satisfied that you can proceed with a sense of purpose and trust. It is not a satisfactory negotiation if clients are manoeuvred into accepting an outcome, only to feel conned or ripped-off later. Obvious analogies might be negotiations over a house sale or salary package where you thought you were getting a good deal, but on later reflection come to the conclusion that you had been subtly (or not so subtly) manipulated. The therapist's aim is not to 'sell' clients a predetermined framing of their concerns but to negotiate descriptions that continue to be both meaningful and engaging for clients, *and* allow therapists the opportunity to utilize the skills that constitute their professional strengths.

Orienting versus influencing

Thinking of our conversations as a process of negotiation rather than assessment also points to the tension between the use of *orienting* and *influencing* questions (Tomm, 1988). Orienting questions are used to help the therapist orient to the family's situation in the sense of learning and understanding more about it (for example, asking about the specific events, background and circumstances that have brought them to therapy). Influencing questions are used to invite a change in the family's perceptions and understandings. Though there is often a degree of overlap (some questions can have both effects), the primary intent of orienting questions is for the therapist to change, while the primary intent of influencing questions is for the clients to change. Problem-focused assessment approaches feature a more extensive use of orienting questions as the therapist gathers information that will result in a formulation and treatment plan. By contrast, constructive approaches (especially in the solution-oriented style) might move almost immediately into influencing questions. For example, even the opening question, 'What are your main hopes in coming here?', can be considered primarily as an influencing question, the intent of which is to invite a future-focused theme and a new way of talking about difficulties.

The preponderance of influencing questions over orienting questions has become a hallmark of constructive therapies. The therapist elicits relatively minimal information about client concerns in order to avoid being swamped with problem-saturated descriptions, and acts on the belief that constructing possibilities is a different 'language game' from assessing problems. However, the question inevitably arises as to how far this can be taken. Are there no purely orienting questions that a constructive therapist might wish to ask? Don't you need *some* minimal amount of information about problems before launching into influencing questions? Depending on their preferred style, constructive therapists might differ considerably on this point. My own suggestion is that it is helpful to gain an appreciation of the context in which clients are living and struggling, and the specific circumstances that have brought them to seek assistance. While retaining a minimalist perspective, I am typically interested in the following:

- The specific circumstances of the referral (the sequence of events leading up to the referral, who made the suggestion for counselling and why).
- The timing of the referral (why *now*, and not earlier or later).
- Who wants to be involved and who does not.
- Who else is involved and what is their agenda (for example, other individuals, agencies, stakeholders, etc.).
- What is at stake for the family? (What are family members' fears or main concerns about what has happened or might happen?)
- Whether family members have had similar experiences in the past (and what is different about this situation).
- Family members' views of how change can occur and what needs to be done.
- What they have attempted to do already and how helpful this has been.
- Any other information that family members believe to be important.

These kinds of orienting questions are not necessarily asked in a direct way or in a set format in the first meeting. Rather, they form a backdrop to the therapist's curiosity and may be introduced at appropriate moments. It is also likely that much of this information will emerge indirectly from responses to other questions. Orienting to the context of present difficulties helps us to gain a richer understanding of the unfolding narrative in which we are now a potentially significant character. At the very least, the process of asking some basic orienting questions can serve an important social function in allowing us to join with family members in going over background information that most clients would consider relevant. The process can serve to validate the seriousness of family members' concerns and to demonstrate the therapist's interest in their predicament. But beyond the enhancement of partnership, it may also allow us to achieve a greater appreciation of each person's experience, point of view and struggle. Carefully orienting to these themes helps to prepare the way for identifying and highlighting subsequent changes. It provides a broader canvas for comparing 'before' and 'after', and allows us to be taken more seriously when remarking on new directions or turning points.

An important part of the therapist's craft in the first meeting involves finding a balance between orienting and influencing questions. If the therapist moves too quickly towards influencing the situation, clients may feel that their concerns and distress have been unheard, minimized or disqualified. The therapist may embark on the express route without being totally clear where the client wants to go. On the other hand, if the therapist spends too much time orienting to the situation, the conversation can become mired in problem-focused data-gathering, negativity, and more of the same.

Case example

I will conclude this chapter with two comparative examples demonstrating the importance of balancing orienting and influencing questions in the process of negotiation. In each scenario the therapist is talking with Helen (35), a sole parent of two daughters, Anna (12) and Jasmine (14). The only referral information the therapist has relates to the girls' 'behaviour problems' that Helen believes are linked to her new relationship with a male friend, Martin. The therapist develops an 'individual engagement' pattern with Helen while the two girls listen.

Version 1

[1] *Therapist*: I always like to start by asking what are your main hopes in coming here?

[2] *Helen*: I need to clear the air with the girls, especially Jasmine. I want to know *exactly* why they're behaving like they are, and I want them to tell me directly if it's got something to do with Martin.

[3] *Therapist*: So what would tell you that our meeting today was helpful?

[4] *Helen*: The problem is that the girls are still very loyal to their father … even though they hardly ever see him. They still tend to idolize him – God knows why – and they think I'm betraying him by bringing Martin home once in a while …

[5] *Jasmine*: [*interrupting*] Once in a while! It's every weekend.

[6] *Helen*: They've become extremely rude to him and to me … they keep calling him my 'boyfriend' and sneering [*indicates Jasmine's scornful expression*] … just like that … see. That's how she carries on all the time.

[7] *Therapist*: So you're hoping that by coming here you'll be able to find a way to clear the air.

[8] *Helen*: They've got to understand that my relationship with their father is finished. There is no possibility of the family ever being together again. All of our lives have to move on. Jasmine's the worst. Anna was getting over the situation but Jasmine keeps getting to her and upsetting her.

[9] *Therapist*: Really? So Anna was getting over the situation. What helped her to do that?

[10] *Helen*: Just that she was younger I suppose. But Jasmine was at an age where she really bonded with her father, and she's always blamed me for the family breaking up.

[11] *Jasmine*: I have not!

[12] *Helen*: Yes you have!

[13] *Jasmine*: You just can't understand!

In this segment, the therapist asks only influencing questions in an attempt to shift the focus of the conversation towards the future. However, the necessary process of negotiation does not occur as the therapist's questions are not adjusted to Helen's responses and seem consistently out of step. Influencing question [3] represents too big a jump into the future and is not attuned to Helen's mood. Consequently, she basically ignores the therapist's question and continues to talk about the problem situation [4]. Possibly feeling unheard she also tends to speak in a provocative way that tempts Jasmine to interrupt. The therapist persists with trying to influence the conversation towards the future [7] but this again is out of step with Helen's priorities and she continues in the same vein [8]. The therapist attempts to build on a possible exception [9] based on Anna getting over the situation, but again this seems gratuitous and is summarily dismissed by Helen [10].

Therapists who are new to constructive approaches often overreact to problem-focused assessment by shifting to the opposite extreme and attempting to take the express route from the first question. It is important to remember that negotiating means adjusting to the client's responses and co-ordinating with the client as you move together through the verbal terrain of problems and change. At the beginning of the negotiation process, asking too many influencing questions can impede rather than enhance the process.

Version 2

[1] *Therapist*: I always like to start by asking what are your main hopes in coming here?

[2] *Helen*: I need to clear the air with the girls, especially Jasmine. I want to know *exactly* why they're behaving like they are, and I want them to tell me directly if it's got something to do with Martin.

[3] *Therapist*:   Can you fill me in a bit on exactly what has been happening and how you think this may be linked to Martin?

[4] *Helen*:   I've known Martin off and on for about a year … we're in the same winetasting club. We started going out about three months ago and he's been staying over occasionally. Just by 'coincidence' the girls' behaviour started going downhill at the same time. Jasmine's been having temper tantrums like you wouldn't believe and her latest trick is to suddenly fall 'ill' when Martin's here so she doesn't have to have dinner with us. It's all so obvious and so rude. I thought she was more grown-up than that.

[5] *Therapist*:   Okay … so when you say that you're hoping to clear the air, are you hoping that we can help find a way forward for both you and Jasmine so that you can talk about these issues in a calm way and try to sort things out?

[6] *Helen*:   Yes, that's exactly what we need to do! I just get so angry with her that I lose my temper too. I end up going down to her level.

[7] *Therapist*:   Another question I often like to ask is, why have you decided to come here now, as opposed to, say, last month or next month? What makes it important to clear the air now?

[8] *Helen*:   It's started to affect Anna too and just in the last couple of weeks she's become agitated when Martin is here on the weekend. I don't think she knows whose side she should be on and I think she feels pulled apart. But she won't talk to me about it. I'm angry with Jasmine, but I'm more worried about Anna.

[9] *Therapist*:   I see. So you'd like to find a way to talk differently with both your daughters. You'd like to talk in a calm grown-up way with Jasmine and you'd like to find a way to encourage Anna to take you into her confidence and tell you what's going on for her.

[10] *Helen*:   Yes, especially with the stresses we all have at this time of year, with the end of the school year soon, and my own job coming up for renewal.

[11] *Therapist*:   So it's an important time for the family and you're wanting everyone to pull together wherever possible …

In this segment, the conversation begins with the same influencing question but the therapist adjusts to the tone of Helen's response [2]. Changing tack, the therapist asks an orienting question [3] that allows Helen to say what she thinks is important about the background to the situation. This allows the therapist to respond with a more effective influencing question [5] that helps to clarify Helen's goal of clearing the air. Helen is able to connect with this question and responds [6]. The therapist asks another orienting question about 'why now?' [7] and gains more valuable information that allows another influencing question to be used [10] drawing a distinction between Helen's goals in relation to Jasmine and Anna.

Here we see a more helpful process of negotiation as the therapist adjusts each question to the tenor of Helen's responses. Through the alternation of orienting and influencing questions, Helen feels heard and is able to respond in a more reflective way that does not provoke Jasmine to interrupt. By finding out more about the context of the problem situation, the therapist has more grist for the constructive mill and is able to craft influencing questions that are more specific and discerning, as can be seen from Helen's responses.

In attempting to balance orienting and influencing questions, a useful approach for new therapists may be to alternate deliberately between the two. In constructive approaches the therapist clearly favours themes of preferences and possibilities. However, the evolving path of inquiry may move in different directions and at different speeds. We invite clients to accompany us on the express route, but then adjust our plans to their responses. It is helpful to remember that even on the express route we don't always travel at the same speed.

Expanding the process of negotiation

This chapter has introduced the fundamental principle of negotiating concerns and requests in constructive therapies. In the context of family work it has highlighted the need for the therapist to keep out of trance and avoid conversations for characterizations, accusations and recriminations. In order to do this, I have suggested the importance of choosing appropriate patterns of engagement and staying multiply engaged with the realities of all family members. I also discussed a constructive approach to the question of assessment, ways of starting the process of inquiry and the tension between orienting and influencing questions in constructive therapies. The short case examples above provide a convenient bridge into the next chapter which expands upon these basic skills by outlining a number of 'process interventions' that are particularly helpful in negotiating *who wants what* in family therapy.

Note

1. This approach is based on the preferred 'style' described in Chapter 1. Therapists who prefer to begin with a narrative style will be more inclined to invite the naming of problems. Those preferring a more conversational style may be content for clients to begin where they like.

4 Clarifying 'Who Wants What?'

We believe that clients come in with some sense of desire and that asking them about that desire is a good place to start. (Walter and Peller, 2000: 64)

We understand backwards ... but we live forwards. (Crites, 1986: 165)

We can now return to the key question of 'Who wants what?' One of the difficulties in writing about constructive therapy practice concerns the degree of specificity used. Some practitioners prefer to describe their work using general principles such as 'opening up conversational space' or 'co-constructing new descriptions', while others focus on specific techniques such as scaling questions or well-formed goals that are used in every session. In attempting to enhance flexibility in practice I am hoping to describe interventions that will occupy a middle ground. They will be identifiable and practical processes, but in most cases will not be confined to any specific technique.

Process interventions

Borrowing a term from Neimeyer (1996), I will call these groups of conversational skills *process interventions*. They are particular patterns of conversation that influence the process of meaning-making in particular ways. They are more concerned with conversational *processes* than with conversational *products*, with how topics are negotiated rather than what topics are discussed, or what outcomes are achieved. Process interventions can be defined in terms of the therapist's intent in using them at a particular time. They occupy a 'middle' level somewhere between specific techniques and abstract principles and may be thought of as rhetorical strategies that can take a number of practical forms.

My particular concern in this chapter is to define a number of process interventions that I have found to be particularly helpful in family meetings. The aim of these process interventions is to invite people to articulate what they are wanting in ways that enhance the possibilities for collaborative inquiry. Even though we may often work from an 'individual engagement' pattern, speaking with one person at a time about their hopes and goals, we maintain the sense of being involved with all of the relationships in the room. In this sense, the process interventions are relationship-oriented as therapists invite speakers to voice their hopes and concerns differently, and also invite listeners to hear differently. They are another contribution towards minimizing the hazards of conjoint relationship therapy, while maximizing the opportunities.

Process interventions are conversational strategies based in the practice of *rhetoric*, which Neimeyer defines as 'an artful use of discourse to accomplish pragmatic ends' (1996: 382). When I think of 'pragmatic ends', I would hope that by the conclusion of the process:

- All family members will feel that their individual concerns, experiences, hopes and points of view have been heard and acknowledged.
- All family members will feel equally supported by the therapist.
- A less constraining and more constructive way of talking about concerns and requests will be developed and shared.
- Where possible, there will be a sense of shared or mutual purpose among participants.
- A reflective emotional climate will be maintained, so that people can respond rather than react to each other.
- There will be provisional agreement on the initial focus and direction of the meeting.

Following Neimeyer, I will describe process interventions in the form of *verbal nouns* (ending with -*ing*) to emphasize process. I will then provide a one-sentence definition of each (Box 4.1) before discussing them in turn using case examples. It is also important to note that many of these interventions can be used in combination, though they are separated below for purposes of exemplification. I have adapted several concepts and interventions from the work of Bill O'Hanlon (Bertolino and O'Hanlon, 2002; Hudson and O'Hanlon, 1991; O'Hanlon and Wilk, 1987), who remains one of the few constructive therapists to have specifically discussed skills for conjoint work.

Box 4.1   Process interventions

Channelling: Diverting the focus and energy of the conversation from present or past experience to future hopes and goals.

Filtering: Reflecting, 'translating' or adding to client comments about other participants in ways that may encourage more reflective postures among listeners.

Specifying: Focusing the discussion of desired change to encourage 'well-formed' goals.

Box 4.1 (Continued)

Theming: Widening the lens to explore the thematic significance of desired change.

Interrelating: Inviting clients to consider and express desired change in relationship or interactional terms.

Mutualizing: Identifying commonalities or shared stories in people's experiences and hopes.

Tracking and Linking: Monitoring and connecting each person's hopes and goals in an inclusive way.

Prioritizing: Clarifying which issues and requests need most immediate attention, and identifying a starting point for change.

Case example

To lend a sense of continuity, I will use segments of conversation with the same set of clients to exemplify each process intervention. This family session involves James (aged 40), Ellen (aged 38), their son Tim (aged 17), and their two daughters Casey (14) and Joanne (12). The parents have sought consultation because of Tom's increasingly erratic and 'bizarre' behaviour. He is in danger of being suspended from school and has become increasingly uncooperative at home, refusing to participate in household activities or duties unless he is allowed to come and go as he wishes, and has been 'terrorizing' his sisters to a point where they refuse to interact with him any more. Several family members are reporting stress-related symptoms and family therapy was recommended by Ellen's physician. The unfolding session conforms to a typically occurring scenario where complainant-type relationships are apparent and the 'identified problem person' is reluctant to participate. At the beginning of the meeting, therefore, the therapist is likely to use an 'individual engagement' pattern of engagement with James and Ellen while Tim and his sisters listen.

Channelling

The aim of channelling is to invite a shift of attention from past or present experience to what family members may be wanting in the future (Hudson and O'Hanlon, 1991). The aim is not to minimize or ignore people's concerns but to 'channel' the energy of these concerns in a new direction by placing a metaphorical fork in the river in order to divert it towards future-oriented hopes. The therapist attempts to maintain the delicate balance between acceptance and change, acknowledgement and possibility: 'You're experiencing X *and* you're wanting Y.' The effective use of channelling can result in family members more clearly articulating their hopes and desires, and making specific requests of others. Such a focus may also provide a different experience for listeners, who may be expecting 'more of the same'.

James: Tim is uncontrollable at home, it's becoming scary. None of us can predict what he'll do next. It's gotten to a stage where we're on edge all the time, just waiting for the next crazy act to occur. He's not capable of listening to reason and he doesn't give a damn about anyone else's feelings. As soon as he doesn't get his way on something, he loses it. It's obvious that he's got serious problems but he's got no right to give *us* problems like this. Ellen has had to take time off work this week to help the other kids cope, and I'm coming home every night to a war zone. He has no right to do this to his family!

Therapist: This sounds pretty desperate. You'd like to help everyone, but you've reached the end of your tether, and you can't work out where to go from here.

James: [*nodding*] What gets to me most is that he doesn't seem to *care* about the effect he's having on any of us. We're not important. We're just like objects he can annoy for a bit of fun.

Therapist: That must be very difficult to get through ... very difficult. So ... am I right in guessing that you've decided that something different has to happen if your family is going to hold together, and that's why you've come here?

James: We have to do something, or someone will get seriously hurt. We've never had much time for counsellors. So you can see how desperate we are.

Therapist: Desperate, yes ... but I also get a sense that you're *determined*. You're determined to try anything (even counselling!) that might offer new ideas for keeping your family together. And you seem determined not to give up on your relationship with Tim, even though it's about as strained as you could imagine. And from what Ellen said a few moments ago, she's also determined to keep trying. So I'm wondering, how can we help to build on this determination so that you can put it to use?

In this interaction the therapist is trying to say to James: you're feeling understandably angry and desperate *and* you're wanting to find a new way forward. This may help to channel the energy of his anger and desperation into *determination* to persevere and find new ways to interact with his son. The therapist keeps the focus on James and avoids joining him in any analysis or criticism of Tim who is sitting away from his parents, but listening carefully. As Turnell and Lipchik (1999) suggest, it is important for constructive therapists to engage with clients at an emotional level. However, this does *not* mean that the therapist needs to focus at length on the emotions conveyed by clients (for example, by reflecting James' underlying anger or inviting him to elaborate on his sense of desperation). Therapists can engage at an emotional level through appropriate pacing, validating clients' concerns, showing interest, and conveying appreciation of their dilemmas. In this example, the therapist hopes that the channelling of anger and desperation into determination will resonate with James at an emotional level, and will also provide a bridge to a discussion of future preferences.

Filtering

The aim of filtering is to influence the way in which a family member talks about others who are in the room. The therapist can work to reduce high levels of reactivity among listeners by acting as an 'interpreter' or 'translator' who summarizes the gist of a family member's complaints but softens them in ways that filter out many of the verbal provocations that can undermine prospects for collaborative work. This might involve selectively paraphrasing what clients have said, deliberately ignoring parts of their communication, or even speaking for the client and adding a constructive 'twist' to their main complaints (Hudson and O'Hanlon, 1991; O'Hanlon and Wilk, 1987). Again, it is important to maintain a balance. If you try to introduce too much change too soon, the speaker may lose the sense of being heard and taken seriously. Therefore, therapists should remain cautious and speculative in their attempts to 'translate' the conversation, checking that they have understood the main points of the speaker's communication. If the speaker persists in making derogatory or provocative remarks about others, it is important that therapists do not echo these sentiments in their own comments. This allows you to distance yourself from what is being said and provides an opportunity to at least model some alternative ways of talking. Filtering can lower the heat of the conversation and perhaps add more light.

Ellen: Tim seems to think that if he can outdo all of us at brinksmanship by always going one step further, and doing something more outrageous, then he'll finally get his way and be allowed to do exactly what he wants. Well I'm sorry, but he's got to understand that if he wants to be part of the family there are responsibilities as well as rights. You can't treat your home like a hotel and just come and go when you like, and treat your family like housemaids and cooks. You have to contribute to running the household and earn the right to have the freedom you want.

Therapist: I get a sense that what you're trying to say to Tim is … 'Look, we really want you in the family, you're a vital part of it, and – despite the anger we show at times – we really love you. But please try to understand that family life is incredibly hard to organize these days, especially when both parents are working, and it really depends on a strong team effort, and a willingness to help each other out. And the more everyone contributes the less any individual has to do, and the less stress there is for everyone. Because the way things have been going recently, nobody wins, and everyone loses.' Have I got that right?

Ellen: That's exactly it! We're all losing. We're all suffering. Just look at everyone. It's like we're all casualties in a war. A war of attrition.

Therapist: They say that the first thing you should do when you find yourself in a hole is stop digging! I wonder what you could all do to help conserve the energy you've got left, so that you don't waste it on any more conflict.

In this example, the therapist deliberately puts words into Ellen's mouth and speaks for her, 'translating' the gist of what she has said into a less censorious communication that might enable Tim to listen differently. Rather than directing all blame and anger at Tim, this message shifts the focus to how everyone is suffering, and suggests that everyone can contribute to helping. Ellen's response to the filtering of her statements seems to indicate that she finds it acceptable. Filtering the personal criticism of Tim results in Ellen developing the metaphor of a war of attrition, focusing on shared distress and the need for everyone to do something to conserve the energy of the family. Tim may be more responsive to these ideas when the therapist talks to him later in the conversation.

Specifying

Specifying includes many of the questions used in solution-focused therapy to invite 'well-formed goals' (Berg, 1994; de Jong and Berg, 2002; de Shazer, 1991). In relationship difficulties people often make requests in ways that come across as confusingly vague or global, as all-or-nothing demands, or as couched in negative rather than positive terms (stopping something, rather than starting something). The lack of specificity about exactly what people are wanting, from whom, in what context and to what degree, is a major stumbling block. Sometimes, in fact, family members may be satisfied with relatively small changes but the way their complaints are expressed comes across to the listener as a demand for a total attitude transplant or personality make-over! Predictably, this is seen as unreasonable or is taken personally, and triggers counter-complaints. Specifying invites family members to talk about their preferred future in particular ways:

- as action requests (changes in specific behaviours, and in specific contexts, rather than in personality, attitude, etc.);
- as positive rather than negative (what is wanted, rather than what is not wanted);
- as the beginning of something rather than the end of something;
- in small steps or signs of change (rather than all or nothing);
- as something that is changeable and within the client's influence;
- in the client's language;
- in interactional terms (see 'Interrelating' below).

Therapist: [*to James and Ellen*] What specific changes are you wanting to see?

James: Well, the first thing is that Tim has got to start showing some respect for his family.

Ellen: Exactly. His attitude has to do a complete 180-degree turn. There's no respect at all at the moment.

Therapist: Okay. 'Respect' is one of those important but difficult words to define. It often means different things to different families. Let me ask both of you this question. Suppose, after coming here, Tim decided that he wanted to behave in a way that showed more respect to the two of you. Let's say it takes a couple of weeks to happen, and then suddenly you notice it. Something is different. How would you first become aware of it? In what part of everyday life would each of you first notice the change?

James: For me, it would be when I came home from work. I can tell as soon as I open the door what kind of atmosphere there is. The tension just hits you.

Therapist: So what would be different? What would be the first sign that something was different?

James: Well, Ellen and the girls wouldn't be telling me what Tim has been up to. They usually give me 'front-line briefings'.

Therapist: What would be happening instead?

James: They probably wouldn't need to tell me anything at all, because there'd be no problems to report.

Therapist: So if you came home and there were no problems being reported, what would happen next? What would be the next sign that things were different?

James: Tim might actually appear at dinner and take an interest in the conversation.

Therapist: Okay. What about you Ellen? What would you notice first that would tell you something was different and better?

Ellen: Tim usually picks a fight with one of his sisters and that starts things off. They get upset – which is really unfair because they're younger and easily hurt – and it all starts from there and just spirals. So what I would notice is that the girls weren't suddenly screaming out as soon as Tim gets home after school.

Therapist: So it would be in the afternoon that you'd first notice the change?

Ellen: Yes. The mornings aren't too bad because he usually gets up so late that there's no one around to annoy.

Therapist: So in the afternoons, if there was calm between Tim and the girls, what else might happen? What else might you notice that would tell you things were better?

Ellen: Tim might acknowledge my existence and actually reply when I say 'hello'.

In this segment, the therapist invites a specification of James' and Ellen's requests in ways that progressively clarify what they are each wanting Tim to do differently. The conversation moves from the vague notion of demanding more respect to a discussion of what specific behaviour they would each like Tim to change, in what actual context, with which specific people, in what order, and with what starting point. This conversational change of direction may enable Tim to listen differently, as he hears specific requests rather than general criticisms. This difference may encourage him to consider the requests as more reasonable and achievable.

Two other useful methods for specifying include *videotalk* and *multiple-choice questioning* (Hudson and O'Hanlon, 1991; O'Hanlon and Wilk, 1987). Videotalk involves the therapist asking clients to imagine a video showing family members performing the changes they have requested. They are then asked to state what they would see and hear on the video that would tell them that these changes had occurred (what exactly would a video of Tim arriving home from school show him doing?). As video is such a common medium in contemporary life, family members of all ages can relate to this method and may be more likely to take an interest in the exercise. We can invite clients to pause the video, replay particular sections, fast-forward it, and so on. By focusing on a particular scene or context, this can add greater texture to the search for 'well-formed' goals.

Multiple-choice questions are also useful in helping clients break down generalized complaints into more context-specific requests. The therapist can suggest a number of different options that might match what the client is wanting – all of which are couched in terms of future-oriented actions. For example, 'I've heard lots of parents say that they want their sons to "show more respect", but they often mean different things by this. Some parents are wanting him to pay more attention to household rules and obligations, others are wanting him to show more interest in family events like going out together (or even appearing at dinner). Sometimes parents are mainly wanting him to be more polite on occasions, or to listen more when they speak to him, or to take more time to communicate what's bothering him. Do any of these match what you're most wanting, or is it something else again?'

Theming

This process intervention involves drawing out the *significance* of a client's hopes, and acts as a complement to specifying. Though it is a routine practice for solution-oriented therapists to invite specification of hopes and goals, it may not always be helpful (Walter and Peller, 2000). In conjoint meetings, a client's hopes, wishes or requests (no matter how 'well-formed') may be heard by others as unrealistic, unacceptable or unreasonable, leading to a conversational stalemate. However, if we can invite clients to expand progressively on the meaning or significance of their hopes, and what difference these changes would make to their lives (and by implication to the lives of others), we may see that the original hopes were not *ends* in themselves, but *means* to more important ends. This may evoke a different response from listeners. Whereas specifying focuses on identifying preferred actions, theming reveals the intentions or desire behind these actions.

Therapist: Let's take a leap of faith, and imagine that Tim did decide to do some of the things you've requested. For example, let's suppose he didn't get into fights with the girls, he did manage to say hello to Ellen in the afternoon, and he did make the occasional appearance at the dinner table. How would that be different?

James: For me, it would show respect for the family, and especially for the authority of his parents. The way he treats his mother is just disgraceful.

Therapist: So you'd be especially pleased by anything Tim does which shows respect for Ellen. What about yourself? What would it mean for you?

James: Well, Tim and I haven't been close for a number of years. He's lost interest in the things we used to do together. So I suppose if we could even talk at the same table occasionally, it would mean that we still have some kind of relationship going.

Therapist: And that's clearly important for you?

James: Very. I probably didn't realize how important until all this began to happen.

Therapist: It sounds like you'd like your relationship with Tim to become stronger again.

James: Yes, I would.

Therapist: Thanks James. What about you Ellen? How would these positive changes make a difference for you?

Ellen: Well, when you mentioned them I didn't think so much about respect, but about getting my son back. We were very close a few years ago. At the time he was growing away from James, he was confiding a lot more in me. And he had a terrific relationship with the girls at that time. I was very proud of him.

Therapist: So these changes might help to revive your sense of pride in your son and your sense of connection with him. And it would help remind you of some of his qualities.

Ellen: Exactly. I feel I've just lost him. He suddenly became a totally different person, almost overnight. And my deepest fear is that he's gone for good.

Therapist: So it's very important for you to maintain some sense of connection with Tim, no matter what particular issues you're struggling with. You'd like the reassurance that there's still a strong relationship there, that will survive these current setbacks.

By extending the inquiry to consider the personal significance of the changes James and Ellen are wanting, it is possible for all participants to hear something new and different. The emerging themes of rebuilding the relationship (James) and regaining a sense of pride and connection (Ellen) might evoke a different response from Tim than would be evoked by making specific action requests. It establishes a connection between means and ends, and could lead to a consideration of other ways in which these broader ends might be achieved. James, Ellen and Tim could reflect on other ways in which their relationships might be sustained beyond the present areas of conflict. This might also invite Tim to comment on the significance to him of future relationships with his parents. As the name suggests, theming has the potential to provide a central focus for the conversation drawing together a number of different threads. It can result in a *vision* for change, rather than specific and sometimes piecemeal goals (Waters and Lawrence, 1993).

Interrelating

The aim of this process intervention is to introduce a relationship perspective by focusing on interaction and reciprocity. Inviting clients to state their hopes in interactional as well as personal terms is one characteristic of 'well-formed' goals in solution-focused therapy (see 'Specifying' above). Because of its importance in relationship work, this process is worth considering as a separate and specialized process.

The asking of relationship questions invites a shift in emphasis from what family members are wanting for themselves, to what they are wanting for their relationships (what they are wanting to be different *between* themselves and others). There are several kinds of relationship questions. Some straightforward questions might be: 'How are you hoping your relationship with — might be different?' 'If things were going more the way you want, what would be happening between you?' 'How would you start to notice that your relationship with — was improving?' 'If the relationships in your family were to improve in the next week, and I could capture this on video, what would I see that would be different?'

While these kinds of questions expand the focus of an individual client's hopes for change, they still involve only the speaker's perspective. Constructive therapists often ask relationship questions that go further and invite a shift in perspective by asking a person to adopt another's viewpoint and speculate about their perceptions or experience. Ziegler and Hiller (2001) have distinguished two broad categories of these questions: 'outsider-perspective questions' and 'role-reversal questions'.

Outsider-perspective questions are typically used in order to invite Person A to reflect on how others (Persons B, C, D, etc.) might view their *own* (A's) actions. If a client has indicated a desire to change but finds it difficult to articulate how this change would be carried out, the therapist could ask a question such as: 'How would your wife (or son or daughter) know that you were changing? What would be the first sign to them that you were serious about making this change?' These questions help Person A to focus on themselves through others' eyes and can be helpful in specifying actions that they could take. They can also be used to invite a reciprocal perspective when Person A is wanting Person B to change. The therapist can ask Person A to imagine that the desired changes have been made, and then ask: 'If this happened, what would Person B notice about the way you responded? What would tell Person B that the changes they have made have been appreciated by you?'

I will also include in this category questions that elicit an interactional perspective on a person's 'preferred view of self' (Eron and Lund, 1996) and how they would like others to see them. 'How would you like — to see you?' 'What would need to happen so that — could start to see you this way?' 'What would be a sign to you that — was starting to see you in the way you prefer?' These questions can initiate a process of identifying and narrowing the gap between the way clients prefer to be viewed and how they are currently being viewed by others.

In outsider-perspective questions, the focus remains on the behaviour of Person A. However, in role-reversal questions, the speaker is asked to speculate about the behaviour and experience of another. For example, Person A might be asked to imagine the impact of their own behaviour changes on Person B and the possible significance of this for Person B. Or Person A could be asked to speculate about what changes Person B might want to see in their relationship. Role-reversal questions are often coupled with outsider-perspective questions. For example: 'If you were being more relaxed and more approachable at home, how would Sandra find out? What would she notice that would tell her this was definitely happening and wasn't just a fluke?' (outsider-perspective). 'And when she noticed this, what effect do you think it might have on her? What difference will it make for her to see you following through with your plan?' (role-reversal).

Interrelating actions and perspectives through relationship questions can help to expand the perspective of both speakers and listeners and can be particularly helpful when the listener (Person B) is the identified 'problem person' and is an unwilling participant. The listener can be brought into the conversation 'vicariously' and may hear something different: Person A taking the time to imagine Person B's perspective and perhaps even agreeing that both parties need to change. This form of indirect engagement can work to pre-empt reactivity and prepare the way for the therapist to address the listener directly at a later stage.

In the excerpt used to exemplify specifying (above), the therapist used a future projection sequence to draw from James a specific description of where the first signs of his hoped-for changes might occur. James said that one important sign would be that 'Tim might actually appear at dinner and take an interest in the conversation.' This strand of conversation might continue as follows:

Therapist: [*to James*] And if Tim did turn up for dinner and participate for a while in the conversation, what would be different between you?

James: Well, I'd probably be so surprised I'd be lost for words. But at least we wouldn't be at each other's throats.

Therapist: So after you got over your surprise, what would be different between you? How would you be interacting with Tim? What would he notice that was different about you?

James: I suppose he'd see me relaxing more and not constantly on alert for trouble.

Therapist: What would tell him that you were more relaxed? What would he notice first?

James:	I suppose I wouldn't be constantly frowning, and I might say a few funny things. Believe it or not, we used to be quite good at jokes and repartee.
Therapist:	Really? So if Tim decided to appear at dinner and take part in the conversation, what he would notice is that you were feeling relaxed enough to indulge in a bit of humour. What effect do you think this might have on him? Do you think that might encourage him to do the same?
James:	I'd like to think that … but it's been so long? I don't have any great hopes.
Therapist:	I certainly understand that. But in terms of your relationship with Tim, that's what you'd like to see happening between you? More humour and repartee like you used to enjoy?
James:	Definitely.
Therapist:	And if I were to ask Tim what changes he would like to see in your relationship, do you think he might say something similar?

As interrelating may at first seem unusual or unexpected, a degree of repetition and gentle persistence is often required. This path of inquiry might encourage both James and Tim to look beyond a win/lose perspective to one where both parties are seen as changing reciprocally and the *relationship* is the winner. Another suitable opportunity for relationship questions would occur if the therapist sensed that Tim was hearing something new from his parents. If, through the use of the different process interventions, James and Ellen appeared to be voicing their concerns and requests differently, the therapist could ask them: 'What's been different about what you've said today? What do you think Tim would say is different about what he's heard so far? What might have surprised him the most?' This could enable James and Ellen to reflect on the differences in their own behaviour and attempt to experience this from Tim's perspective.

Mutualizing

Mutualizing involves the therapist listening for and reflecting the possibility of shared hopes, experiences and aspirations among family members. This may emerge through conversations with each family member and the use of interventions such as specifying, theming and interrelating. For example, sometimes a more abstract or metaphorical theme (such as promoting harmony, keeping the peace, or rebuilding relationships) can be found to link the specific agendas of conflicting individuals. As Lipchik (2002) suggests, a cardinal rule in family therapy is to avoid too much talk about differences and to focus where possible on what family members share, even though it may be mainly negative at first. A sense of shared experience, vision or values can be a surprising and unifying influence when disagreement and misunderstanding have become the norm. At the very least, finding commonalities, however tenuous they may sometimes appear, is a way of 'buying time' for the consultation to be helpful. A new-found sense of connection may encourage family members to persevere in relationship therapy though little immediate progress has been made.

Therapist: [*to James, Ellen, Tim, Casey and Joanne*] I'm getting a sense that, despite the severe conflict that's been happening, one thing you have in common is that you're all quite shocked at how quickly things have gotten out of hand, and you're all bewildered about what to do next. But at the same time you all know that something has to be done quickly ... that things can't go on as they are. Some of you have talked about the house being a war zone at present ... and though there are a lot of serious issues to work through, it seems to me that you're all wanting some kind of truce, so you can all take a deep breath and try to work out some other way of settling your differences as a family. So maybe the first step is to call a truce so that at least things don't get worse ... .

It is important that the therapist bases any suggestion of mutuality on what people have actually said or implied. If the therapist's comments appear gratuitous or gloss over major differences in an attempt to produce a 'feel-good' atmosphere, a premature attempt at mutualizing can be counterproductive. As always, the clients' responsiveness (verbal and non-verbal) helps to shape the negotiation process. Though the example I have given takes the form of a summary statement by the therapist, mutualizing can occur in much simpler ways through comments or questions offered in the course of the conversation. For example, as James and Ellen expand on their hopes, the therapist might say 'That actually sounds a bit like what Tim just said he was wanting. Do you think you might actually be closer on this, than you first thought?' Another opening for mutualizing can be found in the example used for interrelating (above) where it is suggested that a 'shared humour' between James and Tim might be a sign or change. These kinds of threads lend themselves to the possibility of mutualizing comments and reflections.

Tracking and linking

In the sometimes tense and chaotic atmosphere of a conjoint meeting, the therapist can sometimes lose track of each person's hopes and goals, particularly when these seem unconnected or where one or two people tend to dominate the conversation through their energy or influence. Bertolino and O'Hanlon (2002) suggest that the therapist carefully track each person's goals and link them by using the word 'and ...' in order to give equal emphasis to each person and to encourage a more inclusive way of talking (both/and instead of either/or). It provides a way of summarizing and connecting the varied and sometimes confusing threads of the conversation as they emerge. However, the therapist does not simply reflect what each client has said, but offers a constructive summary, selectively emphasizing hopes and goals. This activity helps to check that the therapist has heard each person's point of view, and encourages everyone to feel attended to, acknowledged, and included in the conversation. It may also convey the possibility that everyone's hopes and goals can be addressed.

> *Therapist*: [*to James, Ellen, Tim, Casey and Joanne*] So let me check that I've got this right. James, you're wanting a much greater feeling of respect in the household, especially from Tim towards Ellen and the other members of the family ... and Ellen, you're also wanting a break from this war of attrition and you're hoping that Tim can find a way to reconnect with the really good relationships that he used to have with you and his sisters ... and Tim, you're also wanting peace to break out, and you're wanting to find a way to get your voice heard more in the family, without ending up in a verbal war each time ... and Casey, you're wanting to be able to go about your business without being hassled ... and Joanne, you aren't exactly sure what you're wanting, but you wish the whole family could be happier again. Have I got it right?

This process intervention has both an influencing and an orienting function. It allows the therapist to influence the way in which family members state their concerns and requests and also helps the therapist to orient to any changes that have occurred during the meeting. In conjoint meetings it is not unusual for new issues, goals and priorities to emerge and for family members' perspectives to change. Sometimes, for example, a person who has voiced particular concerns early in the conversation may change their priorities after listening to others engage with the therapist. Tracking and linking provides a way for the therapist periodically to check in with all family members and make sure he or she is still on track with where each person is wanting to go.

Prioritizing

As we have seen, family meetings often produce a diversity of client hopes and goals. In order both to be inclusive yet maintain a coherent focus, it is often important to prioritize in terms of which issues need to be addressed first. Are there any pressing concerns that need to be addressed before other goals can be achieved? Are there some pivotal concerns that, if resolved, might also relieve some of the others? Once priorities are decided, the therapist will ensure that the remaining issues and hopes are kept on the agenda for later. Therapists may also wish to distinguish between immediate and longer-term goals and formalize this in a therapy contract (Madsen, 1999). If clients are unable to agree on priorities, one possibility is for the therapist to make a provisional suggestion as to where to start, promising to consider other people's priorities at the next session. Prioritizing can often be used in tandem with tracking and linking.

> *Therapist*: We've talked about a number of hopes that you each have in coming here. There are quite a few and it will probably take some time to address

	all of them. What do you think has to happen first? If there was one thing we could agree to make a start on today that might help set the stage for all the other changes you are wanting, what do you think that might be?
James:	I think we've all got to agree to call a truce, and make sure things don't get worse.
Ellen:	I agree. We need some way to stop before things get out of hand.
Therapist:	What do you think, Tim? Is that an important first step? Trying to find some ways to keep everyone from losing it?
Tim:	[*shrugs*] Maybe. But I don't know what I can do.
Therapist:	Well, that might be something we can all work on today – what each of you can do to protect your relationships from permanent harm while you struggle with the other issues. Because it seems that when you all lose it, nobody wins, and none of you has any success in getting the others to change. Would that be a good place to start today?
Tim:	So long as it's not just me who has to do things.
Therapist:	A truce means everybody has to work together. It only needs one side to start a war, but everyone has to work to start a truce.

In situations where some participants are clearly more committed to counselling than others, it is helpful to involve all parties in trying to agree on where to start. There is often a temptation to follow the agenda of the people who have been most active in the conversation (James and Ellen in this example). However, their priorities may be far ahead of where the less motivated members might be willing to go. By attempting to involve all members of the meeting we may reach consensus on a starting point that is less ambitious but more collaborative and realistic. In this example it involves focusing simply on family survival strategies: ways in which everyone (including Tim) can contribute to calling a truce.

Between the shoals and toward the horizon

The aim of these process interventions is not simply to explore 'who wants what', but to do so in a manner that will enhance the possibility for constructive collaboration. They are intended to extend the benefits of the hosting process by maintaining a reflective emotional climate and allowing the therapist to develop a sense of partnership with both speakers and listeners. In training contexts, especially, I have found these interventions to be helpful for practitioners who are attempting to make the transition from individual to relationship work and who tend to 'lose the plot' in conjoint settings. As with all such lists of interventions, however, it is important to stress that they are not all appropriate in any session and are certainly not used in a uniform or sequential way.

Developing a navigational metaphor, the therapist uses these processes to steer the conversation between the shoals of both problem and solution talk. A preoccupation with either can cause the conversation to run aground. At one extreme, it can sink under the weight of problem-saturated descriptions and 'bad trance' interactions. At the other, it can become narrowly preoccupied with pursuing a particular goal or end state (The Solution), or with the relentless pursuit of future-oriented talk, regardless of client responsiveness. In this case, the conversation sinks under the weight of its own irrelevance. We need to navigate between these shoals with one eye on collaboration with family members and the other eye fixed on the horizon of possibilities. Attempting to keep the conversation 'afloat', the multiply-engaged therapist works to achieve a balance between the perspectives of speakers and listeners, between acceptance and change, and between orienting and influencing.

Additional processes and contexts

Using structured question sequences

Constructive therapists who specialize in the solution-oriented style may wish to introduce some of the well known structured question sequences early in the meeting in order to accomplish similar purposes. For example, the therapist could use a future projection sequence involving the 'miracle question' (Berg, 1994; de Jong and Berg, 2002; de Shazer, 1994) to invite clients to imagine life after the problem, and to evoke in detail what would be different. Also, a 'scaling question' sequence (ibid.) might be introduced as a way of specifying desired change in terms of process and small steps. In such a sequence clients might be asked a question such as, 'On a scale from zero to ten, where ten is the point where you don't need to come to counselling any more, and zero represents the worst things have been, where would you say you are today?' Depending on the client's response, a sequence of follow-up questions is used to invite specification of what might need to happen in order for them to move ever closer to ten (or to avoid moving backwards from where they are).

My own experience is that it takes a considerable amount of skill and experience to use structured sequences like these in conjoint meetings. Therapists who are relatively new to family therapy often become confused about exactly who to involve, how and when. There is sometimes a tendency to get lost inside the technique so that it becomes an end in itself rather than a means towards an end. With the principle of multiple engagement in mind, the process interventions I have outlined may offer more flexibility in the early stages of a meeting. They allow the therapist to develop a conversation with each individual as speaker or listener, and may also be helpful in building a bridge to the use of specific structured question sequences later in the meeting. For example, if after talking with James, Ellen, Tim and his sisters, we all agree that a 'truce' needs to be called in the 'war of attrition', the therapist could initiate a scaling question sequence by asking each person to indicate their level of confidence (from zero to ten) that a truce can be achieved in the immediate future. Or I could use a future projection sequence, and ask family members to imagine that a miracle occurs in their sleep tonight and they wake up tomorrow to find that a truce has broken out. As they were asleep when the miracle happened, how would each of them find out that something was different? The use of structured sequences in conjoint meetings is facilitated by a shared sense of purpose and direction, aided by a unifying theme.

Deconstructing problems

The process interventions I have described include an invitation to discuss concerns in future-oriented terms. However, some clients may decline this invitation and may clearly wish to spend more time talking about the history or current manifestation of their problems. Also, some constructive therapists may decide to spend more time orienting to the problem situation, either through personal preference or because they are expected to conduct problem-oriented assessments. Working collaboratively, therapists can attempt to negotiate ways of orienting to problems that help to 'deconstruct' or 'unpack' the problem description in constructive ways.

One way of unpacking problems is to talk about them as *verbs*: as forms of actions or patterns that occur in specific contexts, rather than talking about them as personal afflictions, conditions or personality traits. The question becomes, how does a family member 'do' depression, or temper tantrums? How do you practise conflict in your relationship? Specific information can then be gathered about pattern and context. Bertolino and O'Hanlon (2002: 151) suggest exploring these areas:

- How often does the problem typically happen (once an hour, once a day, once a week)?
- What is the typical timing (time of day, week, month, year) of the problem?
- How long does the problem typically last?
- Where does the problem typically happen?
- What does the client, and others who are around, usually do when the problem is happening?

To balance this emphasis on the predominance of problem patterns, I also suggest exploring how the pattern typically *ends*. For example, how do the temper tantrums subside? What exactly happens? Who does what? What tells you that this is about to happen? Or, how do you make up after a fight? Who makes the first move? How do you know that it is time to call a halt? What skills do you use in making up? These kinds of questions construct problems as specific actions occurring – and ending – in specific contexts, where clients can exercise a degree of personal agency.

Another option is to use the externalizing language of the narrative style in order to focus on the *relationship* between people and problems. For example, Madsen (1999: 80–81) lists questions in a range of areas that allow the therapist to assess problems rather than families. These include:

Context of presenting concerns

- In what situations is the problem most/least likely to occur?
- What is the effect of the problem on you and your relationships?
- How does the problem interfere with your preferred life?
- How do you explain the problem?
- How have you attempted to cope with the problem?
- What broader cultural support does the problem receive?

Relevant history

- What is the history of the relationship between the problem and you?
- When has the problem been stronger in the history of that relationship and when have you been stronger?
- What has supported the problem's influence on you (family-of-origin level, family-helper level, broader cultural level)?
- What has supported your influence on the problem (family-of-origin level, family-helper level, broader cultural level)?

Medical information and risk factors

- What effects has the problem had on your physical health? Has it exacerbated existing medical concerns for you and others?
- What, if any, interactions has the problem had with suicidal ideation, violence, substance abuse, sexual abuse or neglect in your lives?

Formulation

- What constraints stand in the way of you getting the future that you want?
- What strengths, resources and knowledge do you have, to deal with those constraints?

I have selected these areas from Madsen's assessment scheme to illustrate ways in which traditional content areas can be reworked in constructive ways. By assessing relationships between problems and family members, we can attempt to steer clear of the four problematic stories of blame, invalidation, determinism and impossibility. As a contribution towards this, Madsen prefers to speak of 'multi-stressed' families rather than 'multi-problem' families.

Using different media and forms of expression

For the purposes of this book, I have focused on the best known medium of constructive therapy conversations: the skilful use of questions and other verbal responses. However, it is important to note that other media and forms of expression are also compatible with the approach. This adds an important degree of flexibility in situations where children or other family members may find verbal expression difficult or threatening. In the narrative style, for instance, forms of expression such as drawing, drama, sandplay, letters and poetry can be used to help clients to map the relationship between themselves and their problems (Freeman, Epston and Lobovits, 1997). In the solution-oriented style, similar forms of expression can be used to evoke preferred futures and signs of change (Berg and Steiner, 2003). For example, a scaling question sequence can be 'enacted', with family members positioning themselves on an imaginary line across the room.

In the context of his work with self-harming adolescents, Selekman (2002) also describes the use of solution-oriented *family sculpting* and *choreography*: methods that are usually associated with more experiential approaches to therapy. Using sculpting, for example, he places an adolescent client in the centre of the room and uses her guidance to position other family members around her in terms of emotional closeness and distance. He then reflects with her on what makes it difficult to move closer to the more distant members. The next phase involves asking the adolescent to sculpt the family as she would like it to be in terms of closeness and distance, and exploring how this new physical arrangement would make a difference for her and the others. In combination with future-oriented questions, this process helps to dramatize how family members will interact differently in their preferred future. Used in this way, sculpting can cast light on both present relationship patterns and preferred relationship patterns.

Working with one client

If some family members refuse to attend or if you have agreed to see one person alone for the first session, the process interventions are still relevant, as is relationship therapy itself. However, there can be a tendency for therapists to 'drop their guard' and be less mindful of their language when working with one client. This can jeopardize multipartiality and may result in the therapist unwittingly joining in the person's characterizations of others. At the very least, therapists need to keep in mind that they may eventually meet the other members and that it is important not to prejudge them or take sides. A helpful way to maintain our vigilance when working with one person is to bring the other family members into the room in spirit and to pretend that they can actually hear everything you say. You can then remain multiply engaged with them as imaginary listeners: you will not say anything about them that you would not be prepared to say in their presence. The process intervention of interrelating can be especially helpful in maintaining a relationship focus with an individual client.

If the person has been coerced into attending or is unsure of the reason for the meeting, they should be hosted as a visitor with no pressure to answer questions or to become a 'customer' for any kind of change. If the person does not wish to state any hopes or therapy goals (other than not having to come again) the therapist's curiosity can turn to speculation about what others might be wanting. This again involves the use of relationship questions:

- What do you think has given — the *impression* that you need to come here?
- What would it take to prove to — that they are wrong and that you don't need to come here again?
- If I were to ask — what they are hoping will be different from you coming here, what do you think they'd say?
- What would be a sign to — that things are changing and that you may not need to come here any more?
- Is there anything that — wants you to do that you actually think might be a good idea?
- Given that you are here and — isn't, is there anything we could talk about that might be helpful to *you*?

When other systems are involved

Sometimes the process of negotiation falters because the views, complaints or expectations of key people are unknown. Families may have been referred by other practitioners or agencies who have a specific involvement with one or more family members. These may include schools or social service agencies. Or the family may be receiving assistance from a number of helpers, each with a different agenda. Sometimes these non-family personnel are the prime movers in the sense of being the people most wanting change, and, perhaps more importantly, the only people who are clear about what exact changes are required. It is not unusual, for example, for a school counsellor to suggest family therapy in relation to a child's classroom behaviour problems or falling grades. However the child and other family members may be unclear about what exactly the referrer is wanting (other than a 'change of attitude'). This is especially important in situations where the referrer is empowered to decide whether satisfactory progress has been made. The referrer and any other key players may need to be brought into the preference-determined system either directly or indirectly. The latter can be achieved by asking clients to contact the referrer and gain further clarity on what is wanted, or by the therapist gaining the family's permission to make direct contact with the relevant person. This person can then be asked many of the same questions that have been asked of family members (for example, specifying questions).

When the going gets tough

Sometimes even the most discreet hosts cannot prevent conflict from breaking out. If family members persistently interrupt each other and engage in conversations for characterizations, accusations and recriminations, therapists can be faced with the dilemma of whether to ignore this and carry on regardless, or whether to intervene in some way.

Firstly, it is important to monitor your own emotional postures, so that you don't react in a fight or flight manner ('I must stop this happening! The session is getting out of control'). Sometimes a therapist's own anxiety about the emotional intensity in the room can prompt extreme reactions: either retreating into passivity or over-reacting. Rather than the therapist becoming increasingly concerned about what to do, it is often better to raise the matter directly with clients. The therapist can work from reflective postures and ask questions from a position of curiosity.

One useful question becomes: Is this kind of conflict a new experience for family members, or is it more of the same? Even though interactions between family members appear distressing, it may, in some ways, be a new experience for them, and one that should be encouraged rather than prematurely nipped in the bud. Perhaps the family have never had the experience of sitting down together and talking through an issue in such an intense way. Though it may be distressing, it could be a positive change and a valuable step towards other changes. If the experience is new, we can explore with clients how it is being *helpful*, and how it is *different* from what they usually do. We can also acknowledge people's willingness to 'hang in there' during a difficult discussion.

If, however, the pattern of conflict is more of the same and part of the problem, our curiosity can turn to other matters. Have the clients come to therapy to do exactly what they usually do at home? Or were they hoping to learn to do something different? If they are wanting things to be different, how would they like the therapist to help them avoid falling into old habits? How does the presence of the therapist affect the conflict habits?

Does it strengthen them or weaken them? Is anything different about the way they are experiencing the conflict here? These kinds of questions can often break the 'bad trance' patterns by inviting clients to reflect upon their own behaviour in a non-threatening way. Sometimes humour can be helpful. I sometimes thank family members for their vivid demonstration of the problems they have been talking about, but indicate that I'm a reasonably fast learner and probably won't need to see it again. By working from reflective postures connected with a stance of curiosity, the therapist can avoid blaming or directly confronting family members and potentially making things worse.

Until things become so reactive that conversation becomes impossible, it is often preferable to simply ignore negative interactions. For example, if you are attempting to develop an individual engagement pattern with Person A, and Person B keeps interrupting, you can remain focused on Person A, and simply resume the conversation when the interruption is over. At the very least, you are modelling an alternative way of responding. Also, if family members do become involved in a 'free for all' it is often useful to sit back and observe for a time, rather than responding immediately. Apart from giving yourself valuable time to calm down and think, this provides opportunities to notice signs of potential resourcefulness that could be utilized later. For example, you might notice that some family members are particularly skilled at calming others down, or that family members seem to know when they are on the brink of going too far, or that occasionally they show some signs of appreciation even in the heat of the moment. Therefore, rather than thinking that you have failed as a host if things start to get out of hand, it is preferable to return to one of the principles of brief therapy: that everything can be utilized in some way.

But what if agreement on goals and priorities cannot be reached? Is there any point in continuing with conjoint meetings if they are likely to prove a draining and futile experience for everyone? Would it be better to offer individual sessions to family members or see them in different groupings?

My own preference is to invite clients to persevere with conjoint meetings for several sessions before suggesting a change of format. It has been said that one of the unofficial aims of a first session is simply to secure a second session, and when I am struggling to invite collaboration on goals and priorities, I shrink my own goals down to inviting the clients to return. A week can be a long time in both politics and family life, and sometimes clients are more prepared to compromise in subsequent sessions. Sometimes, the very 'failure' of the first session produces change. I remember expressing surprise to a family that they seemed so willing to co-operate when the first session had proved so difficult. The mother replied that because the first session had been so 'disastrous' (a more accurate description), they had realized that I couldn't help them, and that they would have to 'pull up their socks' and start to do it themselves!

I find it helpful – and humbling – to remind myself that family meetings can be 'therapeutic' in ways that are largely fortuitous. For example, it has been suggested that the key stimulus to change often comes from events that occur outside of therapy (Duncan and Miller, 2000). An unemployed father may suddenly find work, a child may change teachers or schools, or a mother may recover from a debilitating illness. All of these events have the capacity to transform relationship difficulties, and sometimes the most important contribution of family meetings may simply be to *contain* the present conflict and keep people talking until such external events can 'kick in'. Another fortuitous effect may come from the everyday process of observational learning. Intentionally or otherwise, therapists typically model forms of interaction that are different from those occurring in the family's usual environment. Over time, family members may acquire new options for interaction simply through observation and reflection. For example, parents who observe the therapist engaging their teenage son in a respectful and reflective conversation may note the very different kind of response that he gives when this occurs, and decide to try it for themselves.

These examples remind us of the non-specific, incidental, and ironic aspects of family therapy. Sometimes the resources that clients eventually utilize have no connection with the focus of our conversations. Sometimes we are helpful in ways that have nothing to do with our specific intentions at a particular moment. Sometimes we are helpful despite our models. When the going gets tough, these reflections can encourage us to persevere with family meetings and to avoid being too hard on ourselves, our clients or our favourite models.

From preferences to possibilities

The central contribution of this chapter has been to describe some process interventions that help to elucidate a sense of purpose and direction. It is important to remember, however, that the initial consideration of 'who wants what?' is merely an effective way of *starting* the process of inquiry. It does not set a permanent direction or establish fixed goals or targets for intervention. To emphasize this, Walter and Peller (2000) have chosen to use terms like goal*ing* or, more recently, preferenc*ing* to describe this ongoing process rather than the more conventional term goal-*setting*, which implies that the activity is limited to a particular phase of the conversation, and that particular goals are set in concrete. Similarly, Lipchik (2002) describes an ongoing process of clarifying goals rather than a task of defining goals. Though the initial process of negotiation may seem relatively structured, it continues to evolve as family members refine their preferences. This ongoing inquiry into preferences acts as a bridge to the next phase of inquiry into possibilities.

5 Evoking Possibilities

Every new affirmative projection of the future is a consequence of an appreciative understanding of the past or the present. (Cooperrider, 1990: 120)

A self without a story contracts into the thinness of its personal pronoun. (Crites, 1986: 172)

Constructive therapists are well known (often to the point of parody) for their rigorous attention to identifying episodes of client resourcefulness and hope, and attempting to weave narratives of possibility from these. The best known and most typically used approach takes the form of questions that invite clients to notice and appreciate exceptional or unique experiences[1] that defy the pattern of identified concerns and fit with their preferred futures. Therapists will be intently curious about these experiences: How were they accomplished? How was a particular action planned? How exactly was it carried out? How did the client prepare for it? Who else noticed? What did they see? What might this say about the client's determination or commitment? What might it suggest for the future? The aim is not to persuade the client, or to 'point out positives', but to evoke an experience of hope, curiosity and possibility.

The major principle underlying all of these approaches is that *the therapist's expertise lies in crafting questions that evoke the client's expertise.* This simple principle guides our curiosity and the paths of inquiry that are pursued. Having created a space for inquiry (Chapter 2) and begun a process of inquiry into purpose and preferences (Chapters 3 and 4), the therapist listens for opportunities to inquire into *possibilities* based on the identification and appreciation of competence, differences and change. As the conversation evolves, the therapist continually invites clients to explore and define two central matters: what they are wanting to be different in their lives, and what strengths and resources they can bring to bear on making these desired differences a reality (Berg and de Jong, 1996). Arguably, much of the conversation consists of variations on these themes as the therapist finds different ways of asking clients to elaborate on what they are wanting from the consultation, and on what they are already doing (or have done, or could do) that might be helpful. By shifting back and forth between these converging themes, the therapist helps to bring the conversation to the *threshold of change*. The clients do the rest.

As many enthusiasts have discovered, however, the principles may be simple but the practice is not easy. In family consultations there are hazards and pitfalls in trying to evoke and develop publicly a *shared* narrative of client competence and possibilities. There are also, however, distinct opportunities. In this chapter I introduce two additional process interventions (*eliciting* and *storying*) that are used to evoke possibilities, and discuss some important 'lessons from the field' relating to their use in conjoint sessions. I then describe different forms of inquiry that are typically used to evoke possibilities. The major focus of the chapter is an attempt to demonstrate the most important lessons learned in adapting these approaches to conjoint work.

Eliciting and storying difference/change

The most typical inquiry into possibilities involves the identification of differences or changes that emerge from the immediate focus of the conversation. The ongoing elaboration of 'who wants what?' provides a rich backdrop for the identification of clues to possibilities. In relationship therapy, especially, this form of inquiry makes more sense when conducted in the *wake* of articulating desired change and describing a preferred future. If the process of clarifying 'who wants what?' has been achieved in a way that enhances collaboration and mutual hopes, it can also serve to orient other family members to notice events that are consistent with these hopes and priorities – events that might have been 'off the radar' before. Rather than simply asking an 'exceptions question' such as 'When does the problem not occur?' – which can often be experienced as too abrupt or unusual – the path of inquiry now takes a more extended form along the lines of 'What are you wanting to be different … how are you hoping counselling might help … how will these changes be different for you and your relationships … what would be some signs that this was happening … and *is any part of this happening already?*' In relationship therapy, where clients may be ambivalent and a reactive emotional environment may be apparent, this more 'leisurely' path often proves more effective.

Some of the best known methods in constructive therapy practice involve drawing clients' attention to instances of difference or desired change that have occurred. Before proceeding further, it is important to distinguish between 'difference' and 'change'. Sometimes a client may immediately recognize an event as a *change* in the sense of a positive development or success, but sometimes a client may see it only as something *different*, that may or may not have significance. For example, a client who is struggling to barely cope each day may agree that they have done something different by making a cup of tea for their partner, but may not see this as a meaningful change. A common pitfall for new therapists is their eagerness to see every difference as a positive change or 'success' and to try, prematurely, to persuade clients of this. In order to maintain this distinction, I will use the hybrid term 'difference/change' in the following sections.

Here are two important process interventions that most constructive therapies would identify with their practice.

Box 5.1   Process interventions for evoking possibilities

Eliciting: Inviting clients to notice and identify instances of difference/change that are consistent with their preferred future.

Storying: Inviting clients to 'plot' instances of difference/change into an evolving narrative of competence and possibility.

The skills associated with these interventions are germane to constructive approaches such as solution-focused therapy and narrative therapy, and have helped to define the territory associated with these styles. Therapists consistently seek to draw clients' attention to unnoticed or overlooked areas or episodes of personal knowledge, skill, experience and imagination that may enhance possibilities for change. The process intervention of *eliciting* is used to identify or highlight these events. The related intervention of *storying* is then typically used to invite clients to 'perform meaning' around these events so that they attain significance in shaping a client's narrative. Though these two process interventions may seem to go hand in hand, it is not always the case that eliciting is followed immediately by storying. In the example given above where a client is barely coping, eliciting a difference may be all that is possible at the time – the storying may come later. For this reason, the two interventions are best considered as separate but related activities.

A map for storying difference/change

When therapists manage to elicit exceptional or unique experiences they can utilize many different paths of inquiry in encouraging clients to story these events. In order to orient the therapist's curiosity I have found it useful to conceptualize a map based on two dimensions: a *temporal* dimension (where the conversation moves between past, present and future) and an *actions/meanings* dimension where the conversation shifts between sharpening the focus on actions and widening the lens to incorporate

Figure 5.1 Two-dimensional map for the storying of difference/change

	PAST	PRESENT	FUTURE
ACTIONS Individuals	1	2	3
Relationships	4	5	6
MEANINGS Individuals	7	8	9
Relationships	10	11	12

the thematic significance of these actions. These dimensions cover some essential elements of narrative: movement through time, character, actions, themes and reflections. The map is presented in Figure 5.1 and is similar to that often described in narrative therapy, where the 'landscape of action' is contrasted with the 'landscape of consciousness' (for example, Payne, 2000: 109). However, I have made one change to the way these ideas have been previously presented. In order to emphasize the dimension of relationships in conjoint work, I have divided the actions/meanings dimension into sub-categories of *individuals* and *relationships*. This encourages paths of inquiry that may focus at different times on individual and relationship actions and themes.

Here are two examples of potential paths of inquiry originating from the elicitation of difference/change. You might like to trace the way in which they zigzag across the dimensions of the map, utilizing the different cells. Please note that in the temporal dimension of the 'Present', I include the recent circumstances surrounding the current situation, while using the Past to refer to a more distant time when things were different or better.

Example 1: From the identification of difference/change occurring in the present

One typical path of inquiry might result from the process intervention of *specifying* a client's preferred future: What would be a clear sign that things were improving? A client answers that her adolescent son would begin to show more consideration in a number of areas, including consulting with her before asking his friends over for the weekend, and making an effort to interact with the family in the evening instead of disappearing into his room. The therapist then asks if any of these things are happening already and the client replies that, somewhat to her surprise, she had noticed that he was making an effort in the last week and on several occasions had seemed genuinely interested in making conversation. This might produce a storying sequence as follows:

How exactly did he go about making conversation? Who did he speak to and about what? (2) How did the other members of the family respond? (2, 5) Were people pleased? What was most pleasing about it? (8) How do you think he managed to do this in the present circumstances? (8) What might this suggest about his attitude towards family relationships? (11) When you look back over time, has there always been a thread of connection between you, even in difficult times? (10) What has sustained this thread in the face of adversity? (4, 10) What might this suggest for your relationship in the future? (6, 12).

Example 2: From the identification of difference/change occurring in the past

Sometimes it is easier to locate opportunities relating to more distant times or events. For example, a couple who have been 'caught up in parenting' seem to have lost the ability to communicate in an intimate way. The therapist uses the process intervention of *theming*: What would it mean to you if you did start to do more things as a couple and began to share more of your lives again? The clients reply that they would feel a sense of *closeness* and *intimacy* again. Taking up these themes, the therapist might ask the couple to think back over the history of their relationship and explore the ways in which closeness and intimacy were present then:

What did you do then that was different? (4) How did doing those kinds of things help you feel close and intimate? What was special about them? (10) As your relationship developed over time, how did you go about preserving closeness and intimacy? What new ways did you develop in order to do this? (4) Can you recall a time when you noticed that closeness and intimacy were starting to disappear from your relationship and you decided to do something about this? (4) How did you do this, and how did it make a difference? (4, 10) Would any of these ideas be helpful now, or will you need to find new ways to achieve closeness and intimacy? (5, 11) If you were committed to finding new ways to sustain your relationship in the future, so that it still felt special, how might these positive memories help? (6, 12) What kinds of things would you like to look forward to doing together in the future? (6, 12) What might be the first step in deciding how to bring this about? (6).

These possible paths are by no means exhaustive but suggest the way in which the map provides scope for the therapist's curiosity to move backwards and forwards through time, and between sharpening the lens and widening the focus. It is important to note, of course, that these sequences of questions would not necessarily follow one after the other. They are more like progressive thematic developments that build over the entirety of a conversation. Also, in many instances, the path of inquiry might shift only one or two cells in the figure. Remember that the aim is not to attempt a conversational tour de force by crisscrossing the entire grid in every session, but to use the grid as a backdrop to guide the choice of possible paths at particular moments.

Lessons from the field

As well as learning from trial and error in my own practice, I have had the opportunity over a number of years to observe and supervise practice by graduate students and other practitioners. This has been an invaluable experience in highlighting the most typical pitfalls for constructive rela-tionship therapists. Perhaps *the* most typical hole into which beginning therapists fall is that of trying to highlight client competence and resource-fulness too quickly. At the beginning of this chapter, I implied that con-structive therapists have sometimes become objects of parody in their relentless search for strengths and competence. Particularly in the early years of solution-oriented therapies, it was not unusual for zealous thera-pists to pursue an inquiry about resources almost from the beginning of a meeting. In reply to a client's initial statement about feeling depressed, for example, a therapist might respond almost immediately with 'When have you felt a bit less depressed in the past few days?' This would be routinely followed by 'How did you do that?' and so on. As time-effective thera-pies have become more collaborative and conversational, we have moved on from there. However, when confronted with the complexities of family concerns and the tensions of a reactive emotional climate, it is not unusual for therapists to try to pull out all the stops in an effort to find exceptional or unique experiences. This typically results in a frustrating 'yes–but' interaction as family members counteract the attempt to elicit and story positive changes. When this happens, therapists may find them-selves resorting to persuasion or debate, pointing out positives rather than evoking possibilities. I would like to offer a number of 'lessons from the field' that may assist constructive relationship therapists to avoid situations like this.

Self-awareness

Evoking possibilities is an activity that is best pursued when reflective emotional postures are the norm. In an attempt to counter family conflict or negativity, we can easily try too hard to introduce new perspectives. Often this is because our own emotional postures are reactive (we are in fight/flight mode) and we want to do something immediately in order to be 'helpful'. I remember the time when I first started working with families in a dark and deserted university building at night where I was the only occupant together with the clients I was seeing. As a beginner to family therapy, I can remember the feeling of being utterly alone and unsupported as I listened to families consumed with conflict, negativity and hopelessness. I tended to react in one of two ways. Sometimes I would be drawn into the family's demoralization so that I almost felt like I was becoming a family member, and would emotionally withdraw, retreating into stock expressions of empathy. Or I would react in the opposite way and try to counter feelings of helplessness by energetically 'convincing' the family that things were more optimistic than they thought. My own emotional postures of mobilization or reactivity were influencing me to either withdraw or 'counterattack' in an attempt to do something quickly. With more experience I have learned to monitor my own emotional postures, and to try to shift myself into a reflective position of curiosity so that I can resist the temptation, out of my own anxiety or desperation, to 'help'.

Patience and timing

We need to make a careful distinction between *noticing* opportunities to highlight changes and competencies, and choosing when and how to *act* on these. The therapist listens with a 'constructive ear' for any episodes or suggestions of client competence (Lipchik, 1988). These can be thought of as 'clues' to alternative narratives (Payne, 2000). However, they are only clues at this stage, not *cues* for immediate action. When a client says something significant, there can be a temptation to see this as a cue to jump in immediately with questions such as: 'Was that different?' 'How did you do that?' 'What steps did you take?' 'Who else noticed?' Beginning therapists, in particular, often try to force open every window of opportunity that presents itself. In relationship therapy it is important to take the mood of the audience into account. If you sense a prevailing emotional climate of reactivity (in yourself as much as in others), it is often more helpful to silently *note* or *log* potential clues for future reference when the evidence may be stronger and the audience more receptive to their significance. There is no point in opening windows of opportunity until people are ready to look through them. I remember a situation where two parents were mortified that their teenage son had suddenly run away from home after a period of conflict with themselves and his younger sister. The mother happened to say that the only positive thing that had come out of the experience was that his sister had been absolutely stunned and speechless when she found out. This, her mother assumed, was because she realized for the first time how much she actually cared about her brother. Taking this as a clue to a positive development, I immediately turned to the girl and asked what went through her mind when she first realized her brother had run away. She thought for a moment before replying: 'I was thinking, can I have his room?!'

Sequencing: preferences before possibilities

I have already mentioned that effective eliciting and storying of difference/ change often occurs in the wake of an extended discussion of hopes, goals and signs of change. The more that clients elaborate on these preferences, the more they are likely to be 'primed' to notice and appreciate relevant changes or differences. Furthermore, in relationship therapy, an exploration of each person's preferences may be needed before focusing on any one person's competencies and accomplishments. If some family members' concerns and requests have not yet been heard and acknowledged, they may be unwilling to respond to an invitation to appreciate changes made by others.

Shared goals and mutuality

It is usually easier to evoke possibilities when these relate to shared goals and a mutual sense of purpose. If a family member expresses hopes and goals that are largely personal, a therapist's attempt to highlight success is likely to be appreciated by that individual alone. These changes will be meaningful in personal terms but not in relationship terms. It is often preferable for a therapist to again be patient and wait for an opportunity to highlight an episode that relates to shared or relationship goals.

Curiosity rather than enthusiasm

As I suggested previously, therapists sometimes mistake differences for positive change and move too quickly into 'cheerleading'. When therapists uncover what appears to be an exceptional experience, they can become prematurely enthused about its significance and try to sweep others up in their enthusiasm. Clients, however, are often less enthused about such episodes and can be reluctant to credit them with importance. In order to avoid a 'yes–but' interaction, it is prudent to consider these episodes, at least initially, as differences rather than successful changes, and be curious rather than overtly enthusiastic. For example, if parents have longstanding complaints about their son's lack of attention to study, they are unlikely to see one episode where he goes to his room without being ordered as a great success, and may react against a therapist's enthusiastic attempts to imply this. However, they may be prepared to acknowledge the event as something *different* from the usual pattern and be willing to engage with the therapist's curiosity about how it happened. While this is an important lesson in all therapy, it is especially important in relationship therapy because of the potential for significant others to contribute to the storying process.

Detail and verisimilitude

A potential opportunity of relationship therapy is the potential for inviting other voices to participate in the storying of change. At various points, therapists typically switch from an 'individual engagement' pattern to a 'reciprocal engagement' pattern, directly asking listeners to comment on what others have said ('Have you noticed this too?' 'Are you surprised by the changes that — has made?' 'What does this suggest about his concern for the future?' 'How might this change of direction affect your relationship with him?' etc.). However, there can be a temptation to invite reflections too quickly before a detailed and credible account has been developed. Whether speakers are describing changes that they or others have made, it is often more helpful to stay in individual engagement with the speaker until sufficient details have emerged to substantiate the account and establish its verisimilitude. 'What exactly did you do differently?' 'How did you manage this in the face of these difficulties?' 'What was it that finally helped you decide to take this step?' 'Can you recall the exact moment when you came to this decision?' 'How would other members of the family guess that something important has happened?' These kinds of detailed questions allow new descriptions to emerge with greater credibility, and increase the likelihood of a corroborative response from others.

An emerging theme of these lessons from the field is that therapists can easily find themselves working too hard and depleting their energy in fruitlessly trying to inveigle clients into noticing and appreciating each other's qualities and changes. As in many aspects of relationships, timing and mood are paramount considerations. Relationship therapy can be confusing and chaotic and therapists can easily slip into reactive emotional postures that trigger increasingly desperate actions. They may seize upon any apparent opportunity for an 'exception' and reach for any available technique that might help shift the talk from deficits to strengths. But in doing so they may lose the perspective of multiple engagement, narrowing attention to one small part of the relationship matrix in the room.

Though relationships between partners or family members may continue to be strained, it is important that the 'I–Thou' relationship between the *therapist and each person* remains collaborative. The therapist needs to remain a good host.

Possibilities emerging from the conversation

We can now examine some practical ways in which constructive therapists attempt to evoke possibilities. As the therapist listens with a constructive ear, opportunities to elicit and story difference/change may emerge at various points in the conversation. I will focus the discussion on the following situations:

- where differences/changes are mentioned spontaneously by clients;
- where they are implied by client comments;
- where they follow from a discussion of preferences or signs of change;
- where they occur during the meeting itself.

In each of these situations we have to decide whether, when and how to build upon these opportunities. In the following sections my aim will be twofold: to provide examples of how possibilities can be evoked in these situations, and also to convey some of the dilemmas faced by the therapist. In each example I will compare two possible paths, drawing on the lessons from the field in deciding which is to be preferred.

To anchor the discussion, I will use examples from hypothetical conversations with the Edwards family, who were introduced in Chapter 2 to demonstrate the use of a resource-oriented genogram (Figure 2.1, p. 49). Before proceeding further, you may wish to review the description of the family (Kevin, Sandra, Jessica and Daniel). Let us assume that we have proceeded beyond the initial hosting process to the negotiation of concerns and requests.

Highlighting changes and differences
mentioned spontaneously

Sometimes, at various points in a conversation, family members mention differences and changes without any particular prompting from the therapist. A typical example may occur early in the conversation when someone describes changes they have noticed prior to the session. This is like a spontaneous version of the 'pre-session change' questions used in solution-oriented approaches (where therapists specifically ask if clients have noticed any changes that have occurred in the interval between the making of the appointment and the first meeting). For constructive therapists, these kinds of comments may appear to be manna from heaven and there is an understandable temptation to pursue them immediately. However, in relationship contexts, as we have seen, this can be premature, especially at an early stage where we may still be working in the dark regarding people's agendas and priorities.

Example

During the initial discussion of concerns and requests, Sandra speaks first, talking about the tension that has filled the home since Kevin's redundancy, and her increasing frustration at his moodiness and lack of initiative. She believes that this is the main reason for Daniel's problems at school, and is hoping that family counselling might be a way of getting Kevin to see what is happening. She talks about her difficulty in even persuading him to attend the meeting, but mentions that, much to her own surprise, he has shown greater interest in coming to counselling in the last couple of days …

> *Therapist*: Really! What exactly has he done that shows greater interest?
> *Sandra*: He's asked me a few questions about what counsellors actually do, what kinds of qualifications they have and what kinds of problems they can help with. That kind of thing.
> *Therapist*: And that was a pleasant surprise to you?
> *Sandra*: It sure was. He even reminded the kids this morning about the appointment.

At this point, the therapist considers switching the focus of the conversation to Kevin …

Path 1

> *Therapist*: [*turning to Kevin*] That's interesting, Kevin. When did you start to have second thoughts about coming to counselling?

The therapist is hoping that Kevin's sudden interest in counselling might constitute a significant pre-session change that could be storied in a number of ways. What helped him to change his attitude? What might this say about his concern for his family and their future?

However, in pursuing this path at this early stage, the therapist may well be presumptuous in assuming that Kevin has had second thoughts about counselling. Though this apparent change fits with Sandra's goals for the meeting, we have no way of knowing whether they fit with Kevin's goals, as we have not yet discussed these with him. For all we know, Kevin may have asked questions about counselling out of a desire for self-protection (to gain information about those whom he is up against) or for some other reason. By inviting an immediate response from Kevin, the therapist may simply prompt him to undermine Sandra's perspective. At this early stage, it would probably be better to maintain an individual engagement pattern with Sandra.

Path 2

Therapist:	[*continuing to talk to Sandra*] That's interesting. What do you think has encouraged Kevin to ask these kinds of questions in the last few days?
Sandra:	I'd like to think it's because he realizes that we all need help, and he's wanting to take part.
Therapist:	And if he did, that would be important to you?
Sandra:	That's what I most want. To see him doing something active to help himself and all of us ...

In this segment, the therapist acknowledges Sandra's observations but does not yet assume they are shared by Kevin and does not seek to verify them with him. It may be better to note Sandra's observations for potential development later. If Kevin does indicate that he wants to make changes and sees counselling as potentially helpful, then we can return to the pre-session changes and explore with him how they came about. By then, we could be more confident of a shared perception of positive change, and a shared endeavour in storying the change.

Inquiring about changes and differences that are implied by client comments

As therapists listen with a constructive ear, they often hear comments that suggest, imply or hint at differences, changes or resourcefulness. These are possibilities that can be read between the lines and prompt us to consider alternative lines of inquiry. Here are some examples (paired with the alternative paths they prompt): 'Things have been so bad this week that we almost decided not to come back.' (*So you did decide to keep our appointment, even though it's been a tough week. What helped you decide it was still worth the effort?*) 'When he gets into this mood, it's almost impossible to get through to him.' (*Almost impossible? Do you mean that you are still able to get through to him to some degree, even though it's very difficult?*) 'When we have a fight, we really have one. I mean we don't make up for days afterwards.' (*When you do make up, how does it happen? How have you learned to know when it's time to make up?*) 'I nearly lost it with the boys last night. I was at the end of my tether, and came this close to hitting them.' (*And yet you didn't? What did you do to keep everyone safe?*) Again, therapists are faced with sudden decisions about how, whether and when to elicit and story the differences/changes that are implied.

Example

We are at a later point in the discussion about who is wanting what. Though Kevin appears willing to participate, he continually reacts to Sandra's attempts to 'blame' him for Daniel's misconduct at school. The therapist discovers that, since things have been tense at home, Daniel has been taking some of the tension with him to school and this has made it harder for him to avoid provocations – especially about his father not having a job. Daniel says that he doesn't know what he can do about this because every time he goes to school in a bad mood, he ends up in a fight, and he is in a bad mood 'just about every day'.

Path 1

Therapist: *Just about* every day? You mean there are some days when you don't go to school in a bad mood?

Daniel: Not really, but some days it's worse and I know I'm going to get into a fight.

Therapist: Tell me about the days when you don't go to school in a bad mood. How come those days are better?

Daniel: There aren't many.

Therapist: I know. But on those days, you don't get into fights. Is that right?

Daniel: Sometimes I still do.

Therapist: But they're not so bad?

Daniel: No.

Therapist: That's terrific. How do you manage to avoid the fights on those days?

Daniel: I don't know. Sometimes I still fight.

Therapist: But some days you don't?

Daniel: [*shrugs*] I suppose so.

Therapist: That's great! So what helps you get into a good mood in the morning so that you're able to avoid the fights?

Daniel: (*shrugs*) I don't know.

Therapist: Can you have a guess for me?

Daniel: When Dad isn't shouting at everyone, and making Mum get upset.

Kevin: [*reacting*] Daniel you know that isn't the case. We don't get into fights all that often, and even when do, that's no excuse for behaving like a hooligan at school. (*To therapist*) This attempt to blame me is a total red herring. What's happening is that he's gotten in with a gang at school and they're enemies with another gang. It happens all the time these days, and the school just pussyfoots around it …

In this exchange, the therapist's intentions are clear, but the chosen path of inquiry hasn't yielded many useful possibilities, and has ended with Kevin interrupting in a reactive way. Conscious of the obvious tension between the two parents, the therapist has become over-anxious to find an exception that might produce a positive focus. This has resulted in an attempt to develop prematurely an implied difference into a success story. As you can see from the 'yes–but' pattern that develops (notice how many therapist responses begin with 'but') the therapist appears much more enthused about the differences than Daniel is. The therapist is moving too fast and too far ahead of the clients. This results in Daniel's answers becoming more reluctant and he reacts by slipping into 'more of the same' as he blames his father. This, predictably, threatens another round of characterizations, accusations and recriminations, as Kevin reacts against being painted as the villain.

Path 2

Therapist: Just about every day? You mean there are some days when your mood is different?
Daniel: Not many.
Therapist: No, I guess not. Can you think back over the last week and tell me how many days you didn't go to school with a bad mood?
Daniel: About two, I think.
Therapist: Really? And what two days were they?
Daniel: Monday and Friday.
Therapist: Isn't that interesting. The two end days. Do you find that interesting too?
Daniel: I suppose so.
Therapist: Can you think back over the last few weeks? If I asked you the same question about those weeks, would you say that Monday and Friday were the days when you went to school in a different mood.
Daniel: Yes. Probably.
Therapist: I'm really interested in your thoughts about what makes most Mondays and Fridays a bit different. Any ideas?
Daniel: It must be the weekend.
Therapist: Yes, that occurred to me too. I wonder what it is about the weekend that helps you go to school in a better mood on the day after the weekend and the day before the weekend?
Daniel: I don't know. Everyone's happier on the weekend.
Therapist: So the tension isn't so powerful on the weekends? It doesn't get to you as much, and you're more relaxed?
Daniel: Yes. Dad goes fishing and Mum plays the piano.
Therapist: I see. And this helps you to relax.
Daniel: It's more normal, like it used to be.

In this sequence the therapist paces the conversation more carefully, and spends more time orienting to Daniel's responses. The therapist takes care not to let the reactive emotional postures in the room (especially between Sandra and Kevin) result in a premature push for progress. The tone is one of curiosity about difference rather than enthusiasm about change, and seems more appropriate to the emotional climate of the meeting. This seems to engage Daniel whose responses may be newsworthy to the listeners – especially the fact that he is in a happier mood on the weekend, when he feels that the family environment is more like it used to be.

Eliciting difference/change from a discussion of goals or signs of change

This is probably the most systematic path to the elicitation of difference/ change. There is a systematic progression along the lines of: What are you hoping will be different in the future? What will be some signs that this is happening? Is any of this happening now? How can we make sense of this? What implications might this have for the future?

As in most conversations, however, the 'logical' path will take unexpected twists and turns. Once we have elicited an exceptional or unique experience, how should we attempt to story it? Consider the map of possibilities in Figure 5.1. Should we go forwards or backwards through time? Should we focus on actions or meanings, on individuals or relationships? In the context of conjoint meetings, an additional question concerns who we should attempt to involve in the process, and how? For example, should we stay with an 'individual engagement' pattern, or switch to 'reciprocal engagement' or 'collective engagement'? There is, of course, no prescriptive answer to these questions, but we can consider some of the factors that might influence the path we choose to follow.

Example

Later in the conversation, there is still no agreement between Sandra's and Kevin's views about Daniel's school situation, and there seems no point in pursuing this possibility any further at the moment. However, everyone seems to agree that while the family is working through these issues it is important that they at least try to communicate more constructively and lessen the hold that the current tension has on their daily lives. A tentative common goal emerges of trying to 'get back to normal' in the sense of identifying some simple and valued aspects of family life that might still be available, despite their changed circumstances. The therapist asks, 'What would be some signs that the family was beginning to get back to normal in some small but important ways?' Sandra suggests that Kevin would be enjoying his fishing trips more, and talking about them when he gets home. Daniel says that Sandra would be enjoying her music, playing the piano more. Kevin says that he and Daniel would be playing computer games together, and Jessica says that she would be inviting her friends around to the house. The therapist then switches to a 'collective engagement' pattern and asks whether any of these activities are starting to happen already? There is not much immediate response, but then Jessica mentions that on the last weekend she heard her mother playing the piano and singing in a way that she hadn't done for months. Prompted by her recollection, Daniel also says that he noticed this too. She played for longer and sang and played some of the happier sounding songs she used to like.

Path 1

Therapist:	[*to Jessica and Daniel*] Really! And what was it like for the two of you to hear your Mum being more like her old self again?
Jessica:	I was really surprised. These days she only plays a bit on the weekend and not for very long.
Therapist:	And what effect did it have on you, to hear her playing like this again? Were you pleased as well as surprised?
Jessica:	Yes. I actually kept my door open for a while so I could listen.
Therapist:	[*turning to Daniel*] And what about you Daniel? Were you pleased to hear your Mum playing happier sounding songs again?
Daniel:	Yes. She was in a good mood for a while that day.
Therapist:	And what effect did this have on you? Did her good mood rub off on you?
Daniel:	I think so.
Therapist:	Do you think this might have been one of the things that helped you relax more at school on Monday?
Daniel:	Probably.
Therapist:	[*to Kevin*] Kevin, I'm wondering whether this is news to you? When you got home from fishing did you notice that there was a different mood in the house?
Kevin:	I didn't think about it much at the time, but things did seem a bit less tense on Sunday night.
Therapist:	[*to Sandra*] Sandra, I wonder whether you're surprised to hear what's been said? Did you realize that Jessica and Daniel had noticed the difference in your music on the weekend, and that this might have helped the mood at home?

In this segment the therapist manages to involve everyone and to touch on a number of interesting themes. However, the storying process is rather scattered, moving from person to person and with a changing focus. Who should we speak to, and where should the focus lie? When clients describe differences or changes that *others* have made, should we remain focused on the experience of the observers (Jessica and Daniel in this case), or directly engage with the person who has made the change (Sandra)? Both perspectives are valuable, but in this case the focus should probably be switched to Sandra earlier, rather than involving her at the end. For one thing, this will help to check if she agrees about what happened (otherwise we could expend a lot of energy involving others, only for Sandra to discount their observations). Indirect engagement might be preferable if Sandra appeared to be an unwilling participant, or if the changes seemed unrelated to her own stated preferences.

Path 2

Therapist:	[*to Sandra*] Sandra, were you aware before now that Jessica and Daniel noticed a difference in your music on the weekend?
Sandra:	No, I was a bit surprised that they'd noticed. But I suppose I did feel a bit more relaxed on the weekend, especially Sunday.
Therapist:	So what was different about last weekend that helped you relax for a while and enjoy your music again?
Sandra:	I suppose it was the fact that Kevin seemed more committed to coming to counselling and I didn't feel that I had to make all the running and carry the whole burden of getting everyone organized.
Therapist:	I see. You had a greater sense of the two of you working together, like you used to.
Sandra:	Yes. It was more relief than anything else, and a sense of hope I hadn't felt in a long time. A feeling that maybe he did care about the way things were going and maybe he was going to get involved.
Therapist:	And that sense of relief and hope came out when you were playing the piano?
Sandra:	Yes, I tend to show my feelings through music. I like to sing a bit as well. I used to be in a choir.
Therapist:	When Jessica and Daniel say it sounded more like it used to, what do they mean?
Sandra:	They meant that when things were better in the family I had much more time to enjoy my music, and sometimes I'd play for ages – I'd lose track of time. It became a bit of a joke in the family because someone would have to remind me what time it was.

Here the therapist takes a different tack, focusing closely on Sandra's experience and the significance of her musical expression. This may result in a more detailed understanding of what has helped her feel more hopeful in this instance, as well as identifying a general resource for her and one that may be important interpersonally as part of a 'family tradition'. Noting that Jessica and Daniel were the ones who identified the change, the therapist intends to pursue the question of how Sandra's musical expression may be significant for them. However, unlike the example in Path 1, this will be done after eliciting Sandra's account.

Identifying difference/change occurring in the meeting

Sometimes constructive therapists become so focused on listening for and eliciting differences/changes that have occurred in the past, that they can fail to notice clues to possibility that occur in front of their eyes. Quite often, as the therapeutic process unfolds, clients behave differently in the session from how they behave in their own social contexts, defying the very problem patterns that they are talking about. Couples who talk about their constant bickering may actually listen to each other during the therapy session, or children who are being criticized by their parents for being disruptive and uncontrollable might stay focused for a large part of the meeting. Therapists who remain alert to the processes of the meeting can utilize the immediacy of the situation, often by sharing their own perceptions of the changes/differences that occur.

Example

The therapist notices that, despite being criticized consistently by his parents, especially Kevin, Daniel has remained relatively calm during the session and appears to be closely following the thread of the conversation. Though at first he seemed reluctant to engage in the process, he has become more relaxed and has responded to the therapist's questions with apparent willingness. His demeanour seems to belie the various descriptions of him as sullen, undisciplined and oppositional. The therapist wishes to utilize this observation.

Path 1

Therapist: [*to Daniel*] Daniel, I'd like to share something with you. I'm really impressed by the fact that you've been able to sit here for such a long time tonight, and really make an effort to answer my questions? Are you impressed by that too?

Daniel: Not really.

Therapist: So you know you have the ability to concentrate and really apply yourself?

Daniel: I can sometimes.

Therapist: And I also notice that you've remained calm most of the time, even when your parents were saying some pretty critical things about you. That must have been difficult. Are you impressed by how calm you've stayed?

Daniel: Not really.

Therapist: Well I'm very impressed. [*To the others*] Are you impressed that Daniel has been so calm and concentrated so well during this meeting?

Kevin: Not really. It just proves what I've been saying. He can apply himself when he wants to – like when he's coming here and wants to put on a good face – but when he's home it's a different matter.

Sandra: You've just seen the 'public' Daniel tonight. He's like this when I take him to the doctor or dentist too. But I wish you could visit us at home, because then you'd see the other side of him.

Therapists need to be suitably cautious when using their own observations of family members as the basis for amplifying difference/change. As an outsider who has just become acquainted with the clients, the therapist is unfamiliar with the 'culture' of the family in terms of the typical ways they interact and present themselves in other social settings. What might seem new or different to the therapist might be seen as more of the same to clients. If therapists try to make too much of their observations, they can easily be overruled or 'corrected' by other family members whose perceptions carry the weight of experience.

Path 2

Therapist: [*to Daniel*] Daniel, can I ask you about something that really interests me? I can't help noticing that you've been sitting still and concentrating for almost an hour now, and you've been answering all my questions in a thoughtful way. And I'm a bit surprised because the picture I originally had of you was that you were someone who found it hard to do this. Are you a bit surprised too?

Daniel: A little bit.

Therapist: I've talked to lots of young men of your age, and I've noticed that many of them fidget or get angry, or go silent, especially when their parents are saying some pretty critical things about them. And I'm wondering what's helped you to stay so calm and focused?

Daniel: I just concentrated.

Therapist: I'm wondering what's been different about the way the family has talked tonight, compared to what happens at home or school? What's been different or interesting that's helped you to stay calm and concentrate and answer questions?

Daniel: When you stopped talking about me all the time, and talked about everyone else as well.

Therapist: That was different?

Daniel: At home, it's mostly having a go at me.

Therapist: I see. So talking about the whole family has been helpful?

Daniel: Yes.

Therapist: I'd really be interested to ask everyone else if they've noticed that you've been concentrating tonight. And I'd also like to ask everyone whether they think the family as a whole has talked in a different way tonight and whether that's been helpful …

This path of inquiry is different in a number of ways that may invite a more reflective and appreciative response from family members. Rather than taking an overt position of cheerleading (I'm *impressed*), the therapist takes the more cautious path of being *curious* and *surprised* which is less likely to invite reaction or disqualification. Furthermore, the therapist is careful to ground the observations in the context of previous experiences with young people. This may make the therapist's observations more interesting and credible to listeners. The therapist also explores in some detail Daniel's experience of the conversation, including the key question of what was different about the therapy context as a whole. This also serves to concretize the therapist's observations and to invite a consideration of how the whole family has been different tonight.

Looking elsewhere

So far we have looked at paths of inquiry emerging from the immediate focus of the conversation. In the situations described above the therapist 'seizes' and develops opportunities that are presented, implied or observed, and invites clients to perform meaning around these. But sometimes, for a number of reasons, there may be no obvious clues for evoking possibilities. In a reactive emotional climate family members may not be motivated to notice, let alone appreciate, other people's changes or competencies. Clients who are not attending voluntarily may refuse to engage in the conversation. Even if family members share common hopes for change, their immersion in problem-saturated stories may make it difficult to identify any exceptional or unique experiences. However, we can also look elsewhere in order to 'create' opportunities for eliciting difference/change.

Endurance, resilience and coping

If family members remain pessimistic about future change, the therapist can switch the focus of inquiry to the ways in which they are struggling to endure or cope with the situation. What do they do in order to survive through these difficult times? What new skills have they had to learn? How do they prevent things from getting worse? These questions can be addressed to the family collectively and/or individually. How has Kevin learned to maintain his morale during this period of unemployment? What does Sandra do in order to protect herself from the effects of stress?

Even though family members cannot identify positive changes, they may be able to identify *differences* in the form of coping or protective behaviours, and appreciate the efforts that they and others are making. Focusing on the themes of endurance, resilience and coping can result in other conversational opportunities. For example, we can be curious about how family members learned to cope with adversities like this. Who taught them? Do Kevin or Sandra come from families with a tradition of sticking together during hard times? How have they used this knowledge in the present situation?

As always, these questions must be introduced carefully and responsively – not as a last throw of the dice when all other options have failed. Wording can be particularly important. For example, if you ask, 'How are you coping with the situation?', this carries the implication that family members *are* coping. However, if they feel that they are not coping (which is probably the case since they are coming to counselling!) this suggests that the therapist has not heard and appreciated their difficulties. You may get a reply of, 'We *aren't* coping, that's why we're here!' Preferable wordings might be: 'What do you do to try to keep going? How do you try to get through each day? What do you do to hold the family together? What do you do to make sure things don't get worse?' These questions carry the suggestion that clients are actively struggling, rather than the presumption that they are already coping.

Overcoming urges and temptations

Even though family members may not be able to identify instances where they have acted in accordance with their goals, they may be able to identify occasions when they overcame urges and temptations to act in ways that would have made the situation worse (de Shazer, 1988). For example, even though Daniel may still be provoked into fights on some days of the week, have there been recent times when he was provoked on those days but overcame the urge to retaliate? Even though Kevin is having a difficult struggle with impatience, have there been any recent times when impatience almost got the better of him, but he was able to outmanoeuvre it? These questions can identify small but significant steps that might not register as major successes but can still be appreciated as worthy starting points involving *choices* and *skills* that can be storied. How did you decide not to retaliate that day? What did you decide to do instead? Is this a new skill you have been developing? Who else might have noticed this?

These kinds of questions are most effective when a sense of collaboration and shared goals has been established. This helps to engage other family members in the search for small steps or differences that may often go unnoticed. For example, though Kevin may struggle to identify any examples of resisting impatience, Sandra or one of the children might have noticed an example which they can bring to everyone's attention.

Transferring competencies

In the discussion of problem-free talk in Chapter 2, I mentioned that one aim of this form of inquiry is to identify potential areas of client competence that might be *transferred* to the problem area. Sometimes clients compartmentalize different parts of their lives and do not make a connection between different contexts. Transferring competencies allows the possibility of harnessing a 'natural resource' that can be taken from a number of areas including personal interests, fields of expertise, talents, leisure activities, special life experiences and intellectual skills (Lamarre and Gregoire, 1999). For example, from the Edwards family resource-oriented genogram (Figure 2.1) we have learned that:

- Kevin is good at explaining technical things, and likes to go fishing as a way to relax.

- Sandra plays the piano and enjoys bushwalking and other outdoor activities.
- Jessica is an excellent student, is very popular, and likes animals.
- Daniel achieves high grades in art, is a good soccer team player, and likes computer games.

These areas of 'natural resources' suggest a number of potential lines of inquiry:

- Kevin agrees that he loses patience with Daniel and that this is a concern to him. Yet who would know more about patience than an experienced fisherman? What are the most important lessons Kevin has learned about patience from his experience as a fisherman? Might he be able to transfer some of these abilities into his relationship with Daniel? Has he noticed this happening already?
- Kevin is also skilled at explaining technical things, and Daniel likes computer games. Perhaps the current tension between father and son is obscuring potential commonalities. Could Kevin use his skills in explaining technical things to help his son appreciate some of the 'technical' aspects of self-control?
- Sandra appears to derive great pleasure from her musical abilities and physical activities such as bushwalking. Given that she is under increasing stress, how exactly does playing the piano help? Based on her experience as a music teacher, and her knowledge of herself, what kinds of melodies, rhythms and harmonies might be most helpful to play in times of stress? If she were trying to explain to one of her own students how to use music as a form of therapy for stress, what advice would she give?
- Jessica is keen to avoid both the family drama and having to take sides in the conflicts at home. Yet her evident popularity suggests that she may have good 'people skills'. Might Jessica's interpersonal skills be an under-utilized resource in the present situation? Might she have any thoughts on how her father, mother and brother could interact differently? If she could offer one suggestion to each of them, what would this be? Also, could her interest in animals provide an interesting perspective on the current tensions? If asked to identify each family member as a particular animal, how would she depict each person at the moment? Might this provide some interesting, and possibly humorous, new metaphors?
- Daniel likes soccer and appears to be a good team player on the pitch. What skills and experiences has he learned at soccer that might be helpful in keeping his cool at home and school? How has he learned to avoid provocation on the field and to maintain a focus on his own game and on the final result? How has he learned to avoid

the red card, to dig deep, think ahead, put the team first and outsmart the opposition?

Knowledge about contexts of competence in clients' lives can provide a rich backdrop of skills, concepts and metaphors that can enrich the evocation of possibilities. Though it may not be relevant in every case, and should not be reduced to a predictable technique, transferring competencies can be a useful component of constructive approaches, supplementing and enhancing the differences/changes emerging from the conversation.

Reflecting on the process of the meeting

Sometimes when it is difficult to evoke possibilities throughout a meeting it can be helpful to reflect on the process of the meeting itself. What has it been like for the family to share their story with a professional stranger? Did it match their expectations? What exactly has been different and possibly helpful about the experience? How has it been different from other conversations they have had? If they were to return for another session, would they prefer anything to be different?

Though little apparent progress may have been made on resolving the *content* of specific issues, these kinds of questions often elicit differences/changes in the *process* of the family's attempts at problem-solving. By reflecting on these questions, family members may appreciate that they have engaged in a conversation that has been different, rather than 'more of the same'. For example, they may have talked about difficult issues in a more sustained, respectful and productive way. This itself can be appreciated as a positive step, and can help to sustain hope for persevering in therapy.

Linking the major groups of skills

So far in this book I have focused on three major conversational activities: hosting, negotiating, and evoking. As suggested in Figure 5.2, these groups of skills tend to be cumulative in that each provides a platform for the next. Hosting provides a reflective emotional climate for the negotiation of purpose and preferences. This, in turn, provides a context for evoking possibilities through eliciting and storying difference/change.

I have found this way of linking the groups of skills to be especially helpful for practitioners who are new to family therapy. It helps to remind us that the *ongoing* hosting process remains the foundation on which the other processes are built. As the lessons from the field have demonstrated, jumping the gun in terms of attempting to evoke possibilities prematurely

Figure 5.2   Three groups of skills in constructive therapy

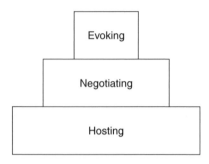

can be unproductive, especially in conjoint meetings. And even a straight-forward inquiry into who wants what can prove difficult if the emotional climate is reactive. Of course, as therapists become more confident and experienced, they learn to improvise and to act on their hunches and intu-itions. For example, you may suddenly sense the opportunity to evoke possibilities even though you have not systematically completed the other processes. One of the hallmarks of experience is that you have enough skills to be able to 'recover' if your hunch proves misguided. Therefore, the sequencing of skills in Figure 5.2 is not a rigid formula, but rather a general guide for systematic practice that helps us to proceed with caution in conjoint meetings.

It can be particularly helpful in situations where new paths suddenly open up or unexpected twists occur. For example, one or more family members may suddenly raise a new issue that is obviously very important for them. Rather than be drawn into pursuing this immediately, we need to remain effective and inclusive hosts, attentive to the emotional envi-ronment of the meeting. We would need to check in with other family members to see if they are comfortable with this change of direction and, if so, to reassure them that their other needs and priorities will also be addressed in the meeting. Assuming family members agree to a change of direction, the new issue will be carefully negotiated in terms of who wants what, before any attempts are made to evoke possibilities. This sense of process and pacing may assist us to remain multiply engaged, and to resist the temptation to get ahead of ourselves and our clients.

Towards the threshold of change

> Acceptance and change. Acceptance and change. Remember these two words, because they are the essential components of therapy. (O'Hanlon and Beadle, 1994: 15)

Having provided these general guidelines, one is frequently asked how much you should attempt to achieve in a first meeting (or, for that matter, any other meeting). How do you know when to end a meeting, and how should it end? In other words, is there a typical session plan or checklist?

Several factors make it difficult to specify a plan that can be followed in entirety. One obvious factor is the time available in a session. Another is the number of clients in the meeting and the degree of conflict or disagreement on hopes and goals. If you review all of the activities I have described so far in this book, how many could you hope to include in a single first meeting, even if you have an hour or more at your disposal? In an ideal scenario you might hope to maintain a hosting role, negotiate concerns and requests, and evoke some meaningful possibilities by the end of the meeting. However, depending on time and circumstances, hosting alone, or hosting accompanied by negotiating may be the most important processes to achieve. In some situations, simply providing a safe environment and listening attentively may be the most important activity.

Rather than specify the completion of a session in terms of a particular outcome or checklist of activities, I am more inclined to think in terms of the prevailing emotional climate and the importance of achieving a delicate balance between *acceptance* and *change* (O'Hanlon and Beadle, 1994). Too much emphasis on acceptance (focusing on present circumstances, past experiences, causal factors or feelings of despair) can result in the conversation becoming mired in present or past difficulties, and problem-saturated descriptions. Conversely, too much emphasis on change (future projections, goals, positive changes, etc.) can leave clients behind in the sense of being too far removed from their current experience and needs. As Cooperrider (1990) puts it, affirmative projections of the future are linked to appreciative understandings of the present and past. I like to think of a constructive conversation as ending at a point where clients are poised on the *threshold of change*, where they experience a heightened sense of possibility that is tempered or balanced by acceptance of the challenges ahead. If we assume that people are 'multi-storied' and 'multi-voiced', the aim is to redress the balance of stories and voices, to create possibilities where none seemed to exist before. Family members are encouraged to go as far as they can, but no one is pushed to go further than they wish. The next step is up to them.

Therapists often build towards the threshold of change through the careful use of constructive feedback and reflections at the end of the meeting. Whether this feedback is prepared during a formal break in the session (a procedure typically followed in solution-focused therapy) or is improvised in the session, it typically comprises several elements:

- an acknowledgement of the difficulties faced by family members and of the differences between their perspectives;
- compliments to each family member about their contribution to the session and their efforts in the face of present circumstances;

- a review of any constructive differences, changes and resources that have emerged from the conversation, and the potential implications of these for future change;
- reflections on what has been different, helpful or unhelpful about the meeting;
- ideas or suggestions for activities between sessions.

Suggestions for between-session activities are often based on the final balance that has been achieved between acceptance and change. If the scales are tipped towards change (for example, family members have reached agreement on a particular goal and seem relatively optimistic), practical ways of achieving this could be discussed. If the eliciting and storying of change reveals that positive steps have already been taken in this direction, the therapist might simply suggest that the family member keep the new direction going and do more of what works. If, on the other hand, the scales are tipped towards acceptance (there is still disagreement over what should happen, or a reactive emotional environment persists), the therapist might simply suggest an 'observation task', asking each person to observe times when things are going more in the direction they would like, and to note these for discussion at the next meeting. Clients who believe that others should change, or who feel pessimistic about change, are more likely to follow through with observation tasks than with action tasks.

Constructive therapists differ considerably in terms of the relative importance they place on between-session activities. While some (for example, Bertolino and O'Hanlon, 2002; de Shazer, 1988; Friedman, 1997) appear more likely to utilize various categories of tasks or action plans, my own inclination has been to move in the opposite direction towards a greater reliance on the conversational process itself as the vehicle for change (see also George, Iveson and Ratner, 1999; Walter and Peller, 2000). Hence, the clear emphasis I have placed on identifying *process interventions* as major skills in a constructive framework.

In Chapters 2–5 I have developed the three major groups of skills that form the practice base of our constructive framework. In practical terms, they are the most essential items in our luggage, enabling us to travel light and to do a lot with a little. It is now important to consider what else we might need to take in order to supplement and support these processes.

Note

1. I prefer the terms 'exceptional experiences' and 'unique experiences' to 'exceptions' and 'unique outcomes' as found in the solution-focused and narrative therapy literature. The latter terms seem to emphasize conversational products rather than processes.

6   Working Constructively over Time

I begin therapy with new clients assuming it will be brief, and I let my clients teach me how long it will be. (O'Hanlon, 1990: 49)

In assembling a simple but robust constructive framework, I have suggested that the processes of hosting, negotiating and evoking are the most characteristic skills that you will use on your professional journeys. These skills will often enable us to take the conversation along the express route – so long as clients are happy with both the direction and the speed. However, journeying with family members over time can be an unpredictable and sometimes disconcerting experience. Sometimes the conversation falters or drifts, diverges on to various scenic routes, reaches an impasse or simply gets lost. At various points, family members may join or depart, so that those who alight at the final destination may be a quite different group from those who began the journey.

I remember a family therapist once bemoaning the fact that most video demonstrations and workshop role-plays only featured the first session. As a way of conveying the reality of an approach, he argued, this was highly misleading because 'as we all know, anyone can do a good first session'. While in one sense this is obviously an exaggeration, it is easy to see what he was getting at. Irrespective of the model being used, the first session will usually appear more structured, coherent and theoretically 'tight' as there is a more specific map to follow. Also, both clients and therapist may be more attentive, focused, and motivated, with everyone being on their best behaviour. The 'messiness' of relationship therapy often reveals itself in subsequent sessions as conflicting reports of change are received, new issues and priorities suddenly emerge, membership of the meetings changes, motivation fluctuates, and the very experience of coming to therapy loses its novelty. It has been said of Christopher Columbus (when he sailed 'accidentally' from Spain to the West Indies while thinking he was heading for China) that he set out without knowing where he was going, arrived without knowing where he was, and returned without knowing where he'd been. As a description of a confused journey in relationship therapy, this is very apt.

One difficulty is that, because many constructive therapists have aligned themselves with brief or time-effective therapy, there has been little emphasis in their training on conceptualizing longer forms of involvement.

There is often an implicit assumption that, if therapy is done well, only a few sessions should be required. However, though constructive therapists may prefer philosophically to approach each session as though it may be the last, they will sometimes find themselves in situations that require several or many additional meetings. How can we approach the prospect of longer-term involvements – of conversations extending over time – while maintaining a constructive orientation? To what extent is the same conversation continued from session to session? How do we respond if the therapy becomes stuck or chaotic, if no consistent theme or purpose is established, or if membership of the meetings keeps changing? How and when is it appropriate to end therapy? Therapists who are trained to expect brief involvements can sometimes feel uncomfortable or disoriented as they move into the uncharted waters of longer-term work. The aim of this chapter is to identify some additional concepts and skills that can help us to work constructively over time. We need to stay focused on our constructive principles and skills while responding flexibly to the vicissitudes of relationship therapy. This can help us to avoid a Columbus-like experience.

Continuity and novelty: serial or series?

When working with clients over time (and regardless of the number of sessions that may ultimately be needed), constructive therapists do not regard themselves as doing long-term therapy, but as doing *briefer therapy with longer-term clients* (Kreider, 1998). This is not an oxymoron but an important distinction, as it retains a commitment to consistent therapeutic principles while recognizing that some clients – for a variety of valid reasons – will require more time than others to achieve their therapeutic goals. Working from this perspective, constructive therapists continue to approach their work on a *sessional* rather than a *stage* basis. In other words, they tend to plan session by session rather than proceeding through planned stages of therapy and developing long-term treatment plans. Decisions about whether and when to schedule further sessions, and about who will attend, are usually negotiated at the end of the current session. Sometimes clients may wish to take things one session at a time in order to deal with a current and specific difficulty. At other times they may wish to pursue a longer-term goal and commit to a number of sessions in order to achieve this. Often, they may change their priorities as the sessions progress.

In working constructively over time, there is another delicate balance to be achieved, between attention to *continuity* and attention to *novelty*. Thematic continuity is obviously important in providing a sense of therapeutic purpose and identifying progress. But it can also be restrictive if it encourages a 'rearview' focus that constantly looks backwards to where people were, rather than considering where they are and what they are wanting, now. As a general rule, it is important to avoid the extremes of being locked into a fixed storyline (and seeing every session as a link in a chain) or, on the other hand, simply treating each session as though it was a first meeting, with no connection to what has gone before. When supervising students or other practitioners who are struggling in their ongoing work with families, I have noticed that they can easily slip into these two extremes: either reverting to a deficit-oriented long-term therapy perspective (where they become pre-occupied with assessing the 'deeper' problem that they must have missed) or, on the other hand, falling into a kind of ad hoc therapy, where they simply respond to the issues of the day, on a session-by-session basis.

Using the analogy of television genres, we could see these extremes as being akin to the distinction between an episode in a serial and an episode in a series. In a television serial you have one continuous story being told over a number of episodes (Part 1, Part 2, Part 3, etc.). When each successive episode in a serial is screened, it is often preceded by a condensed version of 'the story so far', showing clips from the major scenes of the previous episodes. This helps to prime the viewer to remember certain themes, to plot developments and to focus on selective events. We re-live the climax of the previous episode and become interested in the question of … what happens next? By contrast, in a television series (for example, a weekly 'sitcom') you have the same group of central characters appearing in each episode, but each episode is a self-contained story, with no reference to other episodes. You can understand an individual episode without having watched the show before.

One difficulty with successive therapy conversations is that they may well exhibit some of the features of both a serial and a series. Adopting the conventional sense of therapeutic progress, there might be an obvious focus on continuity, with each session being seen as contributing in a cumulative manner to an overall plan or goal. However, there is also a sense in which each conversation can be considered as an episode in its own right, with its own themes and priorities. In some meetings it might be important to focus on continuity across time, in others it might be more important to address a self-contained issue or strike out in new directions. Ongoing therapy becomes confusing when you are not quite clear which genre you are working in. Are we still in the same story or is this becoming a separate episode, or perhaps the beginning of a new serial? What has happened between meetings to change the script? By balancing attention between continuity and novelty, we can consistently return to the themes of *where we've been, where we are,* and *where we're going.*

Beginning successive sessions

Here are some typical ways in which therapists might begin successive sessions. They range from an emphasis on continuity to an emphasis on novelty. At one extreme we begin by recounting 'the story so far' with a view to extending it; at the other we begin by starting a new story:

- You could begin by reviewing your notes from the last session, pointing out the major themes and priorities that emerged, and reminding clients of any suggestions or plans that were made at the end of the meeting. You could then ask clients to take up the story from that point and indicate what happened next. *Can you fill me in on the developments that have occurred since the last meeting? How did you go with the ideas that we discussed? Did you follow through with the plan you were considering?*
- You could begin by inviting clients to think back to the last session and tell you what they recall from it. *What do you remember about our last session? What thoughts or feelings stayed with you? What were the things you went home thinking about? What thoughts have you had since? What difference has the last session made?*
- You could begin by presupposing that change has occurred. *What's been better or different since we last met? What else ... what else?*
- You could begin by asking about priorities for the present session. *Where would you like to begin today? What are your main hopes for this session?*

Each of these openings might be appropriate in particular circumstances and, rather than deciding on a personal favourite and using it rigidly, it is more useful to consider the factors that could influence our choice. One major factor, of course, will be the importance of maintaining our hosting role, and re-establishing a climate of reflective emotional postures at the beginning of each session. This may require a few minutes of problem-free talk that will allow the therapist to reconnect with all clients and gauge the emotional climate in the room. If reactive postures are evident, beginning with a presuppositional question like 'what's been better since last time?' might seem too abrupt or presumptuous, and might prompt a negative pattern of responses. In more reflective emotional environments, however, it might be perfectly appropriate. As usual, it is important to begin by meeting clients where they are, rather than where you would like them to be.

In what circumstances might it be better to begin by emphasizing thematic continuity with previous sessions? One relevant factor concerns the recency and frequency of sessions. If sessions are infrequent, or considerable time has elapsed since the previous session, it can be usual for both clients and therapist to reconnect with the previous developments in their work together. At the very least it is a simple act of courtesy to let clients know that you indeed remember them and have taken the time to review your notes before the meeting. A related factor may be the degree to which clients are multi-stressed. Some families may be experiencing circumstances that are highly stressful or chaotic, involving many over-lapping issues, crises, and contacts with different helping professionals. Emphasizing continuity at the beginning of each session may help these clients to refocus on their main hopes and goals, to appreciate progress that has been made (so that the story does not get lost amidst everyday dif-ficulties), and to differentiate clearly the contribution of therapy from other forms of assistance they are receiving. On the other hand, if you are seeing clients regularly (for example, on a weekly basis), and everyone seems clear on the general direction of the work, there is less need to establish connections, and opening with 'what's been better or different?' might be more appropriate.

A related factor concerns the degree of consensus on themes, goals and priorities. If there is general agreement among clients on the purpose and priorities of therapy, and a particular theme or mutual goal has emerged, it makes sense to connect successive sessions by referring back to these. When consensus appears tenuous, however, and individual priorities seem likely to diverge, the multiply engaged therapist would be wary of 'pushing' the relevance of these connections for all clients, and of locking in the session to a narrow thematic focus.

Building from this discussion about the dilemmas of continuity, we could adopt the general position that, however therapists decide to begin successive sessions, the priority is to ensure that the themes of continuity and novelty are both addressed: that clients are provided with an opportu-nity to 'plot' new developments in the story so far, and also to divert into a separate episode or begin a new serial.

Storying developments

When eliciting and storying client reports of progress I have found the following brief guidelines to be helpful (further examples can be found in Bertolino and O'Hanlon, 2002; Milner and O'Byrne, 2002; and Selekman, 1997).

When clients agree that things are better ...

In this situation, it is important to avoid simply praising or applauding positive developments. While appreciation from the therapist may obvi-ously be valuable, it is preferable to go beyond this and invite clients to appreciate their own and each other's achievements. Therefore the thera-pist's stance will be one of curiosity about how the changes occurred and what significance these might have for people. The therapist will invite clients to attribute change to their own qualities rather than to external influences or random chance, and will be persistently curious about how the changes were achieved, who noticed, and what this might mean in terms of the major themes of the therapy.

When clients have mixed opinions on change ...

In this situation, family members may disagree over the extent or attribution of change, or may indicate that things have been up and down, so-so, or one step forward and two steps back. Therapists can normalize the fact that changes fluctuate and can take time to consolidate. It is also helpful to acknowledge and validate client frustration or disappointment. Sometimes, in these situations, therapists may have moved too far ahead of their clients, perhaps emphasizing change at the expense of acceptance, and unintentionally raising expectations that the problem would be solved quickly. It is important to elicit and story any changes or differences that have occurred, and for this information to be shared among clients. A useful working assumption is that *all clients may have noticed more changes and differences than they remember, and that each client has noticed something that others have not*. On this assumption, we can discuss each person's perception of developments, remaining gently persistent in inviting accounts of difference/change, and hoping to encourage a snowball effect of selective attention and appreciation.

When clients report that things are the same or worse ...

In these situations, the therapist acknowledges family members' frustration and disappointment, but will be careful to avoid trying to cheer clients up or to persuade them things are getting better than they think (which will probably result in a 'yes-but' exchange). It can be helpful to explore any changes and differences that have been noticed, even if they appear negative. If clients report setbacks, we can be curious about whether things have gone all the way back to square one, or stopped short of this? If so, how was this achieved, and how have they prevented things from getting worse? It is also important to check with each person about their perception of change. Sometimes one influential family member (often a parent) will state their perception that things are no better, and other family members will tend to fall into line. However, a careful process of inquiry may reveal that other people have noticed significant changes, but have not talked about these.

As always, we can try to select realities that maintain possibilities even in the face of disappointment. For example, consider the connotations of the terms 'relapse' and 'setback'. A change for the worse could be described using either term. However, to me, a relapse suggests that clients have gone all the way back to square one, and that there is an underlying issue or problem that has to be addressed before lasting change can occur. A setback, by contrast, is a less 'heavy-duty' term that draws attention to the context or circumstances of the event itself, rather than to presumed underlying deficits. We could say that every relapse is the same, whereas every setback is different.

Beyond 'progress': transitions over time

Because constructive therapists tend to proceed on a sessional basis, they may find it difficult to 'map' therapeutic involvements occurring over longer time spans. In brief and solution-oriented styles, especially, the emphasis has been on encouraging progressive narratives of ongoing change. While this is undoubtedly useful, I have found it important to look beyond a session-by-session response and to consider some broader transitions that can occur over time. If we are to respond to the vicissitudes of relationship therapy it is necessary to think beyond an investment in immediate or linear progress.

In order to provide more options, we can usefully start by characterizing some typical developments that can occur in our conversations. When I reflect on my own experience, I find that, on some occasions, I would describe the conversation as 'progressing', but on others I would describe it as 'evolving' or 're-forming'. Doubtless, there are other possibilities, and more fine-grained descriptions, but I will focus on these broad categories. My suggestion is that these distinctions are not a semantic exercise, but can be usefully explored as a way of broadening our conceptions and – hence – our options.

When I think of a conversation as *progressing*, I am relating progress to family members' stated hopes and priorities for therapy. We are making progress in the conventional sense that clients agree that they are getting what they came for and are moving in the direction of their preferred future. Though the progress may not be smooth sailing (it may, at times, be more like one step forward and two steps back), there is a consistent thread of shared purpose and continuity from session to session, however long the therapy takes.

When I think of a conversation as *evolving* over time, I think of a transition from the initial focus to broader or longer-term goals that may be more significant to clients. There is the same sense of shared purpose, but there has been a shift to more salient themes. For example, a family may wish initially to focus on an immediate crisis, but once progress has been made on this front, the conversation may shift to longer-term hopes extending further into the future. Sometimes the successful experience of making progress with the immediate problem may encourage clients to address more longstanding difficulties. Or clients may present initially with a safe 'calling card' issue in order to test the water. Once they feel comfortable and confident in working with the therapist, they may reveal a more significant issue that is troubling them. For example, a couple may initially present with that perennial calling card, a 'communication problem', but the conversation may evolve into a focus on sexual intimacy. When therapy evolves over time, there is a relatively seamless transition from initial goals to more salient goals. Therapists can then attempt to facilitate *progress* in relation to these new priorities.

When I think of a conversation as *re-forming*, however, I am thinking of transitions that are more sudden or unexpected, and that may result in the process of therapy starting over in a quite different direction. There is no seamless transition here, but a more fundamental break with the focus of previous sessions. This may involve changes in issues, format or membership as the preference-determined system re-forms around a different purpose. One example might be a situation where the initial focus of family sessions is the behaviour of children. As this is explored, however, intense conflict between the parents becomes apparent and the conversation changes direction and re-forms as couple therapy. Another scenario may involve a sudden event that precipitates a major change of focus (a partner leaves, a son runs away from home, a family member falls ill, a daughter reveals she is pregnant, a parent reveals an affair). Regardless of whether such an event is linked to the themes of previous sessions or comes out of left field, it necessitates a major change of direction at least for the immediate session. When a conversation re-forms there is a sense of starting over, with different priorities and, perhaps, different people. Having re-formed, however, the conversation can then progress, evolve … or re-form again.

Mapping conversational transitions

Using the transitions I have just described, here are some examples moving from straightforward to more complicated forms. We start with a conventional brief therapy involvement that elicits progress between sessions. We then move to more variable forms where different transitions affect our conception of 'progress'. The sequences depict movements over time, rather than specific numbers of sessions.

Example 1

Conversation Begins → Conversation Progresses → Conversation Ends

In this scenario, the conversation 'progresses' in the sense that the same thematic focus is maintained throughout, and the clients move closer to their preferred future. There may be ups and downs along the way, and a number of sessions may ultimately be required, but no major new elements are encountered, and the conversation remains on the same directional track.

Example 2

Conversation Begins → Conversation Progresses → Conversation Evolves → Conversation Progresses → Conversation Ends

In this situation, the therapy at first follows a similar path but then broadens its focus. For example, in the Martin Family, Angela, aged 15, is experiencing difficulties coping with academic pressures at high school, and her falling grades are associated with a gradual withdrawal from social life. Her mother, Jill, and step-father, Ron, fear she may be developing 'teenage depression'. The other family members (her step-brother, Alex, and step-sister, Kerry) are concerned but do not know how to help. There is a shared goal of finding ways to help Angela through a difficult time, and this becomes the immediate priority. A theme of *getting back on track* is developed and, over the next few sessions, Angela's progress is apparent. By the beginning of session four, Angela scales her confidence about being able to study effectively at eight on a ten-point scale. However, there still seems to be an atmosphere of 'unfinished business' about the conversation, as other problems in the family are hinted at without being stated. The session becomes unfocused and begins to drift.

The therapist then utilizes a reflecting team process in order to gain additional perspectives on the situation (this is described in Chapter 7). Consequently, at the next session, Jill discloses that she and Ron have been thinking about what has been happening with Angela, and now believe that when the 'blended' family was formed two years earlier, they made a mistake in trying to 'carry on as normal' in the hope that things would take care of themselves. They tended to avoid noticing difficulties and to adopt a 'wishing and hoping' approach. But there has been a build-up of resentments and conflicts over parental loyalty, differing assumptions about family life, and differing styles of discipline. Jill and Ron now believe that this may have contributed to Angela finding it difficult to approach any member of the family with her problems. They believe that the family didn't 'come together properly' and are now paying the price. Until now, they have never openly shared these concerns with the children. A new focus for therapy is then negotiated: *how to work out what kind of family they want to be*. Several sessions are then devoted to this new thematic focus and the conversation progresses towards this newly defined preferred future.

Example 3

Conversation Begins → Conversation Progresses → Conversation Re-forms → Conversation Progresses → Conversation Evolves → Conversation Progresses → Conversation Ends

Terry and Sue, a couple in their forties, seek counselling in the hope of 'reinvigorating' their marriage, especially as they are at a point where their teenage children are beginning to lead independent lives. The first session involves taking up the couple's theme of *reinvigorating their relationship* and focuses on what this would look like, how it might be achieved, and what past feelings and actions could act as a platform for shaping their preferred future. Over the next few sessions, the therapy appears to be making progress, though Sue appears keen while Terry becomes more ambivalent. He no longer thinks they have a problem, while Sue thinks they need to go further. At the next session, Sue turns up alone, and is clearly distressed. She relates how she discovered by accident that Terry has been downloading pornography from the Internet and making 'virtual contact' with women through a number of chat sites. When confronted over this, Terry became both aggressive and defensive, accusing Sue of invading his privacy and indicating that he no longer had a sexual interest in their relationship and had only attended therapy in order to spare her feelings. The ensuing escalation has resulted in Terry leaving on a work-related trip, and making veiled suggestions that he won't be returning. The therapy session involves validating Sue's distress and helping her to clarify her priorities. She is still in a state of shock over what has happened and is concerned about what to tell the children. The conversation re-forms into a focus on coping in the immediate future, and imagining herself handling some specific events in the next week. At the next session she reports progress in the sense of coping better than she thought. As Sue suspected, Terry has begun a new relationship with a woman he has met via the Internet. The therapy begins to focus on Sue's future, and evolves into an exploration of her life goals which have been pushed aside over many years. Over a number of months, progress is made towards achieving them.

Example 4

Conversation Begins → Conversation Re-forms → Conversation Progresses → Conversation Evolves → Conversation Progresses → Conversation Ends

Another couple, Ray and Toni, who are in their early thirties, indicate in the first session that they want to give their relationship 'one last chance'. They have broken up and reconnected a number of times and, because they have two young children, want to decide once and for all if they have a future together. The first session focuses on clarifying what they are wanting from therapy, and developing some conception of how they can find out if their relationship is viable in the long term. In the second session, however, there is no sign of progress. There seems little motivation to work at the relationship, and a theme of *if it wasn't for the kids we'd break up* emerges. The therapist wonders aloud if there is a piece missing from the puzzle. Toni indicates her suspicions that there is something in Ray's past that makes it difficult for him to experience intimacy in relationships, and mentions her own impressions of his family as being overly distant and cold. At the next session, Ray divulges that his father was physically and emotionally abusive of his mother and the children with the result that he and his siblings have never been able to feel close or committed in a relationship. So ingrained has been the family habit of silence and secrecy that he has not revealed this until now, even to his wife. The therapy then re-forms around a focus on Ray's struggle with the legacy of his past. The therapist discusses the option of individual therapy but Ray indicates that he would like Toni to be present. Progress is made in the sense that he is gradually able to accept that what has happened has not scarred him for life, and that he has been able to take significant steps towards being a different kind of man from his father. Toni, who has been an audience to these changes, experiences greater understanding of Ray's struggle and the effect this has had on their relationship. Both partners now feel able to recommit to a longer-term goal of rebuilding their relationship, and the therapy evolves in this direction. Progress towards specific hopes and goals is then achieved.

In reviewing these examples, my aim has been to provide constructive therapists with a broader range of options for mapping longer-term work with family members. Constructive therapists do not engage in long-term therapy in the sense of a planned approach that requires a conception of major client deficit and prolonged remediation. Nor, at the other extreme, do they simply engage in a series of ad hoc sessions each tacked on to the previous one and based on a narrow sense of progress. The amount of time spent with each family cannot be prejudged. A seemingly 'straightforward' case might take any number of unexpected twists and turns. Conversely, a multi-stressed family in crisis may only require one or two sessions if new understandings or resources can be identified. As the case vignettes demonstrate, there can be a variety of valid reasons why some clients require more sessions than others. However, each time the conversation progresses, evolves or re-forms, the fundamental processes of hosting and negotiating are utilized and a new sense of purpose is found. This is vital in establishing a vision for the work instead of a series of goals (Waters and Lawrence, 1993). A vision provides a more unifying and energizing theme that focuses the family's involvement. To emphasize this point, Waters and Lawrence ask their trainees to imagine that, in the street outside the clinic, their supervisor happens to meet a family they have been seeing. The supervisor asks the family what they are currently working on in their therapy. Can the clients give an answer in terms of a core thematic focus, or are they likely to reply 'Whatever problem comes up on the day'?

Ending constructively

When and how should constructive therapy end? While copious attention is paid to the importance of beginning well, relatively scant attention is paid to the importance of ending well. For constructive therapists there is a familiar dilemma. On the one hand, if we take the express route we may alight at the destination before anyone has had time to reflect on the journey, to process their learnings or to decide if they wish to go further. For example, it is not unusual to meet couples or families who have been in therapy previously and who now regret that they ended their involvement so quickly. 'If only we'd kept on in counselling, we might have pulled through' is not an unusual refrain. On the other hand, we can find ourselves making detour after detour, taking in more and more scenery, but losing sight of a final destination. In this case, clients are certainly 'in therapy' for longer, but it is doubtful if their hopes and priorities are being usefully addressed. At one extreme, therapists can err on the side of 'seeing' success too early; at the other, they can fall into the habit of becoming overly protective or perfectionistic, perhaps giving an implicit message that there is still more to do or that clients can't yet be trusted to function on their own (Lipchik, 2002).

In considering our approach, it is helpful to review some ideas that have been mentioned in previous chapters. One of the assumptions of constructive therapy is that an appropriate ending point is not necessarily when clients feel that their relationship problems have been finally solved or resolved, but when they no longer require professional assistance to help them achieve these ends. In a sense, ongoing therapy ends when clients have started to become their own therapists. Professional therapy can be an important temporary catalyst, but it is assumed that personal and social resources located in the family's own setting will be more significant in the longer term. As the conversation progresses, and if no further evolution or change of direction occurs, the process of inquiry turns increasingly to the question of *what the most helpful role for therapy is at this time.* Family members may be asked to reflect on the way in which the contribution of the therapist has changed during their work together. A typical development might be that, in early sessions, the therapist was needed to lower the emotional temperature and maintain a sense of direction, whereas in later sessions the therapist has become more of a consultant to the family's own initiatives. At this point, what part can the therapist best play in the life of the family? To orient clients to the final transition out of therapy, several possibilities might be suggested. One option is to space the sessions further apart in order to allow family members to consolidate the changes they have made and gain experience in handling setbacks. If clients are ambivalent about ending therapy, another option is to make a provisional appointment for three or six months down the track. This maintains a tangible connection while giving clients the opportunity to cancel the appointment if they decide they don't need it.

In approaching final sessions, constructive therapists will try to host an ending that *echoes* (Ziegler and Hiller, 2001), so that while therapy may have been relatively brief, the benefits will be enduring. This typically involves several components:

- *Reviewing progress and developments.* Clients are invited to reflect upon what has been different and helpful about the experience of therapy, in order to consolidate the perceived benefits, and to appreciate their own (and others') contribution to change. *What will you remember most about coming here? What has surprised you most about the experience? What have been the most important things you have learned about yourself or your relationships*?
- *Projecting change into the future.* Clients are invited to discuss how they will continue to put the benefits of therapy to work in their everyday lives, and how they will maintain these into the future. *How will you put your new knowledge and understandings to work when you leave here? What will you need to put in place to make sure that these hard-won changes are maintained? How will you keep the ball rolling*?
- *Troubleshooting and pre-empting setbacks.* The therapist normalizes the unpredictability of everyday life and the challenges of maintaining change when stressful events occur. Clients are invited to look ahead and anticipate future events that might lead to setbacks, and to speculate about how they might respond. *Is there anything on the horizon in the next few months that might be a real challenge? What could happen that might make it hard for you to remember what you have learned through coming here? If this begins to happen, what will you do to make sure that the hard work you've put in here doesn't get wasted?*
- *Discussing future contact.* Though it is hoped that clients will be able to respond to setbacks, they may be unsure about this. Maintaining an 'open door policy' is preferable to the implied finality of 'termination' (Bertolino and O'Hanlon, 2002). It can be helpful and reassuring to consider with clients when it might be advisable to seek further

consultation. This normalizes the possibility, and invites family members to distinguish times when they are able to assist each other from times when outside help might be needed. *What would be a sign to you that it might be a good idea to make another appointment? When would you know for sure that it was a good idea to see me again?*

- *Marking transitions.* Particularly after longer-term involvement with clients, or after a struggle with particularly difficult issues, it can be rewarding to mark symbolically the end of therapy as a transition or rite of passage into a new phase of life. Constructive therapists might celebrate these transitions in a number of ways, including the use of farewell or congratulatory cards, the reading of a final therapeutic letter, the holding of an informal 'party', or the conferring of certificates of achievement. It is important, of course, to tailor these possibilities to clients' wishes. Some may prefer a simple farewell, and be embarrassed by an overly staged ritual. Another way to mark the transition is to invite clients to become consultants for your work with any future clients presenting with similar issues. As well as providing a potentially valuable resource, this process marks a family member's transition from being a client to being an informal colleague.

- *Personal reflections and appreciation.* In the same way that therapy began with problem-free talk – with the participants meeting first as people rather than as therapists and clients – it can end in a similar vein, with therapists sharing their personal experience of working with the clients. Where appropriate, this may include what narrative therapists call 'taking-it-back' practices (White, 1997) in which therapists acknowledge the contribution that working with particular clients has made to their own lives.

In preparing to end therapy, we can also return to Griffith and Griffith's reminder that one of the therapist's main hopes is that clients 'will learn how to ask fruitful questions that bring answers to future problems without the intervention of a professional' (1994: 155). If we believe that human systems grow toward what they persistently ask questions about, to what extent have we managed to interest our clients in the kinds of questions we ask? We can explicitly ask clients to reflect upon these themes – What is different and helpful about the kinds of questions that have been asked? How are they different from the kinds of questions that they have asked themselves previously? Have family members begun to notice themselves asking any similar kinds of questions? When clients express frustration that they only seem to be able to talk constructively when they are with me, and are concerned about what will happen when they end therapy, I sometimes ask them to imagine that I am present in their home when they are experiencing relationship tensions. What difference would my 'virtual presence' make? More to the point, *can they imagine the kinds of questions I would ask?* If they learned to ask the same kinds of questions themselves, how might that be helpful?

This chapter has addressed a neglected area in the constructive therapy literature: approaches to working with longer-term clients. As Kreider (1998) wryly puts it, constructive therapists have often felt a need to shuffle their feet and avert their eyes when admitting that they see some clients over extended periods. The argument developed in this chapter is that this need not – and should not – be so. We can continue working with clients for as long as they have therapeutic goals and believe that we can be helpful. Perhaps the challenge is not only to find useful ways of working over time, but to see this as a valid and valuable part of our identity as constructive therapists. Therapy is not intrinsically better for being briefer or longer. Instead, the therapist attempts to achieve a balance between continuity and novelty, combining a conventional interest in therapeutic progress with attention to different kinds of shifts or transitions that can occur in the conversation. This way of thinking can help us to avoid a Columbus-like experience by routinely raising with our clients the question of where we've been, where we are, and where we're going (and, for that matter, who is coming along for the ride).

7 Using Inner Conversation

Talking to other(s) can be described as 'outer talk', and while we listen to others talk we talk with ourselves in 'inner talk'. (Andersen, 1995: 18)

Selecting the reality, rather than *enforcing the action*, is the more therapeutic path to follow. (Griffith and Griffith, 1994: 92)

Constructive therapies have sometimes been characterized as 'technique-driven' in the sense that they are often associated with the practice of asking carefully sequenced questions. In describing and analysing therapeutic conversations, the emphasis is usually placed on events occurring in the observable 'outer' conversation. As they progress through training, therapists 'stock up' on different varieties of questions that can potentially be called into use. However, all participants are simultaneously engaging in an 'inner' conversation (Andersen, 1995; Rober, 1999, 2002), which informs and is informed by the outer conversation. The inner conversation takes place as we listen to others talk. Until recently, the inner conversation has been neglected as a significant factor and resource. In an attempt to develop a framework that looks beyond a preoccupation with techniques, I use this chapter to look at ways of expanding the repertoire of the *inner conversation*. While the co-ordination of inner and outer conversation is important at all times, I will focus the discussion on situations of therapeutic impasse where therapists and clients appear constrained by reactive postures and 'more of the same' interactions. In particular I look at two processes that work to expand the inner conversation: the practice of reflecting team work and the cultivation of 'constructive understandings' in the therapist's inner conversation. These processes work to maintain reflective emotional postures and can help us to access further possibilities for the outer conversation. At the conclusion of Chapter 1, I mentioned the enduring challenge of creating conversations that enable both clients *and* therapists to access their creativities. While the previous chapters have focused largely on evoking client resourcefulness, this chapter also looks at ways of assisting therapists to respond more flexibly and creatively. This involves more than simply pulling another group of questions out of the hat.

Using reflecting team processes

If, over time, the conversation falters or reaches an impasse, it is possible that both therapist and clients are constrained by patterns of 'more of the same'. One stimulating way to free up the creativity of all participants is to bring other voices into the room. This is one of the characteristics of the 'conversational' style in constructive therapy, and one of its most useful applications involves reflecting team processes. The use of a reflecting team can be enormously helpful for both clients and therapists and I would recommend its consideration in any family therapy context (and particularly in training contexts). Some therapists may be in a position to use a team on a regular basis. Others may be able to use a team on specific occasions where their work with particular clients becomes 'stuck'. Reflecting teams are also extremely useful when therapists are seeking supervision. I will briefly describe the 'classical' use of reflecting teams and then discuss some adaptations that may be more practically useful for many therapists.

As mentioned in Chapter 1, the reflecting team format involves a group of observers (usually from three to five people) watching the session from behind a one-way screen. After the initial conversation, which might last for 35–45 minutes, the therapist and clients change positions with the team and become observers as the team members converse and offer reflections on what they have seen and heard. During the team reflection (which lasts about 10 minutes) the family members are invited to listen and to make notes if they wish. After the reflection, positions are reversed once more and the therapists spends the final five minutes or so inviting client reflections on what they have heard. In developing reflecting team discussions, I like to emphasize the following guidelines:

- The team members develop a *conversation* among themselves. They don't simply take turns making observations, but draw each other out about what they have noticed.
- Rather than talking generally about what they have seen, the team members ground their observations in their own experiences and reactions.
- The reflections are based in curiosity and offered in speculative and non-expert ways (I wonder if … could it be that … when that happened I couldn't help wondering if … I felt myself change as I listened to the family talk …).
- The aim is not to arrive at consensus but to increase the range of voices and views, and widen the potential repertoire of expressions about the situation.
- The team members build on the most helpful themes developed by the therapist, and may expand the conversation in directions that have not yet been explored.

The use of a team is not imposed on clients and is presented as a way of gaining access to more people with more potential ideas. It is helpful for the family to meet the team members briefly at the outset, so that the team does not appear as a group of anonymous professionals. More extensive guidelines for reflecting team processes are available from a number of sources (Andersen, 1991; Friedman (ed.), 1995; Friedman, 1997).

Though the aim is not to reach consensus and team members may have quite different perspectives, I suggest that it is helpful for team members to be 'theoretically aligned' at least to the extent of focusing on possibilities and resources rather than deficits and explanations (Lowe and Guy, 1996). It is important that the reflecting process is based on the same constructive principles as the therapy session itself. Indeed, the very rationale of the approach is to enhance the use of these principles and to help family members and therapist to access their creativity and resourcefulness. If the reflecting team's discussion is consistent with constructive principles it can assist in the processes of hosting, negotiating and evoking. As 'outsider witnesses' (Payne, 2000; White, 1997) they can serve to validate the family's struggles while affirming and appreciating their hopes and achievements in the face of difficulties.

In many ways, the reflecting team process remains a method in search of a theory. While many therapists (including myself) attest to its benefit, there is no clear or uniform view on how it works. In fact it was developed almost serendipitously from one particular situation where a therapist was struggling with a family (Andersen, 1991). As Payne (2000) notes, it is difficult to give a precise name to the team's contribution:

> It is part reflecting back of the person's story, part discussion, part inter-member questioning, part sharing of personal experience, part musing on possible questions around meaning for the person of elements in his story, part tentative 'floating' of unique outcomes. (2000: 166–7)

When clients are asked about the benefits of the experience they typically focus on the value of hearing different ideas and suggestions. Certainly, a range of different ideas is presented in speculative and respectful ways. However, it is the process rather than the content that seems unique to the method. If presenting multiple perspectives was all that was involved this could be achieved in more conventional ways (by having a general discussion involving the team and the clients, or by having the team meet behind closed doors and script a communication delivered by one person). Andersen believes that the shift of perspective makes it possible to go back and forth between the inner and outer conversation. The two kinds of conversations provide different perspectives and different starting points for new developments. The reflecting position enables family members and therapist to consider ideas and make connections free of the pressure or necessity to respond. Andersen emphasizes the French and

Norwegian meanings of reflection: 'something heard is taken in and thought about before a response is given' (1991: 28). As he also notes, conversations need pauses:

> And they should be slow enough to let the mind select those ideas it likes to be attached to, and to find the words that can express that attachment. (Andersen, 1991: 32)

No matter how 'collaborative' a therapy session becomes, there is still a sense in which clients and therapist are in the 'hot seat', needing to perform in various ways. The typical turn-taking, question–response style of the conversation makes it difficult to achieve a consistently reflective emotional environment. Adopting the reflecting position offers the unusual social experience of listening without responding as others 'gossip' about you. It engages the listeners' inner conversation, and may help them to consider possibilities they may not have been able to 'hear' before. Reverting to Andersen's suggestions, perhaps it provides time and space for the mind to consider and select ideas and find appropriate words for the outer conversation. In a sense it is a more formal extension of the 'individual engagement' pattern that I have mentioned in previous chapters, where the therapist maintains an indirect engagement with listeners (who could be described as 'reflecting participants'). In the formal team situation, the multiply engaged team members converse directly with each other, and indirectly with the listening clients.

Here is a brief example showing the use of a reflecting team process where a conversation has reached an impasse. It is based on the situation described in Chapter 6 (Example 2 in 'Mapping conversational transitions'). The therapist (Yvonne) has been working with the 'blended' Martin family (Jill, Ron, Angela, Alex, and Kerry) in relation to helping Angela get back on track with her studies. This has been achieved but there is a sense of incompletion, with other conversational threads hanging in the air. Yvonne has sought the family's permission to include a reflecting team in the next session because she feels the conversation has reached an impasse. The members of the reflecting team discuss the session while Yvonne and the family members observe …

Team Member 1: As I listened I had the impression that everyone was on the verge of saying something new … that they were weighing up the pros and cons, trying to decide whether this was the right time.

Team Member 2: I had a similar feeling. What's your guess about what that 'something new' might be?

Team Member 1: As I listened to how pleased everyone was with the really impressive changes that Angela has made, I got a sense of relief but also sadness … how sad it is that this had to happen, and what can we take from this that might help us all as a family …

Team Member 3: That ties in with something I was going to mention. I was struck by Jill's comment that this was a new experience for the family … sitting

Team Member 4:

Team Member 3:

Team Member 1:

Team Member 2:

Team Member 3:

down together and talking about something that concerns them all. I'm curious about what this experience has been like for them and whether they think it's worth pursuing.

Ron also made the comment that this is the first time some things have been said in the open. I was wondering what he meant by that.

I thought that he might be referring to what the children said about not always knowing where they stood with the two parents, and wanting some way of knowing that they were all being treated equally and fairly.

I know how hard that is to achieve in *any* family. But in step-family situations, it almost comes with the territory. And yet, I'm wondering if the success Angela's had, and the new experience everyone had in pulling together, might have served to give them a glimpse of what's possible.

I can relate to situations like this in my own life. You've struggled to make a change, and it's been difficult. Then you have to decide ... do we just leave it here and go back to our usual routine ... or should we use this as platform to try to go further?

It's like a door that's been half-opened. Do you close it again or push it open further? There are big risks both ways and I can understand any hesitation that people are feeling ...

These kinds of reflections may help to crystallize the dilemmas that family members are experiencing and can often provide a useful metaphor (the door being half-open). The team members can speculate in constructive ways about what has been implied or left unsaid and can also offer the listening therapist some clues about where to take the subsequent conversation. Working with the support of a team provides valuable support for the therapist who is able to feel less pressured to notice everything and respond to everyone in the room – having confidence that their colleagues will notice what they do not. In this example, the team reflection assists the therapist and clients to widen the lens and take in a broader perspective before focusing on a new phase of their work. Yvonne may have become so focused on helping Angela in her daily struggles that she has not had the time in her inner conversation to contemplate the broader picture. As described in Chapter 6, the team's reflection assists Jill and Ron to take the step of voicing their concerns and regrets about the way the family came together. The conversation subsequently *evolves* into a longer-term goal of working out what kind of family they want to be. Using the image offered by the team, they have decided to keep the door open rather than close it again.

To assist practitioners who are relatively new to reflecting team practice, I would suggest some additional options. One option is to have a designated member of the reflecting team act as a 'monitor' of the reflections. The monitor's role is to balance the focus of the conversation between different family members and to balance the mood of the conversation between acceptance and change. Teams, like therapists, can be swept along in particular directions, focusing too narrowly on particular family members or becoming too optimistic or pessimistic about the family's possibilities. The role of the monitor is to be alert for this and to 'correct' the balance ('I'm wondering if we might be getting carried away in our enthusiasm for the family's resilience. We have great optimism for them, but it's important to recognize what they've been through and what they are still up against'). Another option is to designate a particular team member to focus on a particular family member with a view to speaking about that person at some point. It is important for *all* family members to be mentioned during the reflection (especially, perhaps, those who have been relatively silent during the session) and this option ensures that no one is left out.

Obviously, there may be logistical constraints on the use of reflecting team practice. However, the process can be modified to fit different contexts. A team can be used occasionally rather than routinely, and can consist of only one or two people. Even if only one colleague is available, that person can be joined by the therapist to form a reflecting 'duo' as the family members observe. If one-way screens are not available, the team can sit in an unobtrusive part of the counselling room. The reflecting process can also be conducted via video using a delayed process. For example, a therapist can videotape a session with a family in one venue and convey the tape the next day to a reflecting team in another venue. The team then record their reflections on the same tape which is then conveyed back to the family for viewing and further reflections with the therapist. When using 'delayed' reflections it is important to minimize the delay and to provide the team's reflection within a day of the original session.[1] Finally, particular kinds of team members can be recruited to work with specific client groups. For example, Selekman (1996) describes the use of peers in reflecting teams for adolescent clients. Also, specific significant others (extended family members or longstanding friends) can be invited to attend at a particular point as outsider witnesses to change (Payne, 2000).

Constructive understandings

In pursuing a stance of multiple engagement, we can become preoccupied with trying to engage with everyone in the room, and forget to remain engaged with ourselves. We can work to promote a climate of reflective emotional postures for clients, and neglect to notice our own fight/flight reactions. In relationship therapy, amidst competing claims, swirls of information and fluctuating tensions, the monitoring of our inner conversation is even more significant, as there are more potential buttons that can be pushed – and more people available to push them. When the outer conversation appears to falter or reach an impasse, we can profitably turn to our inner conversation for clues. My working assumption is that constructive therapy is effective *to the degree that our inner and outer conversations are congruent and originate within reflective postures*. Hoffman (2002) uses the term 'connected speaking' in a similar way.

Griffith and Griffith (1994) argue that it is one of the specific responsibilities of a practitioner to enter the therapy room with an orientation of reflective emotional postures. This is because the therapist's emotional postures become 'coupled' with those of the clients, inviting a reciprocal form of relationship. We may do our best to enter the room with the preferred postures but it is often harder to maintain these postures throughout – and to keep entering the same room with the same clients session after session. In our inner conversation we may hear a refrain such as 'Oh no! Not the Johnsons again!' Perhaps the first step in freeing up our inner conversation is to increase awareness of our own emotional postures as we engage with family members. How do you typically find out that you are acting from reactive rather than reflective postures? What part of your body gives you the first signal? What is the first sign in your inner conversation? If we could view a video of you when you are reactive rather than reflective what would be the telltale signs? When this happens, how does it affect your stances of appreciative ally and multiple engagement? How does the nature of your inner conversation show in your outer conversation?

Inner conversation is more than a professionally detached decision-making process. It consists of an ongoing dialogue between different and often competing internalized voices. For example, it may involve a dialogue between the *role* of the therapist and the *self* of the therapist (Rober, 1999), in which personal reactions to the client or situation may be at odds with the defined practice role. If we accept that a major part of a therapist's expertise lies in self-awareness, an important part of this is awareness about our own internalized population of voices. We are all multi-storied and multi-voiced. If our clients appear to be 'pushing a button' which invites us to reply with a voice of judgement or helplessness, we can seek to find another voice from our inner community that embraces a different reality.

Selecting realities

One typical effect is the tendency to blame or pathologize clients when reacting to aspects of their presentation or behaviour. Whatever the immediate stimulus, we can easily slip into the 'bad trance' induction of deficit-oriented language. It is important to make the qualification that I am not talking here about momentary or fleeting reactions to particular incidents, or to negative first impressions of a client. Therapists are neither computers nor saints; they cannot program their emotional responsiveness and expect to transcend the human range of visceral experience. Nor would they want to, because a therapist's reactions are important sources of insight, compassion, and connection. For example, if a family member 'pulls' a certain reaction from us, this may provide understanding of how this happens with others. However, reactive emotional postures become problematic when they are no longer fleeting but begin to *systematically* skew or bias the inner conversation in ways that limit possibilities for the outer conversation. We are in bad trance territory when we begin to engage in inner conversations for characterizations, accusations and recriminations. For example, we may find ourselves thinking of families or family members as being 'difficult', 'demanding', 'dysfunctional', 'in denial', 'aggressive', 'defensive', 'passive-aggressive', 'uncooperative', 'resistant', 'unmotivated', 'lacking insight' or many of the other terms in the expansive lexicon of deficit. When this happens we have ceased to think constructively about clients, and have begun to 'know' too much and too quickly, leaving no room for dialogue. We need to find ways of disengaging from these conversations in order to find more 'constructive understandings' (Sharry, 2001). Developing a point made by Griffith and Griffith, *selecting realities* in the inner conversation is more therapeutic than enforcing an action in the outer conversation. By carefully selecting assumptions about our clients' qualities, capacities, motivations and responses, we can 'literally choose a world whose atmosphere is one of openness, curiosity and respect' (1994: 92). Constructive therapists have often discussed reframing as a method of inviting clients to view situations differently. However, the emphasis is usually on reframing in the outer conversation. What I am talking about here is a kind of *inner reframing* that occurs as therapists invite themselves to embrace more constructive understandings.

At a general level, Griffith and Griffith (1994: 91–2) suggest a number of simple and basic assumptions that can help us to maintain a stance of openness and curiosity towards our clients in relationship therapy. I have summarized these below:

- Family members as human beings share more similarities than differences with therapists.
- Family members are ordinary people living ordinary lives who have encountered difficult and unforeseen life circumstances.
- When family members seek consultation they are struggling with a dilemma or situation where they are unable to have the kind of conversation that is needed.
- Family members always possess more lived experience and more possibilities than is suggested by the available narratives about them.
- Family members in their deepest desires do not wish to harm themselves or others.

- A therapist cannot understand the meaning or nature of family members' concerns until these have been talked about.
- Change is always possible.
- Family members wish to be free of problems and to make changes in this direction.
- A therapist cannot know for certain what actions family members need to take in order to achieve what they are wanting.

Here are some additional assumptions that I find helpful:

- Family problems often develop 'accidentally' through the misunderstanding or mishandling of everyday life difficulties (Bogdan, 1986; Watzlawick, Weakland and Fisch, 1974). This can happen when attempts to solve problems 'accidentally' perpetuate them and/or where a gap between a family member's preferred view of self and how others actually perceive them widens (Eron and Lund, 1996).
- Sometimes a seemingly trivial event can inadvertently trigger the onset of a major problem (and an equally trivial event can end it).
- Family problems often result from attempts to negotiate significant transitions in family life, and the accompanying disruption to routines.
- Families encountering numerous difficulties are multi-stressed, rather than having multi-problems (Madsen, 1999).
- Family members are often ambivalent about the prospect of change, taking time to weigh up the advantages and disadvantages.
- Family relationships are mysteries to be embraced rather than problems to be solved.

Of course there may be occasions when some of these assumptions do not seem appropriate. However, they are suggestive as general starting positions for our inner conversation, and can help us to avoid the four problematic themes of blame, invalidation, determinism and impossibility.

Here are two specific examples, showing the process of inner reframing that might assist the outer conversation. In each situation there is an initial reaction and a temptation to enforce an action in the outer conversation. However, the systematic attempt to derive constructive understandings acts to reconfigure the therapist's emotional postures and to free up the outer conversation.

Example 1

Situation

Stan (aged 45) is berating his sons Adam (18) and Larry (aged 16) over their reluctance to 'take their lives seriously', knuckle down and take responsibility for making a career. This has become the characteristic pattern in each session so far. As the session develops, Stan adopts an increasingly angry and hectoring tone, making long speeches, lecturing his sons and talking over them. Adam's and Larry's reactions switch between retaliatory anger and passivity, while their mother, June (aged 42), attempts to placate and mediate between her husband and sons. About a year ago, Stan was retrenched after many years in a professional career and has had to take on bits and pieces of casual work in order to make a living. June has told the therapist that this has made him even more embittered and aggressive, and that there have been episodes of violence with the boys when Stan has been drinking.

(a) Initial reaction

As Stan gets into full swing, railing against the indolence of his sons, and utterly dominating the 'conversation' I feel increasingly frustrated and reciprocally angry. Something about his loud and hectoring tone evokes the same emotional reaction in me as I can see in Adam and Larry; a tension between aggression and resignation, between wanting to 'take him on' and wanting to switch off and just ride out the storm. Increasingly with each session, I find myself siding with the other family members against Stan.

Part of me wants to challenge him in the outer conversation: to *make* him aware of the effect his tirades are having on his family, to *make* him see that his anger has more to do with his own experience, to exert authority and *insist* that he allow the others to speak, or to simply *ignore* him and attempt to converse with June and the two sons. Another part of me wants simply to switch into empathic mode and just daydream!

(b) Constructive understandings

- How is Stan teaching me to help him? Perhaps he is telling me that I need to respond to him differently from the way his sons and wife do. It is important that I take his views seriously and converse with him in a respectful way, neither mocking him, undermining him, placating him or ignoring him. How can I best do this?
- What can I admire and respect about Stan? What qualities are hidden by the external 'bluster'? Is there another side to him that I haven't seen yet, perhaps one that his family have not seen for a while? How can I create a safe space for this other side to show itself?
- Stan is angry but he is also desperate and fearful. While there is aggression in his face and voice, I can glimpse fear and helplessness in his eyes. Am I the only one who senses this? How can I connect with these hidden feelings?

- Especially after what he has been through, Stan is desperately concerned about the future of his sons. Are they (and for that matter, is he, himself) fully aware of the effects of the retrenchment on his life and outlook? Has this been talked about at length in the family? Who knows and who doesn't?
- He probably has some valid points to make; if these could be put in a different way, free from characterizations, accusations and recriminations, is it possible that other family members might actually agree with some of them?
- What other part of this family's history is being hidden? What alternative stories about Stan's relationship with his sons could be told? Who would be the best person to ask about this?

(c) Responses in outer conversation

Drawing on these new forms of curiosity in my inner conversation, I could remain in individual engagement with Stan, attempting to draw out his concerns and hopes for his family, and inviting him to express these in ways that may be different and more engaging. By focusing on my own interaction with him, I may be able to minimize the tendency for him to lecture his sons directly with the inevitable reactivity this produces. Rather than trying to 'take him on' or withdrawing into passivity, I am now in a more reflective space where I can be curious rather than critical. One option might be to ask what Eron and Lund (1996) call the 'mystery question'. This takes the generic form (using Stan as an example): How did someone with X preferred attributes (wanting the best for his sons and wanting to be viewed by them as a good and loving father) wind up in situation Y (intense and painful conflict with his sons and increasing estrangement from his wife) and being viewed by others in Z ways (aggressive, rigid and bullying)? This kind of question can invite useful insights and connections, but only if asked within reflective postures (otherwise it comes across as an attack along the lines of 'Can't you see that …!'). The constructive understandings in my inner conversation have reconfigured my emotional postures and stimulated my curiosity and my desire to work collaboratively with Stan and the other family members.

Example 2

Situation

Alice (14) has been persistently answering 'I don't know', or a variation on this theme, to most of the questions that the therapist has asked. Sometimes she answers directly, sometimes she shrugs her shoulders or uses a quizzical facial expression. At times she looks at the ceiling, rolls her eyes or drums her fingernails on the side of her chair. Each time Alice responds in this way, her mother Margo (32) glances at the therapist with a knowing expression that says 'See! That's what she does all the time. That's what we have to put up with. Now you can see what she's like.' Alice has become incommunicative at home, spending most of her time in her room. She has begun to neglect her personal hygiene and is being picked on at school because she is considerably overweight. Margo believes that her daughter is being systematically bullied and humiliated because of her appearance but Alice will not confirm this. Margo thinks she is being blindly loyal to her school 'friends' in the hope that they might finally accept her. Her question to the therapist is: 'Can you find a way of getting through to her, and getting her to open up?'

(a) Initial reaction

As the session unfolds, I find myself reacting negatively to both Alice and Margo. Alice seems pleased with her ability to stonewall, and seems to be doing this in a practised way. She does not make any attempt to reflect seriously on my questions but goes immediately into 'I don't know and I don't care' mode. I sense my own frustration, especially as her mother expects me to know how to get Alice to 'open up'. I am tempted to rise to the challenge and try to outwit Alice and 'get through to her' someway. But I also sense that she is increasingly angry and may be feeling humiliated by the way her mother deliberately parades her responses as a way of demonstrating her problems to the therapist. This pulls a reaction from me also, and I feel like confronting Margo with the consequences of her behaviour ('... in the same way that Alice is being humiliated at school, can't you see that you are also humiliating her here?)

(b) Constructive understandings

- Alice's response of 'I don't know' is perfectly legitimate and acceptable. She is choosing to be protective of her right to privacy. It is best for her not to reveal anything significant until she is convinced that she can trust me, and even then I have no right to expect co-operation. If it is a matter of trust, how can I try to earn this, so that she feels she has an option? For example, would she be more willing to talk to me if I saw her alone?
- Having experienced how easily both Alice's and Margo's patterns of interaction can evoke frustration, criticism, ridicule and humiliation, I can learn from this and make sure that I don't 'couple' with these reactive patterns.

- Margo is sincerely trying to help and, behind her obvious exasperation, she may also be feeling humiliated and incompetent as a parent. The last thing she needs is a therapist helping her feel even more humiliated!
- By parading examples of her daughter's behaviour, Margo may be seeking a sense of validation and vindication: 'It is difficult and frustrating – I'm not making it up!' This is a perfectly understandable position. I wonder how much support Margo is getting from her husband and others? Is she carrying the main burden of parenting?
- If Margo felt more competent and confident as a parent, what difference might this make to the way she interacts with Alice?
- If Alice knew that whatever she disclosed would be treated with respect and would not result in further interrogation or humiliation, what difference might this make? Might she be more willing to engage with my questions?
- What other aspects are there to Alice, Margo and their relationship? Who would be best placed to tell me about these? Are there others in the family or at school whose voices could transform the available stories?

(c) Responses in outer conversation

I can thank Alice for her honesty in not making something up just to suit her mother or me, and say that I respect her right to privacy. I could indicate that, if there is something that she might like to share with me, I would be happy to hear it, but it is best to wait until she can trust me. I may then be able to engage indirectly with Alice as she listens to my conversation with Margo. I can acknowledge and normalize Margo's sense of frustration and desperation as a parent, inquire about the degree of support she has, and ask about the ways that different family members have tried to support each other during this difficult period. Have there been any pre-session changes or differences of note? What signs would indicate to her that she could allow herself to worry less? What does she know about Alice that gives her a sense of hope? I could also ask both Alice and Margo about the resilience of their relationship in the face of the present circumstances. What is its history and what are its enduring strengths? Inviting Alice to be a commentator on something else, rather than the direct focus of the conversation, may encourage her to participate to some degree. I might also speculate aloud about the possibility and advisability of my talking to Alice alone. Would this be helpful or not?

There are many more potential examples that could be used. For example, it is not unusual for therapists to label themselves also in deficit-oriented ways ('I can't work with angry men', 'I'm hopeless with young children', etc.). It may be interesting for you to reflect on a recent situation where you have characterized yourself in a similar way and go through the process I have outlined in order to arrive at a more constructive understanding. However, I am not wanting to generate a list of ready-made 'inner reframes' for all occasions. It is more important to suggest a systematic process that therapists can adapt to their own needs and circumstances. In the inner conversation our personal reactions metaphorically 'dialogue' with our professional role as we try to think constructively about what is happening, and what might be done. The more practice we have in processing our inner conversation and articulating this experience, the more likely it is that we will be able to access constructive understandings in future sessions.

Relationship blind spots

Rober (1999) has drawn another useful distinction between different kinds of therapist reactions that occur in the inner conversation. He suggests that some are evoked by aspects of the immediate social context – the outer conversation – while others are related to aspects of the therapist's personal story. Another important part of self-awareness relates to sensitivity to our own biases and predispositions. I am not talking here about professional preferences in the sense of actively choosing one model over another, but about systematic personal biases that may show themselves in family therapy. Returning to an earlier point, because of the complexity of issues and the emotionality that can be present in relationship therapy, there can be more personal buttons to be pushed and more people available to push them. Therefore, if we are to maintain an orientation of reflective emotional postures, awareness of our own *relationship blind spots* is an important part of our expertise. These often show themselves in our tendency to feel underconnected with some family members and over-connected with others. It can relate to bias in terms of gender (do you find yourself typically siding with the man or woman in conjoint work?), age (do you tend to side with parents or children?), values (do you find yourself working to keep couples together or encouraging individual freedom?), or more context-specific reactions (such as a response to a client's display of intense anger). For example, looking back to Example 1 above, if a therapist experienced Stan's anger in a particularly intense way that resonated for several days, this might suggest a connection with the therapist's personal relationship history.

My aim is not to pathologize therapists any more than clients but to *normalize* these experiences and encourage their inclusion as part of our expertise in self-awareness. We can become aware of these blind spots in a number of ways: through monitoring our habitual reactions to particular kinds of relationship issues or clients, through evaluating the efficacy of our work with different problems or populations, or through the observations of supervisors or colleagues.

In processing the various kinds of reactions that occur in our inner conversation, the availability of either formal or peer supervision is a vital resource for family therapists. It is important to note that supervision in its various forms can also be conducted using a constructive framework. In this approach, the emphasis is placed upon supervising the therapist's own self-supervision (Lowe, 2000). It works to enhance the therapist's ability to discern situations in which they can process their own work from situations where they require additional assistance. In group contexts, this can also include the valuable resource of a reflecting team (Lowe and Guy, 1999).

This chapter has continued one of the major themes of the book: a view of constructive family therapy as a reflective and relational stance rather than a disembodied set of techniques. This draws us to a consideration of the inner conversation and of ways to expand its repertoire for both clients and therapists. The shift of perspective between inner and outer conversation can be particularly helpful in situations of impasse. Rather than seeking answers in the outer conversation, the therapist can attempt to cultivate the inner conversation as a resource. This allows for the co-ordination of inner and outer conversation in new forms of connected speaking that produce new possibilities.

Note

1. This suggestion came from Bob Bertolino's 'Breaking the Rules' workshop, Brisbane, 2002.

8   Borrowing from Other Frameworks

Simplicity before understanding is simplistic; simplicity after understanding is simple. (de Bono, 1998: 68)

Oversimplification means carrying simplification to the point where other values are ignored. (de Bono, 1998: 70)

In beginning this chapter I invite you to consider the following dilemma: This is the last chapter in the book in which I will be introducing any major new concepts. It offers the final opportunity to add to our constructive framework before taking it on the road. There is room for only one or two more items of luggage. What should they be?

You may wish to reflect on your reactions to the content of the book so far. In my desire to travel light, what have I left out that you would have included as an essential item in your therapeutic luggage? What would need to be in this chapter in order for *my* constructive framework to be sufficient for *your* practice with families? What additional forms of knowledge do you think might be important – or even crucial? Perhaps you would like to incorporate knowledge and skills from other therapeutic traditions. Or perhaps you possess other kinds of professional knowledge that you think are relevant. For example, you might be an educator, a doctor, a social worker, a clinical psychologist, or any other member of the helping community who might possess specialized knowledge that could be important in family work.

One of the most striking – and perhaps unique – aspects of constructive therapies is that their theoretical foundations are not intrinsically linked to conventional therapeutic concerns. In other words, there is no particular theory about human behaviour, personality, normative developmental processes, healthy/unhealthy family functioning, or even about the nature and cause of problems. Compared to other major therapies, there is strikingly little interest in theorizing about these concerns. For example, in their *Course Notes* on solution-focused therapy, George, Iveson and Ratner state:

> If it has a theory at all it is more a philosophical theory about the nature of knowledge, the social construction of reality and the creative potential of language. These are theories which give clues about how the conversational process works to create change rather than theories about human behaviour and personality. (page 2, no date given)[1]

While this approach helps to identify what is different and often exciting about constructive therapies, it can also be disconcerting for the many therapists who *are* interested in more conventional forms of therapeutic theorizing, who wish to extend their professional repertoire across theoretical divides, or who wish to utilize knowledge from other frameworks.

For example, one dilemma for many practitioners concerns the preference of many constructive therapists to limit their curiosity to what family members actually verbalize as their specific concerns and requests. This is a reaction to the more traditional therapeutic practice of distinguishing between surface and depth: between presenting problems (symptoms) and underlying causes (structural conditions) that therapists interpret. This distinction often produces the very whirlpool of deficit-oriented hypothesis generation that we travel light in order to avoid. However, while this may be a purist's ideal, how literally should it be taken? Can we not both listen appreciatively to the client's story *and* hypothesize beyond it? What if the therapist suspects that progress towards the clients' goals is being compromised by factors such as biochemical imbalances, family secrets, the legacy of personal trauma, or alcohol abuse? To what extent is it 'legitimate' for a constructive therapist to entertain or introduce such unspoken possibilities?

More broadly, the question becomes: to what extent can a therapist committed to a particular framework attempt to access knowledge from other frameworks without losing a sense of identity and direction? Regardless of what this 'extracurricular' knowledge is, can we find a way to include it within a constructive framework? So far in this book I have introduced ideas and methods that seem to fit consistently with constructive therapy principles. An attempt has been made to dispense with much of the theoretical adornment that more general books on family therapy would contain. But is this enough? As I mentioned at the beginning, a persistent challenge for constructive therapists is to distinguish travelling light from being ill-equipped. I want my work to be simple but not simplistic or oversimplified to the point of ignoring other important values and considerations (de Bono, 1998). Therefore, in preparing for an unpredictable journey, knowing that I will need to respond flexibly and to improvise in a wide range of circumstances, I need a Plan B, a way of selectively 'borrowing' from other orientations when a 'business as usual' approach seems ineffective or inappropriate. I cannot carry a weighty encyclopaedia of eclectic knowledge, so what can I pack that is useful and manageable?

Each of us must decide what additional forms of knowledge we might need, and how much room we can make to accommodate them. Rather than specifying content, it is more useful to specify a *process* that therapists can use when considering how and when to include ideas from other frameworks. This is the key item of luggage that we need to take, and is an appropriate theme for this penultimate chapter. My approach may not cover the particular content that coincides with your own 'extracurricular' interests, but it will offer a way of thinking about these areas that may enable you to include them *within* a constructive framework. In searching for concepts that encourage this possibility, I discuss *primary, secondary and rejected pictures* (Wile, 1993) and the *lifting of constraints* (Breunlin, 1999). In this chapter I outline the major concepts and principles, while in Chapter 9 I provide a selective range of examples that we may encounter as we take the framework on the road. The question becomes one of how we can engage with voices from other discourses in ways that are purposeful rather than confusing. While this conceptual juggling act might not always be successful, we may, in many cases, be able to use additional knowledge in ways that enhance our preferred framework rather than detract from it. By switching to Plan B we may actually find a way of improving Plan A.

Beyond purity and eclecticism

One of the most frequently asked questions from students and practitioners concerns the issue of theoretical purity. Do we have to unlearn or ignore all of our other training, and practise in a 'pure' way? Or can we integrate other knowledge in a way that avoids becoming messily eclectic? Is there a place in this framework for concepts X, Y or Z? On one hand, how can you afford to leave these out in a book about family therapy? On the other hand, how inclusive can you become without losing your distinctive orientation and surrendering to confusion?

The question of theoretical purity versus forms of eclecticism, integrationism or pluralism has long occupied therapists. Some wear eclecticism as a badge of honour, suggesting that it is the only rational response, given the complexities of our profession. At the other extreme, others see it as an embarrassing admission that should only be made behind closed doors and between consenting adults. In the latter view, an 'admission' of eclecticism is tantamount to acknowledging that you can't think clearly and don't really have much of a clue about what you are doing. It is relatively easy to state a theoretical or ideological position on this issue, but I am much more interested in how it plays out in practice. If viewed as extremes on a continuum, it seems to me that very few, if any, therapists practise in ways that are consistently pure *or* eclectic. Whether intentionally or not, we borrow or steal ideas from many different places (our history of formal training, reading, workshops, discussions with colleagues and supervisors) and may continue to utilize these even if they are inconsistent with our present professed framework. For example, I trained as a cognitive-behavioural psychologist before becoming interested in constructionist approaches, and still find myself automatically using some of the useful ideas from that perspective. Applying a central tenet of narrative therapy, the story we tell about our therapy framework can never capture all of our lived experience in actually practising therapy. Beyebach and Morejón put it more 'fundamentally': 'Integration happens!' (1999: 25).

But, at the other extreme, I also suspect that very few therapists are actually eclectic in the sense of choosing from an unrestricted menu of approaches in a given situation. I suspect that if we were to watch an avowed 'eclectic' therapist work with a number of cases, we would see a consistency of style in the sense that there would be a number of key skills that were used in every case, and others that were used in most cases. My suggestion is that most therapists have preferred ways of working that define their particular interests, skills and areas of knowledge. As far as possible they try to work within this professional comfort zone. However, they are also likely to have at least some working knowledge of alternative approaches and other forms of additional knowledge that they draw upon in particular circumstances. They are *selectively* eclectic in the sense of preferring approaches that they can more easily accommodate to their preferred style. In the same way that some drinks mix well and others don't, different theoretical discourses may complement each other or simply clash in an unpalatable way. The point to be made, therefore, is that though 'integration happens', there may be a method to it that can usefully be articulated. It is a question of *how* we integrate and whether this is done systematically or haphazardly.

Primary, secondary and rejected pictures

One of the difficulties with generic terms like 'eclecticism', 'pluralism', 'integration' or the 'both/and' position is that they often obscure more than they reveal. What does it actually mean to practise in an eclectic way? For example, let us suppose we start working with a family using Model A. We then decide (for whatever reason) to switch to Model B. Do we take the whole package of theory and practice from Model B, or just parts of it? What happens next? Do we stay in Model B or do we switch back to Model A? How and when do we decide? Supposing we switch again, to Model C. Do we see the case through to completion as defined by that approach or revert to Models A or B? Might we end up doing some combination of Models A, B and C that is not recognizable as any of them? Also, what about the factor of the therapist's own preferences and skills? Are there some models that the therapist prefers and returns to as often as possible, or are they assumed to be equally at home in all? Is a claim to eclectic practice meant to suggest that you know every model in the field and can use them all equally well? Following from this, does the eclectic practitioner use each model in the *same way* as a specialist in that model would use it? For example, if a structural family therapist decides to use some concepts from narrative therapy (or vice versa), will each therapist perform the other's model in the 'classical' way? Or do they adapt it to fit their preferred way of working? These are the kinds of issues that get hidden in the vagaries of 'eclectic practice' and make it difficult to articulate systematic guidelines for moving between approaches.

My suggestion for working in a selectively eclectic way is that this involves identifying our preferred ways of working, and recognizing that we don't simply borrow ideas from elsewhere but adapt them so that they fit more closely with our preferred approaches. One contribution that I have found particularly helpful is the distinction made by Wile (1993) between a therapist's *primary, secondary* and *rejected pictures*. To me, this distinction captures better than any other the moment-to-moment experience of doing therapy. As Wile suggests, and many therapists would confirm, there are periods during a conversation when we lose sight of the major principles of our approach (our 'primary pictures'); when we cannot immediately see how they can be applied to the situation at hand. At such times, we may react to events by shifting to different theoretical pictures (Wile uses the term 'pictures' to indicate the parts of a theory that a therapist actually uses in a consistent way, and which tend to become habitual in practice – as we work with clients, certain pictures or images expand to fill our view and cover our field of vision). Therapists of course prefer to work consistently from their primary pictures and do not like these periods of uncertainty when 'cross-theory leakage' occurs. Therefore, they will work hard to find an angle or opportunity that will allow them to return to their primary pictures as soon as possible.

But this does not happen in a random way. Wile suggests that when we depart from our primary pictures we make a further distinction between those alternative pictures that we are willing to accommodate ('secondary pictures') and those that we actively try to avoid ('rejected pictures'). He goes as far as to suggest that: 'Adopting primary pictures, shifting at times into secondary pictures, and avoiding rejected pictures, is what "doing psychotherapy" *is*' (Wile, 1993: 304). Clarifying and distinguishing our primary, secondary and rejected pictures may help us to achieve a more systematic way of approaching the need for both focus and flexibility. It should help us to develop an understanding as to which alternative ideas we can accommodate and adapt to complement our primary pictures, and which ones do not fit in any shape or form.

Primary pictures

Primary pictures are the basic beliefs that you have about people. They are the theories that you have in your mind most of the time: even before your clients walk into your office, even where there is no immediate evidence – even perhaps when there is *contradicting* evidence (Wile, 1993: 273–4).

As Wile puts it, primary pictures are a therapist's ultimate explanatory principles or rock-bottom ideas. In practical terms, this means that one or more of these pictures is at the forefront of my mind from moment to moment in a session. These are the preferred realities that I select to inform my practice.

You have already been introduced to my primary pictures: they are the central principles or therapeutic vision that I have outlined in this book. My major primary pictures, unlike Wile's, however, are more to do with beliefs about therapy than with beliefs about people. They represent my preferred realities and practices, the lenses through which I view my work. For example:

- the 'collaborative inquiry' picture
- the 'resourceful client' picture
- the 'hosting–negotiating–evoking' picture
- the 'simplicity–parsimony' picture

Even before I meet new clients I make the assumption that our work will take the form of a process of collaborative inquiry that will utilize the processes of hosting, negotiating and evoking in order to assist clients to access their resourcefulness in the most simple and straightforward way. I will work hard to maintain these pictures whatever turns our actual conversation may take.

Wile provides examples of typical primary pictures used by therapists from different orientations. For example:

Psychodynamic primary pictures

- the 'character defects, developmental deficits' picture
- the 'holdover from history' picture
- the 'symptoms serve unconscious purposes' picture

Cognitive-behavioural primary pictures

- the 'skills deficit' picture
- the 'positive reinforcement' picture
- the 'irrational ideas, negative self-talk' picture

Family systems primary pictures

- the 'family homeostasis, identified patient' picture
- the 'pathological boundaries and coalitions' picture
- the 'transmission through three generations' picture

Despite their preference for the comfort zone of their primary pictures, however, therapists are often willing to shift into secondary pictures.

Secondary pictures

Secondary pictures are *not* typically at the forefront of your mind. You do *not* have them even before the client walks into your office. You have them only when there *is* immediate evidence. And you can easily shift out of them. (Wile, 1993: 274)

Wile suggests that therapists snap into secondary pictures when they lack sufficient information, ideas or angles to apply their primary pictures. As soon as there *is* significant information, as soon as they can find a suitable angle, they revert to their primary pictures. Secondary pictures involve concepts and methods originating from other frameworks or perspectives. One therapist's primary pictures are another therapist's secondary pictures. A crucial point is that the therapist is not philosophically opposed to using these concepts and practices in specific circumstances and contexts, though they are not their preferred ways of thinking and working. This means that we borrow selectively from other approaches and use them in ways that are intended to facilitate a return, as soon as possible, to our primary pictures. For example, a cognitive-behavioural therapist may be working on communication skills with a couple using a primary picture of 'skills deficits' when one partner says that her anger toward her husband reminds her of her anger towards her father. The therapist may switch into a 'holdover from history' picture taken from a more psychodynamic orientation. The therapist may shift into this temporarily to explore its significance but will be seeking to find a way back into primary pictures as soon as possible. In this case, for example, the woman might eventually be helped to monitor her internal talk during arguments so that she can differentiate between her husband and her father or between her response as a child and her response as an adult. This may allow a return to the 'skills-deficits' primary picture and actually enhance its effectiveness. By contrast, a psychodynamic therapist working with the same couple may adopt primary pictures such as 'holdover from history' or 'developmental deficits'. However, the therapist may notice that the couple's communication patterns are filled with blaming or 'you' statements, which are impeding progress. The therapist might switch temporarily into a 'skills-deficits' picture and help the couple to discriminate between 'I' statements and 'you' statements and to improve their communication skills. Again, however, the aim is to facilitate a return to primary pictures, and to a focus on historical issues.

Therefore, when therapists switch to secondary pictures and borrow ideas from other orientations, they do not necessarily use them *in the same way, to the same degree or for the same purpose* as do therapists for whom these are primary pictures. Instead, they 'adapt' them in various ways in order to negotiate obstacles to the use of their primary pictures. They do not carry an extensive encyclopaedia of knowledge from other frameworks, but a selective range of ideas that they can borrow where necessary – and return as soon as possible.

Rejected pictures

But there is another category of pictures that is much harder to reconcile with our primary pictures.

> *Rejected pictures* are those you do not snap into even if there *is* immediate suggestive evidence for them. Your therapeutic approach is defined, in part, by your rejected pictures – by the pictures you go out of your way *not* to have, and if you find yourself having, you try to shift out of. (Wile, 1993: 277)

Perhaps we could describe rejected pictures as being our personal and professional blind spots. Whereas secondary pictures can be reconciled in various ways with our primary pictures, rejected pictures tend to be antithetical to one or more of our primary pictures. You reject them despite immediate suggestive evidence. They are not 'wrong' (one therapist's rejected pictures are another therapist's primary pictures) but they do not fit with your preferred way of working.

Here are some of my rejected pictures. As you can see, they represent the 'other' side of the assumptions implied by my primary pictures:

- the 'diagnosis–treatment' picture
- the 'character defects, developmental deficits' picture
- the 'programmed change' picture
- the 'unilateral action' picture

Despite what others might see as clear evidence, I will try to avoid pictures that suggest the need to shift from open-ended conversation to the clinical treatment of objectively existing conditions. I will work hard not to see my work as involving long-term psychological or developmental remediation based on specialized professional knowledge, or as participation in a programmed sequence of change. Likewise, I will tend to delay as far as possible the choice to take unilateral action that is contrary to a client's stated goals or wishes (for example, in the case of a person who threatens harm to self or others).

The distinction between primary, secondary and rejected pictures is summarized in Box 8.1.

Box 8.1   Primary, secondary and rejected pictures

Primary pictures are those you have even without immediate suggestive evidence.

Secondary pictures are those you have only with immediate suggestive evidence.

Rejected pictures are those you reject despite immediate suggestive evidence, because they directly contradict one or more of your primary pictures.

(Wile, 1993: 278)

For the purposes of this chapter, the most significant contribution of Wile's scheme is the relationship between primary and secondary pictures. This relationship encourages the possibility of broadening our horizon by borrowing ideas from other frameworks, but doing so in a way that allows us to maintain our overall sense of direction. It is another way of widening the lens (shifting to secondary pictures) before re-sharpening the focus (reverting to primary pictures).

Identifying and lifting constraints

In what circumstances might a constructive therapist decide to shift to secondary pictures and temporarily to abandon business as usual? In assembling a constructive framework, I suggest that another useful concept involves the identification and lifting of *constraints* (Breunlin, 1999). The concept of constraints will be familiar to family therapists schooled in the cybernetic orientation to human systems. As Breunlin suggests, constraints can be defined as 'anything in a human system that keeps it from solving problems' (1999: 367). In a family therapy context, this might include beliefs/stories, habitual patterns of interaction, organizational structures and broader cultural assumptions that act to restrict family members in various ways. Importantly for a constructive framework, constraints tend to be associated with the concept of 'negative explanation' rather than the more traditional 'positive explanation'. Using negative explanation, problems are assumed to persist because family members are *constrained* from finding alternatives. The key question is then what holds family members back or restricts them in their attempts to find solutions. This contrasts with positive explanation, which assumes that problems are *caused* or propelled by particular forces or motivations (so that the key question is then what causes the problem). As Breunlin notes, positive explanation tends to favour a functional or homeostatic view, which suggests that the family system actively resists attempts to introduce change, or that problems serve functions for the family. However, a negative explanation asserts that family members neither need problems nor wish them to continue. If constraints can be identified and lifted, family members can utilize their collective resources to find a way forward. Constraints, not people, are assumed to be the problem (Madsen, 1999).

This conceptualization allows us to consider a range of constraining influences while continuing to avoid the problematic stories of blame, invalidation, determinacy and impossibility. The language of negative explanation allows us to hypothesize about constraints without pathologizing family members or diagnosing structural deficiencies that are the 'real' problem. We can use this language in both our outer and inner conversation:

> I'm wondering what may be holding you back or restricting you from pursuing the future that you want? Some families who have consulted with me about similar concerns have told me that one thing that often gets in the way is ———. Is this a relevant factor in your lives?

If our preferred approach based on primary pictures appears insufficient to help family members, or we cannot think of the most appropriate way to apply our primary pictures, we can temporarily switch to secondary pictures and hypothesize about potential areas of constraint that are not being currently addressed. This may involve consideration of concepts from other theoretical frameworks or professional perspectives. The identification and lifting of constraints then paves the way for a return to our primary pictures.

Levels and types of constraint

There are a number of different kinds of constraints that could be relevant in family scenarios. Clients may be constrained by biochemical imbalances, by conditioned responses, by longstanding problematic patterns or habits, by a lack of specific information, knowledge or social skills, by the behavioural, cognitive and emotional legacy of past events ('holdover from history'), by fear or intimidation, by unspoken realities. Any of these kinds of constraints can make working exclusively from one's primary pictures problematic. For example, working from the 'heliotropic principle' I may be hoping that a family will grow towards what they (and the therapist) persistently ask questions about. But what if one or more family members are constrained by intense anxiety or anger that effectively restricts their participation in a process of collaborative inquiry? How might this skew the kinds of questions that are asked and the realities that are constructed? Despite my attempt to use the familiar skills of my primary pictures, at what point might I need to suspend business as usual and consider these individual constraints?

Breunlin suggests that therapists consider a number of levels in the 'biopsychosocial' system: biology, person, relationship, family, community and society. I will briefly describe each and give examples of the types of constraint that can act to restrict family members.

Biology

Individuals' attempts to struggle with relationship difficulties can be constrained by biological factors such as physiological disorders, biochemical disturbances or genetic predispositions. Breunlin offers several examples. A simple example might be a marital problem concerning impotence, where a man's obesity and blood pressure medication make it difficult for him to sustain an erection. Another example involves the 'physiological flooding' that men, in particular, can experience during spousal conflict and which impairs their cognitive functioning. Other potential areas in this category could be conditioned fears or the experience of flashbacks or dissociation, where physiology takes over and restricts attempts to converse and connect. Biological constraints might require psychiatric referral or medical intervention, perhaps in combination with individual psychotherapy or psycho-education.

Person

Constraints at the level of the person focus on the psychology of the self: the ways in which individuals characteristically make, interpret and experience meanings and emotions (Breunlin, 1999). When struggling to deal with relationship issues, individuals can be constrained by beliefs, assumptions and expectations that were learned in their own family of origin, and by the habitual behaviours that accompany them. These can include 'recipes' or formulas for good parenting, gender roles and ways to handle conflict in family relationships. By implication, there can be a lack of alternative information, options and skills. Individuals can also be constrained by their own 'childhood survival stories' (Parry and Doan, 1994), the patterns of fight or flight responses learned in childhood in order to cope with threats or abandonment, and which can be re-activated in adulthood in conflicts where rejection is threatened. Another important form of personal constraint is the individual's *theory of change* (Duncan and Miller, 2000), the assumptions made about what needs to happen for family therapy to be successful and change to occur. Therapeutic progress can be constrained by a failure to achieve an accommodation between the therapist's approach and an individual's theory of change. For example, a parent who believes that change can only occur if their teenage children are forced to 'come to their senses' and accept parental discipline, may be disconcerted by a therapeutic approach that appears to take the children's complaints seriously.

Relationship

In family therapy, relationship constraints typically focus on the parental or spousal dyad. Attempts made by family members to resolve relationship difficulties can be constrained by conflict or tension between the adult partners, resulting in a failure to work co-operatively or to exercise leadership in a family. However, relationship constraints can also relate to any other dyad in a family grouping, for example between one parent and a child, or between two siblings. Each dyadic relationship in a family has its own history and dynamics. Dyadic constraints often show themselves in recursive patterns of interaction such as pursue/withdraw; over-responsible/ under-responsible; minimize/maximize; demand disclosure/secrecy and withholding; and correction and control/protest and rebellion (Madsen, 1999). Escalations in these dyadic dances, with their patterns of mutual invitation, can restrict the possibilities for change, especially in the broader family context where multiple dyadic relationships are present.

Family

The family level of constraints has naturally been the main interest area for family therapists. The family, viewed as a human system, becomes a key context for both personal and relational development. Breunlin suggests that when the family 'cannot *organize*, *interact* and *develop appropriately*, its functioning can constrain problem resolution' (1999: 370, italics added). The words I have highlighted point to some major areas of theorizing within the systemic tradition of family therapy (Dallos and Draper, 2000; Nichols and Schwartz, 2004).

- Families can be constrained by organizational structures such as cross-generational coalitions and alliances that do not allow clear boundaries to be established between the parental and sibling sub-system. The failure to maintain clear (but not rigid) boundaries may result in a child being drawn into a conflict between parents ('triangulated') or in family members engaging in ways that are over-involved or disengaged. Maintaining clear boundaries and a hierarchical structure can be viewed as important organizational principles in 'healthy' family functioning.

Lack of clarity about who is in charge, who should be involved, and how decisions are made regarding various issues, can constrain problem resolution.

- Family functioning can also be constrained by triadic (as opposed to dyadic) patterns of interaction between family members. These can form problem-maintaining feedback loops or vicious cycles. More broadly, these observable patterns may be linked to implicit family rules about who is entitled to speak to whom and about what. Sometimes, constraining patterns of interaction can be traced to trans-generational influences and the 'transmission' of family traditions.
- Families can also be constrained by difficulties in negotiating important developmental transitions in the family life cycle (Carter and McGoldrick, 1999). Different kinds of stressors are influential at particular times in a family's life, requiring a significant change in daily routines and problem-solving strategies. For example, Christensen, Todahl and Barrett (1999) suggest that routines are at the heart of family life, and that different kinds of everyday tasks need to be co-ordinated for an infant pre-school family, a school-age family, an adolescent family, a launching family and a post-parental family. Difficulties in negotiating these changes can constrain the family's capacity to resolve specific relationship problems. Carter and McGoldrick describe two major kinds of developmental influences on families. *Vertical* stressors refer to patterns and beliefs passed down from generation to generation. *Horizontal* stressors refer to both predictable life cycle transitions and to unpredictable events such as war, illness or untimely death.

Community

Community level constraints arise from the relationship between a family and the institutions and facilities within their immediate community. These can include schools, social support organizations, recreational and shopping facilities, employment opportunities, public transport, perceptions of community safety, etc. For example, a family's options for resolving their own difficulties can be constrained by particular organizational attitudes (a school's biased perceptions about a particular group of students), by the lack of recreational facilities or employment in a community, or by a concern for safety in the neighbourhood (such that parents are reluctant to allow their children out of the house). These factors may make it more difficult for family members to embark on new activities, obtain extra income, form new networks of relationships – or even to get out of each other's way.

Society

At the broadest level, family members can be constrained by societal trends, transformations and upheavals that can affect well-being and material possibilities (for example, globalization). Therapists, however, are often more concerned with constraints at the level of societal norms and dominant discourses: the taken-for-granted assumptions and characteristic ways of talking that prevail at particular times. These could include assumptions about what is normal and ideal in family life, about appropriate gender roles and relations, about preferred body shapes for men and women, about the causes and nature of family conflict (and what needs to be done), and about the relative value to be placed on individual happiness versus relational responsibility. In a rapidly changing and increasingly heterogeneous society, the variety of competing discourses can, in itself, be confusing and act to constrain possibilities for collaboration.

Qualifications and distinctions

A review of these six levels clearly indicates the manifold ways in which family members can become caught up in what Breunlin calls a 'a web of constraints' (1999: 365). However, when incorporating these considerations into a constructive framework, it is important to draw some distinctions. For constructive therapists who wish to prioritize parsimony and minimalism, there is a familiar dilemma. Where do we stop? Should we routinely analyse every family we see in relation to every conceivable level and type of constraint? If so, even though constraints are couched in negative explanation, might this not slip back into being a de facto version of formal assessment (in which family members are scored on a checklist of 'underlying' constraints)? Are we to assume that constraints are objective realities that form part of the therapist's professional knowledge? Might this open a Pandora's Box of therapeutic 'inventities' that need to be included in the framework?

When hypothesizing about potential constraints, it is important to remember that a hypothesis remains a supposition that is tentatively accepted as a guide for the therapist in a particular session. It remains a construction rather than a reflection of reality, a process of curiosity not certainty, and is used to initiate dialogue, not to foreclose it. In order to engage in 'constructive hypothesizing' (Rober, 2002) therapists should ensure that a hypothesis about constraints not only avoids deficit language but is generally congruent with family members' own perspectives (that is, it should be different but not too different). Constraints are negotiated realities, and hypothesizing is one way of initiating this process. The scheme of six levels, therefore, is a useful guide that helps to stimulate the therapist's curiosity. It is not a blueprint for action.

In addition, Breunlin's theory of constraints is integrationist, linked to broad meta-frameworks rather than a specific orientation. From such a perspective, the levels and types of constraint could be considered as primary pictures that are used to map therapeutic work with every family. However, my suggested use of these ideas is different in two ways. Firstly, I am adapting them to a specific orientation of constructive family therapy. This means that I will selectively focus on particular kinds or constructions of constraint that fit with a competency-based and parsimonious approach (I am more likely to think of individuals as being constrained by childhood survival stories than by intrapsychic pathologies). Secondly, I am using them as *secondary* pictures that can 'back up' my primary pictures on certain occasions. I will not be using them routinely but only in response to immediate evidence and difficulties in applying my primary pictures. In fact, the different forms of constraint neatly complement my primary pictures by acting, as Breunlin notes, as a necessary and sobering balance to more optimistic orientations.

A constructive therapist's pictures

In drawing together the two sets of concepts that I have introduced – primary, secondary and rejected pictures, and the identification and lifting of constraints – we arrive at the scheme depicted in Figure 8.1. I have used my own set of pictures as an example.

We assume that our primary pictures are sufficient to address the major concerns that family members are experiencing, and attempt to keep these pictures continually in the foreground as we work. However, as Wile suggests, there will be times when we lack the 'information, idea or angle' needed to apply our primary pictures (1993: 277). In such situations – faced by immediate suggestive evidence – we may switch to secondary pictures and hypothesize about different forms of constraint. We may borrow and adapt ideas from different frameworks in an attempt to lift these constraints. As soon as possible, however – when we gain the relevant information, idea or angle – we will shift back to our primary pictures. Meanwhile, we will attempt to avoid what Wile calls 'cross-theory leakage' with our rejected pictures, as this would be contradictory and confusing. However, at times we may have to utilize rejected pictures, perhaps by finding a way to shift them into the secondary picture category. For example, we may need to implement unilateral action in the face of specific constraints, but will try to make this as 'collaborative' as possible in the circumstances (see Chapter 9).

Figure 8.1 **Example of a constructive therapist's 'pictures'**

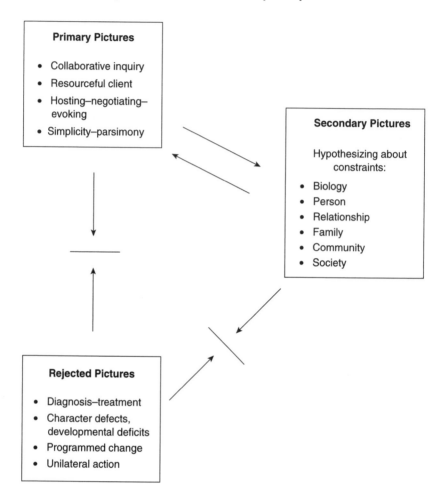

The potential to shift *temporarily* into secondary pictures, adapt ideas from other frameworks, and then shift *back* to primary pictures provides a way of considering many additional kinds of constraint while retaining a clear theoretical allegiance. This is crucial if we are to avoid the confusions that therapists can encounter when borrowing from other frameworks.

Distinguishing primary from secondary pictures

Therapists who routinely use a number of ideas to structure their work may find it difficult to distinguish clearly their primary and secondary pictures. In order to determine whether a concept is a primary or secondary picture in your framework, a simple question can be asked. Do you attempt to use this concept to structure your first meeting with *every* family you see (irrespective of immediate evidence)? If the answer is 'yes', this is probably a primary picture. For example, within the systemic tradition of family therapy, practitioners may utilize a number of primary pictures. Some may map every family's organizational structures, while others may assess every family in terms of life-cycle tasks and transitions. Still others might analyse every family in terms of circular feedback loops or family belief systems, or might use an extensive genogram to map every family's intergenerational patterns and influences. A practitioner trained in systemic family therapy might typically use a number of these concepts as primary pictures. By contrast, constructive therapists are more likely to call upon them as secondary pictures, to be used only with specific families when hypothesizing about constraints. This helps to define my sense of the difference in emphasis between constructive and systemic frameworks. Constructive therapists will borrow and adapt systemic concepts where necessary (in response to immediate evidence) and use them in order to lift constraints and facilitate a return to their primary pictures (see Chapter 9 for specific examples). Systemic therapists, by contrast, are more likely to adopt these concepts as their primary pictures and use them to organize their preferred approach in every situation.

Shifting within the framework

The emphasis of this chapter has fallen on shifting *between* frameworks and using secondary pictures that come from other therapeutic orientations (systemic, psychodynamic, cognitive-behavioural, etc.). However, constructive therapists may also distinguish between primary and secondary pictures *within* their own orientation. In Chapter 1, I distinguished between three styles of constructive therapy – solution-oriented, narrative and conversational – and suggested that I preferred the solution-oriented style as my 'home' or 'default' style. Using this preferred style I will typically begin by attempting to negotiate future preferences and possibilities. However, if this approach reaches an impasse, I may switch to secondary pictures, hypothesize about constraints and externalize these in narrative style, or perhaps utilize a reflecting team process in conversational style. Once the lens has been widened, I will search for a way to return to my preferred solution-oriented style and sharpen the focus once more. However, others within the constructive orientation may have a distinctly different preference, using the narrative style or conversational style as their primary approach, and switching to the others in particular circumstances. In other words, my primary pictures may be another constructive therapist's secondary pictures and vice versa.

Case example

To illustrate the way in which a therapist shifts between primary and secondary pictures, I will return to one of the case examples used to demonstrate 'Constructive understandings' in Chapter 7. The example features Stan (aged 45), his wife June (42) and sons Adam (18) and Larry (16). Despite my attempts to work from primary pictures, the first couple of sessions take on a characteristic pattern with Stan lecturing his sons over their reluctance to 'take their lives seriously', knuckle down and make clear career choices. Stan appears to lose himself in anger, inviting reactions of retaliation or helpless passivity from his sons, while their mother attempts to mediate. As the therapist, my own emotional postures are compromised as I feel that Stan's reactions are way out of proportion to the immediate grievances and I find myself siding with Adam and Larry. I am struggling to maintain a stance of multipartiality, as we become locked into 'more of the same' patterns, with no shared goals and a distinct atmosphere of antagonism.

Shifting to secondary pictures

In an attempt to develop a more constructive understanding of Stan's behaviour, I begin to hypothesize about what factors may be constraining his attempts to communicate effectively with his sons. Observing Stan's reactions, I am struck by the fact that when he 'loses it' in the session and adopts an overly aggressive and hectoring tone, he seems to disconnect from the immediate conversation. It is as though he is engaging simultaneously in *two* conversations, a private conversation as well as a public conversation. Who might the private conversation be with and what might it be about? From what I have learned about the family's situation, I wonder if it might be connected with his own recent retrenchment and some unresolved bitterness about this? Might anger and resentment against his employer, and the shock of losing what had seemed a secure position, be undermining his judgement and intruding into his family relationships? As suggested in Chapter 7, I decide to ask him a 'mystery question'. How did someone like Stan, who wants the best for his sons and wants to be viewed by them as a good and loving father, wind up in a situation of such painful and distressing conflict with them, where they view him as being aggressive, rigid and bullying? Stan reflects for a time and seems somewhat nonplussed. I ask him to ponder this question between sessions.

Wanting to explore this further with Stan, but being careful to avoid pathologizing or blaming him for the conflict, I say to the family members that at the next session I would like to meet separately for a time with Stan and June, and with Adam and Larry. This normalizes the situation as one that might allow us to all to have a break from conflict and for all people to say anything to me that they might find it difficult to say in a conjoint session. In the meeting with Stan and June, I ask what they have been thinking about in the past week. Stan indicates that he has been thinking about the question I asked and says that his own retrenchment brought home to him the 'way the world is going' and how you can't take anything like security and loyalty for granted. The shock and anger have made him all the more determined that his own sons will have good career prospects and marketable skills, and have made him all the more furious at observing their laid-back attitude to the future. June says that Stan has 'cried like a baby' when alone with her, but feels a need to appear strong with his sons, even more so now that he feels a loss of self-respect and authority. Therefore he has never disclosed his own experiences or vulnerability to Adam and Larry and has made a deliberate effort to carry on as before. This is confirmed in my meeting with Adam and Larry who say that their well-meaning attempts to talk to Stan at the time were angrily rebuffed so that after a while they lost all sympathy for him and felt more for their mother who was the 'meat in the sandwich'.

I then share with Stan my sense that when he talks with his sons, he seems to be engaging in two conversations at once, a public one with them and a private one with someone else. When this happens, the two conversations get confused and the extreme emotions tend to derail the conversation with Adam and Larry. This way of talking helps Stan to identify that he still bears a lot of anger and resentment towards his former employer and that he keeps 'playing the tapes' of the retrenchment in his mind. Do these private conversations (with their memories and emotions) work to help or to hinder his conversations with his sons? What happens when he forgets which tape he is playing? Would it be helpful if he could learn to separate these two conversations, so that he could increase his chances of saying exactly what he wanted to say to Adam and Larry? Would this help them to perceive him as he wants to be perceived?

Reverting to primary pictures

This way of talking provides an angle that allows me to shift back to my primary pictures. Having negotiated a description of the constraint as being the intrusion of Stan's private conversations ('inner tapes') into his family conversations, I can help Stan to 'lift' the constraint by reverting to familiar constructive therapy methods. As Stan becomes aware of how powerfully his inner tapes can sabotage his best intentions, he becomes more motivated to exert some influence, and now has a new therapeutic goal. How would he know if he was able to separate the two conversations? What would be a sign that he was learning to ignore or switch off the inner tape so that it didn't intrude? In his struggles so far, have there been any indications that he is already doing this to some extent? Has June noticed any changes? Might Adam or Larry have noticed anything? What are Stan's own thoughts on how he can best proceed to separate the tapes? How would he scale his confidence at this point of time?

This example shows the way in which a constructive therapist attempts initially to work from primary pictures but finds it difficult to maintain a shared sense of purpose and collaboration. Responding to the suggestive evidence of an individual's behaviour, the therapist switches to secondary pictures hypothesizing about potential constraints at the level of the person. By arranging to discuss these constraints in a less defensive context (a separate session with Stan and June) the therapist is able to negotiate a change of focus for the conversation. The therapist carefully chooses a way of talking about the constraint (playing inner tapes) that minimizes deficit-oriented language and avoids blaming the client for the family's distress. With a new goal and direction in place, the therapist can shift back to primary pictures, specifying preferred changes and seeking once more to evoke the resourcefulness of particular family members in attempting to lift the constraint and get the conversation back on track. The conversation could potentially evolve in a number of directions, perhaps involving a resumption of family sessions with a new sense of direction, or perhaps involving some individual sessions with Stan or couple sessions with Stan and June before meeting again with the family.

Reflections, cautions and implications

This chapter has contributed the final – and perhaps one of the most significant – conceptual elements of a constructive framework for family therapy. It has addressed a neglected area in the constructive therapy literature and suggested a way in which practitioners can enrich the potential of their work by selectively drawing upon ideas from other therapeutic or professional perspectives. The question is not one of content (*what* specific ideas should be included?) but one of process (*how* can therapists utilize ideas that they believe are important to their work with families but adapt them in ways that are congruent with a constructive framework?). The key piece of luggage is not an encyclopaedia of family therapy but the concepts of 'primary, secondary and rejected pictures', and 'lifting constraints', which provide a way of selectively *borrowing and adapting* knowledge from other frameworks. There are still probably many concepts that you may think should be added to this book. Hopefully the discussion in this chapter may help to clarify whether these are primary or secondary pictures for you, and how you would like to use them. It has not been my intention to argue for my own specific pictures (they are *a* constructive therapist's pictures, not *the* constructive therapist's pictures). It is more a case of, if I show you mine, will it help you to articulate yours?

The distinction between primary, secondary and rejected pictures may help us avoid the extremes of 'either/or' polemics and 'both/and' confusion. We need not avoid engaging with the 'otherness' of different traditions, but can consider the possibility of incorporating ideas as secondary pictures rather than dismissing them as rejected pictures. In therapy training contexts there can sometimes be a tendency either to ignore other approaches or to implicitly dismiss them. For example, with students whose first exposure to therapy is the constructive orientation, there can sometimes be an implicit message of 'don't bother learning anything else', or 'everything else is incompatible'. In a field as diverse as family therapy, this deprives therapists and their clients of many potential resources.

In this regard it is instructive to return to the theoretical aspect of the constructive framework I have developed: it's basis in construct*ionism*. I believe that a constructionist perspective actually challenges us to consider and engage with other frameworks. It is important to remember that a constructionist perspective does not seek to rule on what is or is not fundamentally real. In fact, as Gergen has stated, constructionism is 'ontologically mute' (1994: 72). In other words, it can say nothing about what actually exists in the world. Its contribution does not lie in trying to identify 'what there is', but in analysing the process of *construction* that inevitably follows. Because once we begin to articulate 'what there is' in the world – what we think is real and significant – we enter the world of discourse and into considerations of social processes, history, cultural traditions, and values (Gergen, 1994; 1999).

Therefore, when considering concepts from different frameworks, a constructionist orientation is not so much concerned with affirming or denying their objective existence, but in analysing the process of construction that inevitably occurs, and how these concepts might potentially be used. How might concepts from diverse frameworks be used in ways that position clients as deficient and add to the professional power of the therapist? On the other hand, how might they be used in ways that position clients as competent and contribute to a more collaborative approach? My suggestion, therefore, is that constructive therapists avoid becoming sidetracked by 'therapy wars' and arguments about which concepts are 'real'. Their approach neither equips them nor requires them to rule particular concepts in or out. Instead, it encourages and challenges them to consider the potential for using these concepts in 'constructive' ways.

Cautions

It is salutary, however, to remember that our ultimate aim is to return to our primary pictures and our preferred vision of therapy. Therapists can easily become 'intoxicated' or sidetracked by the range of therapeutic concepts that are potentially available. Beyebach and Morejón (1999) caution against several possibilities that can occur when 'integration happens' in constructive therapies. The therapist may become preoccupied with problems and resort to 'diagnostic thinking' (when this kind of problem occurs, this kind of constraint is operating, therefore following this recipe). This can prompt a return to prioritizing professional knowledge and shifting the therapist's position in relation to the clients, with the therapist taking on a more expert role. There may also be an associated tendency for the therapist to work too hard and become too active, with the clients becoming increasingly passive. Finally, there is the temptation for the therapy to become unnecessarily complicated so that rather than taking the more parsimonious or express route, we follow the 'road to fanciness' (1999: 39). Facing challenges and uncertainties it is important not to revert to a default setting of 'expertosis' but to return, instead, to the fundamental principles of travelling light.

Professional development

My sense of how therapists develop through experience is that they often begin with a small number of primary pictures and a large number of rejected pictures. Perhaps they are initially enthused by a particular model, are content to stay within its comfort zone, and utterly reject everything else (with no shades of grey in the form of secondary pictures). Over time, however, and as they gain more exposure to different positions, they tend to convert some of their rejected pictures into secondary pictures as they discern ways of using aspects of these approaches. They may also shift some of their original primary pictures into other groups and replace them as they modify their allegiance to favourite models. I suspect that what 'becoming more experienced' means for a therapist is that we learn to operate from a few flexible primary pictures, while increasing our number of secondary pictures and reducing our number of rejected pictures. We can try to take something from every discourse, while using it in our own way and for our own purposes. Perhaps this is what de Bono (1998) means when he suggests that simplicity before understanding is simplistic, while simplicity after understanding is simple. Exposure to a wide range of ideas, while maintaining a commitment to our preferred change principles, may provide the breadth of understanding that enables us to practise a simple approach simply.

Note

1. Solution-Focused Brief Therapy Course Notes were compiled by Evan George, Chris Iveson and Harvey Ratner of the Brief Therapy Practice in London (7–8 Newbury Street, London, EC1A 7HU) and were presented to participants at a two-day course I attended in 2000.

9   Responding to Challenges

Preparing for contingencies

Perhaps the ultimate test for any therapeutic framework is how well it prepares a practitioner to encounter the unexpected. This returns us once again to the dilemma of travelling light. If we try to prepare for every contingency that might occur – and carry information on every kind of family scenario we can imagine – we will be weighed down by excess baggage. However, when we are struggling in unusual or challenging situations, it can be reassuring to turn to some examples that we may be able to adapt to our own circumstances. Though each traveller's experience is unique, there may be a range of situations that are typically encountered and can be generalized across a wide range of contexts.

The aim of this final chapter is to identify a selective range of family therapy scenarios that can enable constructive therapists to plan for contingencies, avoid common pitfalls, and respond to challenges. By carefully selecting these, I hope to complement the generic approach taken in the earlier sections of the book. But I clearly cannot cover the A–Z of family problems even in the most cursory way. So how should I decide what to include?

Selecting scenarios

The approach I have chosen is to identify some particular *types* of scenarios that can prove challenging for constructive therapists. Rather than skimming over the A–Z of family problems, I will build on the concepts introduced in Chapter 8 and develop examples based on major kinds of *constraints* that constructive therapists typically encounter in family work. In selecting the kinds of scenarios to cover I have been guided by my own trial-and-error learning and also by the repeated patterns of frequently asked questions encountered in classes and workshops. The themes of these questions help to identify what is missing in much of the literature, and provide clues to the kinds of contingencies that are typically encountered when we take our framework on the road. We can still travel light, while including a select group of examples that resonate across the broad spectrum of practice.

The scenarios I have selected involve situations where: (i) biological constraints may require the use of medication; (ii) family therapy includes an individual diagnosed with a specific condition; (iii) psycho-educational or other therapist resources may be appropriate; (iv) systemic constraints may be a significant factor; and (v) there are challenges to collaborative practice. With each scenario I discuss the key dilemmas, and then explore ways in which constructive therapists might respond to the challenges.

Biological constraints and medication

Dilemmas

The consideration of biological constraints focuses attention on the therapist's attitude towards the use of psychotropic medication. How does this fit with a constructive framework? Bertolino and O'Hanlon (2002) note that therapists often find themselves in a precarious situation of feeling that they have to be either for or against medication. They suggest that, for competency-based therapists, either extreme is unnecessary and disrespectful. While there is clearly a danger of over-prescription of well-publicized drugs, and the possibility of client agency taking a back seat to the medication, it is also important to recognize that in many situations (for example, involving Attention Deficit Hyperactivity Disorder, depression or extreme anxiety) medication may be helpful or crucial.

Constructive responses

Hoyt (1996, 1998) uses the term 'restoring restorying' to describe the potential contribution of medication in constructive therapies. In situations where medication helps a person to focus their thinking or acts to abate disruptive or debilitating moods, it can enable them to access reflective emotional postures and enhance the process of collaborating with others, clarifying goals and storying change. For similar reasons, Griffith and Griffith (1994) prefer the term 'ethological pharmacology' to the more conventional 'psychopharmacology', to emphasize the connection between medication and the social world of relationships, rather than reducing the focus to the drug treatment of the individual mind. In ethological pharmacology the focus is on 'how medications can create the physiological space for the appearance of new language and new meaning that will be transformative and therapeutic for the patient and his or her social relationships' (1994: 189).

Hoyt (1998) notes that some constructive therapists take a stance of never mentioning medication unless their clients mention it first. This reflects an understandable concern about reductionistic analyses that isolate brain imbalances as the sole 'cause' of a problem and promote medication as the first-choice approach to treatment. However, this extreme position may also restrict the client's access to a potentially important resource. Griffith and Griffith (1994) suggest that therapists try to avoid exclusionary concepts that emphasize either conversational *or* pharmacological approaches while precluding consideration of the other. One alternative, taken from narrative therapy, is to draw a distinction between the relevance of the two kinds of discourse (physiological and psychosocial). Griffith and Griffith (1994: 197) provide some examples:

- When the family is stressed, how much of it seems to come from the schizophrenia and how much from the 'bad habits' that the schizophrenia may have initiated?
- Which parts do the medications help and which parts do they not?
- When schizophrenia dominates the life of your family, what positive aspects of you as a family does it hide?
- Can you tell me about your daughter as you know her as a person, in aspects that have nothing to do with schizophrenia?
- Are there times when she controls the influence of the schizophrenia? How does she do this? (Griffith and Griffith, 1994: 197)

This form of inquiry acts to recognize and distinguish the relevance of both domains without reducing one to the other. Importantly, from a constructive orientation, the physiological domain is presented as influencing but never totally dominating or incorporating the psychosocial domain, so that medications contribute in a circumscribed way while conversational therapies are more relevant in other domains.

Therefore, rather than being for or against medication, it is more important for constructive therapists to deconstruct or negotiate the *meaning* of medication in each individual's or family's life. While recognizing the potential contribution of medication, therapists are concerned to avoid constructions that either position biological constraints as the only relevant factors to be considered, or position clients as passive recipients whose only role in the change process involves following a prescription. Instead, the therapist's curiosity, might turn to the following themes:

- How, *precisely*, does the medication help? As a result of feeling better after taking medication, what are clients able to *do* better or differently?

What difference does this make? Bertolino and O'Hanlon (2002) note that medication can help a client feel better but the individual still must initiate actions – the medication alone does not make someone interact differently with family members.

- In those areas where medication doesn't help or isn't relevant, what have family members learned to do to help themselves? What resources have they drawn upon in order to deal with the challenges they face?
- Are there any relevant family stories about previous experiences of medications? What are individual family members' attitudes towards the role of medication, and how might these be influencing the present situation?
- What percentage of the credit for change should go to family members and what percentage to the medication? Is the contribution of the clients or the medication increasing most over time? How is this happening?
- What other people, events or resources are making a contribution?
- How is the medication helping clients to achieve *their* goals? How are clients *putting the medication to use* in their lives? For example, Berg and Steiner (2003) use the analogy of a car when talking with children about Ritalin, suggesting that the medication is like the oil in the engine that helps to make the car run smoothly. However, the most important factor remains the attention and skills of the driver – who remains firmly in the driver's seat.
- How are family members imagining the future of their relationship with the medication? Will it be a lifelong association or a temporary alliance? What would be a sign that their relationship with medication might be changing?

In a constructive framework, the use of medication to lift biological constraints is likely to be considered as a secondary picture. As can be seen from the questions above, however, there is a clear potential for the therapist to switch the emphasis back to primary pictures and relate medication to themes of client agency, preferences and choice.

Family therapy and Condition X

Dilemmas

At a broader level, effective therapy can be constrained in a family situation in which an individual has been diagnosed with a particular psychological or physical condition. I will use the term 'Condition X' to stand for a wide range of constraints at the level of the person that might include psychotic disorders, learning disabilities, various forms of trauma and addiction, eating disorders, depression, grief, anxiety and physical disabilities – in other words, the gamut of individual problem descriptions that might conceivably arrive at a therapist's door. In such situations, it is not unusual for the focus and purpose of *relationship* therapy to become confused with the individual's struggle with Condition X. Remembering that constructive family therapists do not assume systemic causes or relationship explanations for individual conditions, the relevance of family therapy must be negotiated in each case. Is the purpose of conjoint therapy to assist the individual family member in their struggle with Condition X, to help family members to understand and cope with the individual's condition, or to address relationship difficulties that have evolved indirectly from Condition X? There may also be confusion caused by specialized knowledge and generalized assumptions about the condition. Both the therapist and clients may become experts on *the condition*, but somehow manage to lose connection with specific hopes and goals.

Constructive responses

Clarifying the purpose of family meetings

In negotiating concerns and requests, and discussing who might be involved in the sessions, it is important for the therapist and family members to remain clear about the purpose of conjoint meetings. For example, here are some different ways in which family members could become involved with a particular individual's Condition X:

- One or more parents and/or siblings may attend therapy sessions in order to provide emotional support for a young person struggling with Condition X. For example, a mother attends sessions in order to encourage and support her nine-year-old son who is struggling with debilitating fears and who does not want to work alone with the therapist. In such situations, the individual's struggles with Condition X remain the focus of therapy, with family members staying largely in the background.
- Family members may wish to learn more about Condition X in order to help both the individual and themselves to cope with it. For example, family members may participate in order to learn more about a son's attention deficit disorder or a mother's chronic fatigue syndrome. There is more emphasis here on a psycho-educational role in relation to family members.
- Family members may be struggling to cope with the consequences of a particular person's condition and indicate that *they* need assistance in handling the stress and relationship tensions that have developed. Examples

could include members of a family in which a parent has Alzheimer's disease, or parents of an 'out-of-control' child who won't attend therapy. In such cases, an individual's condition may 'exhaust' family members who seek counselling primarily for their problems in coping.

- Family members (including the person diagnosed with Condition X) attend and the focus is on relationship tensions that originated from responses to the condition but have now taken on a life of their own. In this situation, the focus is on addressing relationship concerns in which Condition X is a contributing factor, but may no longer be the major focus of therapy. For example, in a family where a daughter (Sarah) is struggling with bulimia, a number of relationship tensions develop: Sarah's siblings accuse her of being a 'drama queen' and exaggerating her problems in order to manipulate attention; her parents strongly disagree on how to approach the situation ('she needs special consideration' versus 'stop indulging her and just treat her like a normal child'), which exacerbates some latent areas of conflict in their relationship; some family members feel an increasing degree of frustration with Sarah, coupled with guilt about feeling frustrated; and everyone walks on eggshells around her, feeling inhibited and internalizing their stress.

Conceivably, a therapist's work with a particular family could take on a number of these forms over time. A difficulty arises when the agenda for conjoint work is not clear and the different forms of family involvement become confused. A central principle of collaborative work is that no family member feels blamed or victimized. However, this principle can easily be lost in family sessions, where the individual defined with Condition X becomes the sole focus of attention and is implicitly held responsible for family distress. Conversely, parents or other family members feel that the therapist is shifting responsibility to them. An important task of the therapist is to find ways of talking that avoid either of these extremes. For example, in situations where family members indicate that they have come to provide support for the individual's therapy, the therapist can often make best use of their presence as occasional observers and witnesses of change. Using an 'individual engagement' pattern with the individual, the therapist might switch to a 'reciprocal engagement' pattern at an opportune moment and ask the observing family member a question such as, 'I'm wondering if you or anyone else in the family has noticed this recent development?' However, if the therapist tries to take advantage of the presence of family members in order to shift the focus of the conversation to the topic of family relationships, this runs the risk of alienating the other family members ('We came here to help you help our son, but now we feel as though you're giving us the third degree as though it's our fault!'). As always, it is important to consider each family member's position and relationship with the therapist. For example, are they in a customer-, complainant- or visitor-type relationship?

Perhaps the most challenging situation is the one where Condition X indirectly results in a number of relationship tensions. Family members may ostensibly attend to support an individual's struggle with Condition X, only to disclose a number of pent-up relationship issues that have evolved as the various members attempted to respond to the condition. Alert to these shifts in the wind, the therapist can attempt to normalize family members' experiences and renegotiate priorities both for the immediate session and beyond:

- 'It's not unusual for families to go through all sorts of experiences when they are trying to help someone who is struggling with a particular problem. There can be all kinds of unexpected repercussions and changes in emotions and relationships, and sometimes these become a major part of the problem. From what you've all been saying today, I'm wondering if it might be helpful to change tack for a while and focus on these unexpected developments?'
- 'Is it more important to stay with our focus on helping Sarah struggle with [Condition X], or is it more important to address some of the relationship tensions that have accidentally developed as you've all struggled with stress and uncertainty?'
- 'If we decide to stay focused on assisting Sarah, how can we keep these other tensions from getting in the way? What is the best way for everyone else to contribute? If we focus on addressing the relationship tensions in the house, what should be our main priority, and how might this be connected with our other goal of assisting Sarah?'
- 'Given the tension that has developed between [for example, the two parents, over their approach to Sarah], should this become a focus for future sessions? If so, who should attend?'

These kinds of questions help the therapist and family members to remain alert to changes in relationship concerns and therapeutic priorities. They can enable us to redefine the preference-determined system and help the conversation progress, evolve or re-form in new directions. A failure to clarify the purpose of *family* therapy in relation to an individual's struggle with Condition X can easily result in confusion and frustration for the therapist and clients.

I have known family therapists involved in extraordinarily complicated situations where they were working concurrently with several different children in the same family (who had been diagnosed with different conditions), sometimes seeing the children individually and sometimes with their parents, while also working separately with the parents on couple issues, and occasionally seeing the whole family! Unless a degree of clarity is maintained about the purpose of these different conversations, this can result in another 'Columbus-like' experience of not knowing where we are going, where we are or where we have been.

Uniting clients against the condition

In situations where Condition X has become the central or defining focus of a family's life, the externalizing method of the narrative style can be particularly useful in deflecting blame, frustration and anger on to problems and patterns rather than people. Rather than allowing Condition X to create conflict or divisions between people (Sarah's problem with bulimia divides her parents and creates tension with siblings), we can invite family members to unite against the influence of the condition. Families can work collaboratively against the multiple stresses connected with Condition X. This construction allows us to focus on relationship implications without blaming or pathologizing either the bearer of the condition or the other family members.

Depending on circumstances, the process of inquiry could take a number of paths:

- 'In addition to restricting Sarah's life, how has bulimia restricted other people's lives and relationships?'
- 'How has bulimia gradually strengthened its position in this family? What tactics has it used to take centre stage and become the focus of your lives?'
- 'How has it gone about organizing the family's life? How has it tried to make you dance to its tune?'
- 'What kinds of habits has it produced? How has it tried to trick you into acting in ways that make it stronger and make you all feel weaker?' (For example, creating divisions between family members, inducing conflict, guilt or blame.)
- 'What are bulimia's allies? What is its life support system? What does it depend on to survive?' (For example, secrecy, silence, shame or censorship.)
- 'What does bulimia require you all to do to keep it in the spotlight?'
- 'Is this acceptable to you as a family? What is your position on your relationship with bulimia?'
- 'What parts of your family life belong to bulimia and what parts still belong to you?'
- 'If we thought of bulimia as casting a spell on the family, so that you only see what it wants you to see, what is it trying to hide from you? If we broke this spell, what would you see instead?'

- 'Have there been times when you have worked together to overcome the influence of bulimia?'
- 'If you decided to work together in order to resist bulimia's influence, what is the first thing you would need to do?'

In order to focus on relationships rather than individuals, it is sometimes preferable to shift the externalized description away from Condition X altogether and focus instead on externalizing the particular relationship practices that the condition has encouraged or the beliefs and attitudes that sustain it. For example, with bulimia, we might focus on the habits of *secrecy and shame*, and the way these prevent people from sharing their experiences, trusting each other and working together. Or, we could discuss externalized patterns of 'pursue/withdraw' or 'demand disclosure/secrecy and withholding', which act to strengthen bulimia and weaken family members. These constructions provide a potential bridge for linking the individual's struggle with Condition X to a family's relationship struggles without attaching blame to anyone.

Resources from the therapist's world

Dilemmas

One of the most frequently asked questions concerns whether and when it is appropriate for constructive therapists to contribute ideas, practical suggestions, psycho-educational material or other resources from their own professional world. If the therapist's expertise is defined primarily by the ability to evoke the client's expertise, are these activities theoretically or philosophically inconsistent, and should they be avoided? At a more practical level, what if clients specifically ask for ideas, opinions or suggestions? It has been suggested that imparting information and facilitating skill development plays a greater part in family therapy than most practitioners recognize (Sprenkle, Blow and Dickey, 1999). How then should constructive therapists proceed?

Constructive responses

So far, I have emphasized an approach in which the therapist's expertise is *complementary* to that of the clients – the therapist asks questions so that family members can find answers. The therapist's expertise is based on the process of crafting questions, rather than the content of particular problem areas. However, at times, the therapist's expertise can also be *supplementary*, adding to that of the clients. As I suggested in Chapter 1, the challenge for constructive therapists is not to relinquish professional expertise but to conceptualize it differently – to think of it as a potential contribution to the path of inquiry, rather than a definitive interpretation or intervention. It is expertise without The Expert.

A central principle is that use of resources from the therapist's world remains a *secondary picture* in a constructive framework, and relates to a hypothesis that family members' problem-solving options may be constrained by a lack of access to alternative perspectives, ideas or skills. As suggested in Chapter 8, a shift to secondary pictures is not an end in itself but a means of lifting constraints so that we can return to our primary pictures. By keeping *this* end in sight, we can introduce various forms of content expertise while attempting to support the collaborative, competency-based foundations of our framework.

Psycho-educational resources: coaxing versus coaching

Many forms of psycho-educational material might be considered potentially useful in family therapy: basic communication skills (for example, the use of 'I-language', turn-taking and reflective listening); skills in problem-solving, conflict resolution, relaxation or anger-management; information about individual and family life stages, parenting styles, and communication patterns; or more specific information relating to Condition X, Y or Z. For constructive therapists, the dilemma is one of how to introduce this material in such a way that the focus remains on the clients (their preferred futures and priorities) rather than on their induction into a structured learning process. Sometimes when ideas relating to new information or skills are introduced, the clients can disappear into 'the programme', which starts to take over the session. If psycho-educational packages are simply taken off the shelf and given to clients, the specific focus on client-directed goals can be lost. An analogous situation might be one where a worker experiences conflict with specific individuals, and is told that he has an 'anger' problem and must attend an 'anger-management' course. The link between such a generalized course and the worker's specific context is likely to be tenuous at best. Nor is it likely to be an affirming experience.

Some useful guidelines can be adapted from the practice of solution-focused groupwork (Sharry, 2001). In this approach, a key principle is that the introduction of psycho-educational material is seen as the *beginning* of a solution-building process rather than the end. To introduce the material in a constructive manner, the therapist can begin by inviting clients to state what they already know about the topic, what they have already learned to do differently, and what specifically they would like to learn more about. When the therapist introduces specific ideas or suggestions, family members can be asked to review this information and discuss the degree to which it fits for them. What aspects might they find helpful?

What aspects wouldn't be helpful? How could these ideas be adapted to their specific circumstances? Do they have any other ideas that might actually be more helpful? The material introduced by the therapist is presented as a way of stimulating the clients' own creativity: here are some ideas or suggestions that others have found helpful and that *may* be helpful to you. Rather than being presented with a package or programme, clients are asked to consider the ideas critically, adapt the 'fit' as necessary, and use them as a sounding board for finding better ideas. In this way, constructive therapists prefer to *coax* rather than coach expertise.

Example

In Chapter 5, I described the process of evoking possibilities with the Edwards family (Kevin, 41, Sandra, 38, Jessica, 15 and Daniel, 12). As we saw, the family agreed that they needed to find some ways of 'getting back to normal' during a period of multiple stresses involving Kevin's employment situation, Daniel's difficulties at school and relationship conflicts relating to these circumstances. However, it seems clear that their attempts to focus on this goal are being constrained by difficulties in talking constructively about family issues. When they are at home, family members seem unable to communicate without falling into characterizations, accusations and recriminations that make things worse. They have heard about books and courses on 'communication skills'. What would the therapist recommend?

In response to the family's requests, a therapist might indicate that he or she is aware of a number of ideas that others have found useful, but raise the dilemmas of a 'one size fits all' approach. A central question becomes, 'How can we find out which approach is best suited to this particular family?' The therapist can suggest that the supplementary ideas work best when applied to specific goals, and when they fit with the existing strengths of the family. In this particular case, the therapist might ask family members what they have already noticed themselves and others doing to help keep the peace in this difficult time. To what extent can they draw upon previous experiences and to what extent will they have to do something quite different? If there was one thing that family members would like to learn to do differently, what would it be?

These kinds of questions help the therapist to decide which particular supplementary resources might prove most useful. For example, if family members are already taking steps to keep the peace, the therapist might simply offer some suggestions for noticing these steps and indicating appreciation for change. Might it be useful for everyone to note when something different and positive happens? Might this be a good way to put these changes on the record so that they don't get forgotten when tension is around?

However, if the situation seems different from any previous difficulties the family has faced, and they cannot identify any positive steps, the therapist might offer some more structured possibilities. These might include options such as developing a safety plan (identifying trigger points for conflict and taking action to avoid extreme conflict), using different forms of verbal expression such as being specific about requests for change and avoiding blaming statements, finding ways of undermining the tension by studying the way it works (for example, working out the times when family members may be most vulnerable and becoming aware of the habits that the tension has produced), having regular family meetings that can be structured with an agenda so that problems can be discussed in a calmer atmosphere, or perhaps using the therapy session itself as a safe forum for experimenting with new skills.

In a constructive framework, the therapist does *not* have an investment in the clients accepting any of these suggestions, but uses them as a way of supplementing client resources and stimulating further possibilities. Further, when using psycho-educational material as a secondary picture, the therapist constantly searches for an angle that will facilitate a return to primary pictures. For example, if we discuss with the Edwards family the possibility of holding formal family meetings, we can attempt to relate this suggestion to resources within the family. From their professional experiences, what do Kevin and Sandra already know about the difference between good and bad meetings? How could they pool their experience in order to develop processes for good family meetings? What about Jessica and Daniel? Have they ever been involved in meetings at school or other forums? How could family members adapt the idea of meetings to match their particular style and needs?

If we are talking about specific communication skills, we can again relate these ideas to client experiences and competencies. Do family members already use skills A, B and C in *other contexts* of their lives, for example at work or in the classroom? What is different about these contexts that makes it easier to use the skills? What would help them to transfer these skills to family interactions? Have they observed other people whom they admire use these communication skills? If family members could each select a role model to observe and learn from (for example, a colleague, relative, television personality, sports star, etc.) who would they choose? One of the difficulties in presenting psycho-educational material is that it is often couched in professional jargon that positions clients in a student–teacher relationship with the therapist. The questions I have described above are intended to position the new ideas in the context of family members' *local* knowledge: their existing language, frames and experiences.

In these ways, the introduction of 'new' material – adapted to a constructive framework – may actually help clients to access 'old' (already existing) resources. By viewing supplementary resources as secondary pictures – as a means to an end – we look for ways to revert to a more familiar question: 'Now that you have additional ideas or skills, how does this help, and how does it affect what you are now wanting from therapy?'

Systemic constraints and constructive therapy

Dilemmas

As might be expected, family therapists are particularly interested in con-ceptualizing constraints at the level of the family. Breunlin (1999) relates these constraints to the key systemic themes of family *organization, inter-action* and *development*. However, as I mentioned in Chapter 1, construc-tive therapists remain ambivalent about the discourse of systemic family therapy, particularly in relation to the concept of the family as a system. Wishing to work time-effectively, to encourage personal agency and to remain 'radically particularistic', constructive therapists tend to eschew systemic concepts that have the potential to make family processes mys-tifying, to blame, categorize or pathologize families, or shift attention to presumed underlying realities rather than focusing on client preferences. I have suggested that constructive therapists are more inclined to focus on the dancers than the dance. This is why, for example, I have tended throughout this book to refer to clients as 'family members' rather than 'the family'.

Constructive responses

Yet the discourse of systemic family therapy may also provide insights, metaphors and ideas that can be adapted to the priorities of a constructive framework. By thinking of these concepts as secondary pictures associ-ated with the lifting of constraints at the family level, we can attempt to utilize them as potential resources. In this section I will use several exam-ples to show how systemic ideas can be selectively adapted to construc-tive practice. The examples involve the key systemic themes of organization, interaction and development.

Organization

Example

Paula (38) is the mother of Jack (15) and Sonia (12). She has remarried after five years as a sole parent following the death of her first husband. During this period, the family lived with Paula's mother, Thelma. Now

Paula has married Derek (36) and moved with Jack and Sonia into his house. Within a year she requests family therapy in relation to Jack's increasingly 'out of control' behaviour at home, and concerns about the 'gangs' he is getting involved with at school. The appointment has been triggered by several recent incidents involving under-age drinking and the illegal purchase of cigarettes. Paula also asks that Thelma attend the sessions, because Jack feels more supported in her presence.

Attempting to work from primary pictures, the therapist encounters difficulties in establishing a collaborative environment and negotiating agreement on preferences. Family members persistently interrupt, maintaining a reactive emotional climate. Any attempts to evoke possibilities or appreciation are met by a 'yes–but' response. The therapist observes that Derek appears increasingly isolated within the family; that Thelma supports Jack and criticizes Paula and Derek whenever his behaviour is questioned; that Paula seems increasingly fragile and indecisive; and that Sonia tries to agree with everyone. It is difficult to define a preference-determined system in terms of who wants what and who should be involved.

Switching to secondary pictures, the therapist hypothesizes about potential constraints at the level of family organization. This involves consideration of some of the central concepts associated with structural family therapy (Minuchin, 1974). Perhaps the problem-solving capacity of the newly formed family is being constrained by habits and practices carried over from the previous organization. For example:

- Jack may have had a greater leadership role as the only male in the family when he was living with Paula, Thelma and Sonia. He may have taken on more adult responsibilities so that, in some respects, his relationship with Paula might have been more like adult to adult, than mother to son. His 'status' may be threatened in the new household.
- Paula's sense of identity as a competent adult and parent may have been undermined when forced to 'return home' and live with her mother. By contrast, Thelma's position and authority may have increased.
- In the new household, these factors make it difficult for Paula and Derek to establish a clear sense of leadership as adults and parents. Both Jack and Thelma regularly become involved in 'parental business', blurring the boundaries between the various sub-systems in the family organization. When facing conflict, Paula feels trapped in divided loyalties between her new husband and her mother and children.

The therapist might normalize the difficulties that occur when new families are formed and talk about the ways in which old arrangements can intrude into new arrangements. When people are not clear on what the new arrangements should be, confusion can make it difficult to resolve relationship problems. This may open up a number of paths of inquiry:

- How can the family best work out what the new arrangements should be?
- What would each person like to be included in the new arrangements?
- What are the areas in which the parents should take leadership? What style of leadership should this be? How can others be involved?
- How will these arrangements be different from the old arrangements for each person? In what ways will this be a positive or negative development?
- How can they preserve what was best about the old arrangements in ways that won't undermine the new arrangements? For example, what is the best way to use Thelma's knowledge and experience as a resource for the new family rather than a trigger for conflict? What parts of the old arrangements were strengths and resources and what parts were forced on them by circumstances? What parts of the old arrangements might they be happy to leave behind?
- What particular habits will each person have to challenge if this is to happen?
- If we thought of the therapy sessions as a way of rehearsing the new arrangements, how should they be conducted, what should we talk about, and who should attend?

These kinds of questions and comments allow the therapist to introduce ideas about structural constraints while maintaining an emphasis on collaboration and negotiation. Depending on client responses there may be opportunities to switch back to primary pictures. For example, if family members agree that only parts of the old arrangements should be carried over into the new arrangements, we can explore each person's hopes about what these might be, and ask if anyone has noticed this happening already. We may then arrive at a potentially unifying goal of clarifying the new arrangements for the new family.

This way of utilizing structural concepts differs from some of the conventional methods of structural therapy in which the therapist's hypotheses about structural problems are used to plan more direct interventions. For example, a structural therapist might work to limit Thelma's involvement by simply not inviting her to attend. Alternatively, the therapist might attempt to strengthen the parental system and its boundaries by focusing attention on Derek and Paula and blocking interruptions from Jack or Sonia ('Please keep out of this. This is adult talk'). Or the therapist could deliberately side with Paula against her mother and son in order to unbalance the present dynamics and strengthen her position as a competent adult. In structural therapy, the reorganization of the family is a primary picture and an end in itself. In a constructive therapy framework, it is a secondary picture and a means to an end.

Interaction

Example

In the Walters family, Don (49) and Julie (47) seek counselling in relation to their youngest daughter Kim (16). Don and Julie are concerned about Kim's 'obsession' with fitness training and dieting, believing that she is developing an eating disorder. They have begun to interrogate her about this on a regular basis, to which she has responded with increasing hostility or silence, telling them to mind their own business. They have attempted to monitor what she eats at home, have become experts on ideal weights and nutritional issues for young women and have tried to get Kim to reveal what is 'really' wrong (they believe she has a 'self-esteem' problem, because she is less academically gifted than her older siblings). Kim has reacted by refusing to disclose or discuss her weight and clearly resents her parent's 'interference' with her lifestyle.

At the first meeting, Kim appears hostile, obviously not wanting to be there. It proves difficult to involve all of the family members in negotiating a shared purpose for therapy. In the session, the parents attempt to interrogate Kim about what is really going on, and seem to expect the therapist to find a way to get her to 'open up'. In response to this, Kim retreats into a moody silence. She refuses to attend the scheduled second session and the therapist meets with Don and Julie.

Though the session is more collaborative in Kim's absence, it proves difficult for the parents to focus on future possibilities or to identify any hopeful signs. They remain preoccupied with getting through to Kim and specifically ask the therapist for advice on how to do this. Switching to secondary pictures, the therapist speculates that, in their concern and desire to help, Don and Julie may inadvertently be contributing to making things worse: they may be caught up in a 'vicious cycle' of interaction where the more they pursue, the more Kim withdraws; the more they demand disclosure, the more they invite secrecy and withholding; the more they try to control, the more they invite protest and rebellion. As these patterns of mutual invitation escalate, family members often take increasingly extreme positions that further constrain the possibilities for change.

The therapist invites Don and Julie to reflect on what they have already tried to do, and what they have learned about what *doesn't* work. This helps them to identify the interactional constraints in which they are currently caught up. The therapist discusses the problematic pattern in externalized form, drawing it on a whiteboard, normalizing its appearance, and validating the intentions and experiences of the family members involved. Don and Julie recognize the relevance of the pattern. The therapist inquires about the effect of this escalating pattern on family relationships?

What is it encouraging Don and Julie to do that may not be helpful? How does it invite Kim to respond? How does it distract them from noticing other aspects of their relationships? If the pattern keeps escalating, what is likely to happen in the near future?

This evolving path of inquiry may have a number of effects. It may enable Don and Julie to adopt a more reflective emotional posture by distancing themselves from what has been happening. It may invite them to reflect more on their own experiences of anxiety and desperation rather than focusing solely on Kim. It may lead to a discussion of alternative and preferred interactional patterns, perhaps ones that they have used in other contexts. This may provide the therapist with an angle that allows a switch back to primary pictures. If they could set the undesirable patterns aside, what else could they draw upon? Have there been any times when they have refused to get caught up in the vicious cycle and done something different? How did they do this? What have they learned about Kim's qualities over the years that may give a clue as to how to work with her? What have they learned as parents from their experiences with the older children?

Again, in this example, a constructive therapist borrows and adapts a more systemic concept in order to lift constraints and return to primary pictures. The idea of the 'problem-maintaining solution' and vicious cycles of constraint is often associated with strategic forms of family therapy such as the MRI (Mental Research Institute) model (Watzlawick, Weakland and Fisch, 1974). In such approaches, however, this concept is a primary picture and every family is mapped in terms of these interactions. Also, there is a clear difference in method and style. In the MRI model, for example, a strategic intervention is planned involving a direct suggestion for Don and Julie to do something different and perhaps paradoxical (for example, deliberately ignoring Kim for a week or two and focusing instead on their own social life). In a constructive framework, however, the constraining pattern is more likely to be introduced in a narrative or conversational style as one possibility to be considered and discussed. It is used in order to negotiate a new focus and direction for the therapist's primary pictures.

Development

Example

In the Elliot family, Jerry (35) and Toni (30) are caught in escalating conflict with their oldest child Penny (16) who is 'growing up too fast' and 'thinks she is older than she is'. Sometimes she behaves like a 12-year old and sometimes she behaves like an adult. She is demanding to sleep over at friends' houses whenever she wants to, is retreating into her own peer group, refusing to participate in family activities, and becoming increasingly rude both to her parents and especially to her younger brothers. She has a 'boyfriend' who she refuses to bring home, and who has recently been arrested for shoplifting. Jerry and Toni seek consultation on a number of parenting issues.

In the first session, it proves difficult to negotiate a theme or purpose for relationship therapy. There are several types of concerns, including how to decide how much freedom to give Penny, how to talk to her about this, how to enforce the decisions that are made, and also how to resolve the clear conflict between the parents themselves. Penny seems to get more sympathy from Jerry than from Toni, and tends to play the parents off against each other. It is often unclear whether the focus should be on couple therapy or family therapy. Because of the problems encountered in negotiating a clear focus, the therapist switches into secondary pictures in search of some concepts or metaphors that might provide a new perspective. One possibility is to draw upon developmental concepts relating to adolescent issues in the family life cycle. This might be useful in normalizing the parents' experiences and providing some ideas about working collaboratively.

The therapist talks to Jerry and Toni about some of the dilemmas that typically face parents having their first experience of a young person moving rapidly through adolescence. Christensen, Todahl, and Barrett (1999: 45–6) list a number of these:

- Should parents set limits?
- What behaviours should be taken seriously?
- Should you let him/her try and fail?
- Can you risk letting him/her try and fail?
- Should you ask about his/her friends?
- Should they have a curfew? What should it be? What if they are late?
- Do they need to report their whereabouts? What if they don't?
- What can they wear? Where can they wear it?
- Who can they be friends with? Can they be alone with their friends?
- How much telephone time is enough? What if they want it secret?
- What chores are reasonable, how often, and do they have to do them well?
- What are the consequences for not following the rules?
- Who needs to agree about the rules? How are they known?
- How are rules changed and adapted?

Jerry and Toni can readily connect with these dilemmas and seem visibly relieved to know how 'normal' and typical they are. The therapist expands the discussion by asking both parents to reflect on their own experiences of adolescence and the relationships with their own parents at the time.

How did Jerry's experience differ from Toni's and what significance might this have in the present situation? Now that they have experienced the adolescent 'rite of passage' from both ends, what learnings can they draw upon? How can they combine their experiences to work out a way to relate to Penny?

The therapist also introduces the distinction sometimes used in narrative therapy between parenting to *protect* and parenting to *prepare* (Parry and Doan, 1994). When children are younger, the dominant theme of parenting is often one of protection. However, as children become young adults, the dominant theme tends to become preparation for adulthood. Often, during adolescence, the two themes or stories come into conflict and confusion. Sometimes the habits of the protecting style are so ingrained that they persist even though they may have outlived their usefulness. Parry and Doan (1994: 115–16) list some useful questions:

- How much of your parenting these days is informed by parenting to protect as compared to parenting to prepare?
- Which would be most important to you – to parent to protect or to parent to prepare?
- What would be the differences between the two?
- If we asked your adolescent which she needs the most, protection or preparation, what do you think she would say?
- In your family of origin, did your parents practise parenting to protect or parenting to prepare?
- If you wanted to begin parenting to prepare, what steps could you take to try this out and see if you like it?
- In what ways are you already parenting to prepare? Has this proved useful? How have you managed to do this in these areas?

The selective introduction of developmental themes helps to contextualize Jerry and Toni's experiences as a typically difficult transition in family relationships. Furthermore, the distinction between the externalized styles of parenting helps to shift the focus of conflict away from them, and encourages a more forward-looking focus for the therapeutic conversation: how can they achieve a more productive balance between parenting to protect and parenting to prepare? When introducing developmental concepts, constructive therapists are careful to avoid implications that family members have been deficient in not addressing normative developmental tasks or progressing adequately through sequenced life stages. Instead, selective concepts and metaphors are adapted in order to widen the lens and take in a broader perspective. As can be seen from the questions above, this in turn provides a way of re-sharpening the focus and returning to our primary pictures.

These three examples, all involving relationship difficulties and teenage children, demonstrate ways in which therapists can utilize systemic concepts of organization, interaction and development while retaining a constructive orientation. A variety of well known family therapy concepts and practices can be introduced in similar ways (for example, the use of genograms to illuminate intergenerational patterns and influences). As secondary pictures, these are called into use as alternative *conversational themes* rather than underlying systemic realities. As Bogdan (1984) once noted, it is important to distinguish between the rhetorical or strategic use of a formulation, and its status as a proposition. For constructive therapists, the vocabulary of systemic family therapy is more likely to be used rhetorically – as a different way of talking that might lift constraints. For systemic therapists, however, formulations concerning organizational structures, recursive feedback patterns and developmental stages and tasks are more likely to be afforded the status of central theoretical propositions that need to be considered (as primary pictures) in every situation. When constructive therapists hypothesize about systemic constraints they temporarily position themselves outside of the family system and act as observers (as shown in Figure 3.2, p. 60). However, as the constraints are addressed, they will revert to a position within the preference-determined system (Figure 3.1, p. 59), which may now have a new sense of purpose and direction. Returning to the terminology mentioned in Chapter 3, this involves an ongoing shift between second and first order perspectives.

Challenges to collaborative practice

Dilemmas

Our preferred vision of constructive family therapy takes the form of a cooperative search for the best in people and their relationships. Yet, there are occasions when some of our practice ideals may have to recede into the background. Examples might include situations involving family violence or abuse, issues of child protection, the need for hospitalization in a crisis situation, or revelations of intentions to self-harm or to harm others. In such situations, ethical, safety and legal considerations may require various forms of unilateral action to be taken. For example, we may have to adopt a normative stance and accept that some family practices are unacceptable, we may decide to exclude some family members from the conversation, we may decide that one person's therapeutic goals must take priority over another's, or that an agency's agenda must take priority over a family's wishes. Practitioners who identify with various styles of constructive therapy recognize the dilemmas involved in trying to balance coercion with co-operation (Turnell and Edwards, 1999) and in juggling a

Therapy Hat with a Social Control Hat (Lipchik, 2002). If we have to depart from a collaborative stance, are we effectively abandoning a constructive framework? Is collaboration an all-or-nothing principle, or can collaboration and coercion coexist?

Constructive responses

In addressing these dilemmas, it is important to avoid creating a mutually exclusive either/or distinction between collaborative and non-collaborative practice. This can lead to a dead end whereby if we can't be collaborative in an idealized way, we feel that we must abandon the principle altogether and change frameworks. Arguably, 'pure' forms of either collaboration or coercion are difficult to find in any case. Even in our idealized sense of collaboration, therapists obviously use their leadership position to influence the conversation in a systematic way (are clients given a choice about whether they wish to work 'collaboratively' in the first place?). And in most coercive scenarios, a degree of cooperation, if only in the form of compliance, is usually required. It is more helpful to identify different forms or degrees of collaboration, so that we can try to facilitate the sense of partnership that fits the constraints of a particular situation. I find it helpful to distinguish between *open-ended* and *contingent* collaborative processes.

Open-ended collaboration

In an open-ended collaborative process the therapist has no particular investment in the focus, direction or outcome of the conversation (other than to help clients identify and achieve their aims). There is no predetermined agenda in terms of what has to be talked about or agreed upon in a particular session. The therapist's main concern is with the *processes* of building an experience of partnership and co-constructing preferences and possibilities. The collaborative process is open-ended in the sense that it could evolve in any number of directions and the therapist is happy to 'go with the flow'. The case examples I have used in the early chapters of this book demonstrate this form of collaborative practice.

Contingent collaboration

In a contingent collaborative process, the therapist still works to encourage an experience of partnership and co-operation, but in the context of *therapist-determined* goals and priorities. The collaborative process is not open-ended but is bounded or qualified by the priorities of the therapist's agenda. It is 'contingent' in the sense of being uncertain, conditional and dependent on client responses to this agenda. In situations of contingent collaboration, the therapist's agenda may be directly at odds with some family members' stated wishes, may include a predetermined outcome, may involve the gathering of data for purposes that are not made transparent to clients, and may involve various degrees of coercion.

Contingent forms of collaboration are appropriate in situations where our preferred form of open-ended collaboration is constrained by ethical, professional or legal concerns requiring a change in priorities. Often, a therapist might begin with an open-ended form of collaboration and then, at a particular point, decide to switch to contingent forms of collaboration. For example:

- A therapist is working with a 10-year-old girl and her family in relation to her 'night fears'. At one point, she reveals that the fears are greatest when her mother is on shift work and she is left alone in the house with her father.
- A therapist working with a couple experiencing intense conflict notices what appears to be a bruise on the body of the wife, who tries to cover it with her clothing.
- In a therapy session with a depressed client, family members produce drafts of 'suicide letters' that they claim to have discovered in the last twenty-four hours.
- In the course of a discussion about a child's reported injuries, a child protection practitioner decides that the child needs to be separated from the parents while a more extensive medical examination is conducted.
- In a crisis counselling situation, a client appears to be hallucinating and makes threats to harm himself and family members. The therapist considers the possibility of hospitalization.

In these kinds of situations, in the face of immediate suggestive evidence, constructive therapists may feel obliged to forgo open-ended collaboration and unilaterally to enact an alternative agenda. Depending on the situation and the professional's role, this may initially involve relatively simple steps such as introducing particular lines of inquiry into the conversation or arranging to talk to family members separately. Subsequent activities may include formal or informal processes of investigation, the gathering of risk assessment information, potential disclosure of client revelations to external authorities, decisions about the appropriateness of family therapy versus alternative interventions, and decisions about separating individuals from other family members. Collaboration with family members is contingent upon this agenda being enacted.

When responding to these kinds of challenging situations, it is helpful to have some practice principles at our disposal. I have found a number of the ideas developed by Turnell and Edwards (1999) in their *Signs of Safety* approach to child protection to be helpful in thinking about a range of potential scenarios. Their approach is based on the recognition that collaboration is possible even in situations where various degrees of coercion may be required. This means that the purpose of the conversation need not be restricted to obtaining information or gaining compliance, but can still be viewed as a *forum for change* where important attitudes and skills of constructive practice are relevant. As far as possible, it remains a thera-peutic conversation, rather than reverting to the status of an interview. We can still work to negotiate narratives that avoid blame, invalidation, deter-minism and impossibility. We can still work, within ethical boundaries, to validate client experience, negotiate preferences and elicit competencies. I have summarized my adaptation of Turnell and Edwards' principles in Box 9.1.

Box 9.1 Practice Principles for contingent collaboration

- Cooperate with the person, not with their abusive or dangerous behaviour.
- Create overlap between therapist/agency goals and family goals.
- Focus on the future as well as the past.
- Focus on details.
- Discover family strengths, resources and exceptional experiences.
- Assess willingness, confidence and capacity.
- Use skills selectively.

Cooperate with the person, not with their abusive or dangerous behaviour

In situations of contingent collaboration, the therapist still works to elicit, understand and acknowledge the position of each family member. The therapist can acknowledge each person's viewpoint and emotional expe-rience without agreeing with or endorsing their position or behaviour. For example, we can elicit and acknowledge a person's account of an abusive practice ('I just lost it for a moment, it's only when I'm drunk that I lose my temper, she provokes me', etc.) while still insisting on following a due process of inquiry and gathering relevant information. Similarly, we can acknowledge a person's resentment of our 'intrusion' into 'private' matters while still pursuing our inquiry. Therapists should be upfront about their concerns and the processes involved, explaining their actions, offering family members choices where possible and inviting input ('Given that X needs to happen, what might be the best way to go about it?'). Though the collaborative process is not open-ended, the therapist can work to remain open-*minded* in relation to different people's perceptions and perspectives. We can attempt to be authoritative (to exercise authority) without becoming authoritarian.

Create overlap between therapist/agency goals and family goals

Though the therapist's agenda may appear fundamentally at odds with that of one or more family members, it may be still be possible to achieve a degree of overlap between what all parties are wanting. This may involve negotiating a thematic priority such as 'safety' or 'keeping the peace' or simply the goal of ending professional involvement and the need for future surveillance as quickly as possible. However, the more carefully the therapist goes about eliciting family members' preferences, the greater the prospect of creating a degree of overlap and agreement that will fit that unique situation. As Turnell and Edwards remind us, motivation is a product of interaction rather than a fixed personal quality. If we assume that every client is a customer for something, we can more readily invite shifts between visitor-type, complainant-type and customer-type relationships with the therapist or agency. For example, rather than simply complying with an externally imposed criterion for demonstrating the cessation of violence, a husband may become interested in the more positive goal of exploring new ways of being himself or expressing himself. Another man, in a similar predicament, however, may have no interest in such ideas, but may be motivated to get the agency out of his life as soon as possible.

Focus on the future as well as the past

This principle can be particularly important in situations where accusations and recriminations about past behaviour tend to predominate and clients are implicitly or explicitly urged to accept responsibility for their actions. This may go hand in hand with an expectation that they should be willing to dwell in detail on past events. While this may be desirable in a general sense, it can be a constraining factor if it becomes the therapist's sole aim, accompanied by the belief that this must happen before any 'real' change is possible. Therapists can easily become caught up in exchanges that have the effect of blaming clients for the past, resulting in denial or resistance. It is often more productive to focus on the theme of taking responsibility for the future. By focusing on positive goals (in the sense of starting something rather than stopping something) it is more likely that the therapist will engage the client in the conversation. In many cases, clients are more willing to go into detail about future plans than past deeds, to accept responsibility for safety than for harm. By focusing on the future, and avoiding an experience of blame, therapists may invite clients into a more cooperative relationship. This may increase the likelihood of them ultimately accepting responsibility for both the future and the past.

Focus on details

Whether we are discussing past events or future plans, negative aspects of a situation or positive aspects, it is important to gather specific contextual details about actions, intentions, thoughts and feelings. As Turnell and Edwards suggest, solutions grow out of details, not generalizations. A focus on details can fill out the picture and help us to avoid being caught up in the one-dimensional characterizations that are readily at hand in fraught situations (Perpetrator, Victim, Colluding/Denying Parent, Suicide Risk, etc.).

Discover family strengths, resources and exceptional experiences

To avoid the stultifying effects of problem-saturated accounts, it is helpful to achieve a sense of balance by remaining alert to instances or indications of family members' resourcefulness and coping abilities. This is not done in order to mitigate or minimize the present circumstances, but to acknowledge credible accomplishments and to suggest the possibility that family strengths and life experiences can still serve as the foundation for future change. A person may commit an act of violence but for the first time accept responsibility for their actions and agree to seek help. A person may attempt suicide but later recount the story of how they had successfully struggled for days with suicidal thoughts before finally succumbing. A crisis situation may result in clients revealing their 'secrets' to their extended families and drawing upon a wider network of support. Eliciting these kinds of episodes may not have an immediate effect on what the therapist or agency needs to do, but they add to the potential for future work that may take on a more open-ended format.

Assess willingness, confidence and capacity

In situations of contingent collaboration, practitioners may have to make judgements about the likelihood of clients pursuing particular paths of action. Is a husband sincere when he wholeheartedly agrees that hitting his wife was wrong and that he will never do it again? Or is he saying what he thinks he needs to say in order to jump the hurdle of therapy and persuade his wife to return? Is a person who has been hospitalized after attempting suicide likely to be able to put into place the resources they will need in order to protect themselves from further risk? Turnell and Edwards suggest that therapists discuss and assess clients' *willingness, capacity* and *confidence* to put in place their future plans. They provide examples of the use of scaling questions to initiate this process (1999: 80–1).

Willingness

- On a scale of 0 to 10, where 10 means you are willing to do anything in order to —— and 0 means you are not willing to do anything, where would you place yourself on that scale?
- You talked earlier about the possibility of doing ——. On a scale of 0 to 10, how willing are you to try that?
- What, if anything, would increase your willingness to do something about these problems?

Capacity to take action

- On a scale of 0 to 10, how would you rate your ability to do something about these problems?
- What aspects of these problems do you feel most able to tackle?
- On a scale of 0 to 10, how would you rate your ability to implement the plans we have talked about?
- What parts of these plans would you feel most able to try?
- What or who could help you do these things?

Confidence

- On a scale of 0 to 10, how confident are you that things will improve in your family? What gives you that level of confidence?
- On a scale of 0 to 10, how confident are you that you can do something (to make your child safer, stop the abuse, avoid being hurt, etc.)? What would increase your confidence?
- On a scale of 0 to 10, how confident are you that —— can change his/her behaviour?

Example

A useful example comes from Lethem (1994, Chapter 6) who describes her work with Jason, a man who has been separated for several months from his wife (Wendy) after assaulting her a number of times. The therapist's agenda was to assess the extent to which Jason was willing to accept responsibility for his violent actions and to work on controlling violence in the future. During the session the therapist asks an initial scaling question. 'If 0 is when things were worst between you and 10 is you're back together and confident that no harm will occur in an argument, where are you now?' Jason replies that they are at 5. The therapist then reviews what he has done to help them reach 5. Jason mentions that he has stopped drinking and has been calming himself down. The therapist then asks another scaling question. 'If 0 means you think you will probably hit her again, and 10 means you are completely confident you won't, where are you now?' Jason replies that he is at 9, 'near enough complete'.

The therapist then inquires about what it would take for Wendy to give a similar rating of confidence. At this point Jason begins to blame Wendy's family for blackening his reputation and asserts that they are all wrong about him. The therapist persists with her theme by asking what it will take to prove them wrong? Might one possibility be a scenario where Wendy had 'a really tough go at you, verbally, and you held back?' Jason agrees that he would verbalize without hitting her. The therapist then asks if this would convince her, or would she still worry. Jason admits that she would still back down in the end, out of the fear that shouting can lead to hitting. The therapist asks once more: 'What would convince her, What would it take for her to say 9?' Jason replies that he hasn't got a clue, that he can only try his best and if that isn't good enough, 'it has to sink, doesn't it?' The therapist introduces the possibility of a longer-term commitment to working with Jason on controlling his violence. Jason's reply is: 'I wouldn't mind getting over it.'

To the therapist, this final sentence sums up Jason's attitude to his situation. He wouldn't *mind* things improving but there was a limit to his willingness to examine, identify and take the necessary actions. While convinced of his commitment to his family and his desire to be back with Wendy, the therapist still doubted his interest in taking full responsibility and working to control his violence. He was willing to make one appointment in order to show cooperation with his wife's wishes, but did not take up the offer of longer-term work. He has effectively declined an 'invitation to responsibility' (Jenkins, 1990).

Use skills selectively

Finally, constructive therapists may need to be selective in the way they use their customary skills and may need to modify specific methods. For example, when using a narrative style, therapists are careful to avoid externalizing oppressive practices such as violence or abuse (Milner and O'Byrne, 2002; Payne, 2000). When this occurs, it may encourage lack of accountability for personal actions. If, for example, we externalize violence as a 'habit', or a vicious cycle, or a force which takes over the person, we may collude with a client's claim that they can't help themselves (the habit, cycle or force is too strong). If externalization is appropriate in such situations, it is more likely to be used in relation to *attitudes, beliefs or strategies* that act to support the oppressive practice. The person is then positioned as having a choice in relation to these contributing influences: to cooperate with them or challenge them. If Jason, in the example above, had chosen to work on controlling violence, the therapist could be curious about the kinds of attitudes and beliefs about men and women that help to legitimize his behaviour. How do these beliefs work to help him find excuses and ignore consideration of others? If he wishes to take a stand against violence, what would he have to do to challenge these beliefs? What alternative beliefs might be available? What experiences can he draw upon in relation to these alternative beliefs? The overriding concern is that the externalized entities are not presented as inescapable causes, but only as influences (Payne, 2000).

Therapists using a solution-oriented style may also modify their use of specific methods. For example, it may not be appropriate to take on a cheerleading role at every opportunity when a client reports a change or exception. If a therapist was working with Wendy (Jason's wife) and she mentioned an episode where she was able to influence him by doing something different, the therapist would be cautious about the implications of this. George, Iveson and Ratner (1999) stress the importance of being encouraging but realistic about whether specific changes will lead to increased safety in the long term. The therapist might proceed by inviting Wendy to take a longer-term perspective – 'How much safer do you feel?' 'How will Jason be most likely to react?' 'In the longer term, will this action produce greater safety or greater risk?' 'Knowing the history of your relationship, does it offer realistic hopes or false hopes?' 'How would you know if it offered a realistic hope?' Similarly, if a therapist was working with Jason and he reported an incident where he almost lost control but didn't, it might not be appropriate to cheerlead this development in the customary way. Milner and O'Byrne (2002) warn that this risks tracking men along a conventionally narrow discourse of masculinity: men must learn to control their 'natural' aggressive instincts and depend on women to both nurture and police them. An alternative approach is to introduce the theme of different ways for men to 'be themselves' and to investigate experiences such as compassion, consideration and caring for others. If men respond to these themes in terms of preferred ways of being, the therapist can work to elicit and story exceptions in *these* areas.

Though we may find ourselves shifting back and forth between open-ended and contingent forms of collaboration, we can still identify with the basic priorities of a constructive framework. Indeed, as some of the examples suggest, our constructive principles may be more important than ever in difficult situations. Though we may have to adapt or modify them, it is important that we don't abandon them. When working from a stance of contingent collaboration, our efforts at building a sense of partnership are not intended simply to achieve compliance with our predetermined agenda. Looking beyond the immediate scenario, they are intended to plant the seeds for more open-ended collaborative processes that may be possible later. A switch to contingent collaboration, therefore, need not signify the end of a constructive approach, but may offer the potential for a new beginning.

Final Reflections

I hope that this walk in the world of constructive family therapy has enabled you to reflect on its potential contribution to your own professional journey. Practitioners are often ambivalent about using specific maps and frameworks for therapy. Sometimes these prove to be too narrow and confining, leaving us no room to move or to express ourselves. There is a feeling that if we don't follow the map exactly, then we aren't doing 'the model' correctly. Sometimes they are too vague and inclusive, giving us only general principles with little sense of direction or discernment. Sometimes they are presented in a style that just doesn't connect with our experience. Reflecting this ambivalence, Rober (2002) notes that therapists, like travellers, are never sure if they can trust their maps, or how accurately the maps represent the territory they are crossing. Yet, as he also reminds us, 'without a map the travellers would certainly be lost' (2002: 477).

I have tried to present a framework that offers a clear sense of purpose and direction without being overly prescriptive, one that will allow you to access and expand your own creativity for the benefit of your clients. A therapy book isn't quite like a Swiss Army Knife, a travel guide or a luggage list! But I have tried to use these images to offer a framework that allows us both to travel light and journey well: to minimize the hazards and maximize the opportunities of family therapy. It encourages a commitment to a constructive orientation while defining this in terms of styles, vision and practice principles rather than specific techniques or exclusionary concepts. I hope you now have more tools to accomplish the therapeutic mission, but, beyond this, that you have a way of thinking that will help to stimulate your creativity wherever your journey takes you. I also hope the framework allows you to incorporate your own enthusiasms and areas of specialized knowledge in 'constructive' ways.

One of the most enduring aspects of the family therapy tradition is its willingness to shift between lenses and to entertain multiple viewpoints. Family therapy, through its history and practice, is 'uniquely attuned … to the simultaneous consideration of multiple contexts' (Rambo, 1993: 4). In developing a constructive framework I have tried to respect this diversity of perspectives while providing a sense of purpose and priority. I aspire to the paradoxical vision of a 'comprehensive minimalism', valuing simplicity that is informed by a breadth of understanding. To this end, my aim has been to provide a flexible framework that allows for freedom of movement between primary and secondary pictures, between the express route and the scenic route, between widening the lens and sharpening the focus, between first and second order perspectives, between knowing and not knowing.

The metaphor of travelling light continually challenges us to make important distinctions, and offers an ongoing stimulus for critical reflection. What concepts, images and skills are at the heart of a constructive approach to family therapy? What do we need and use on a day-to-day basis, and what can we do without? What is *really* important to the vision and spirit of our work? A framework is a basic structure that is meant to be built upon and extended, and I hope you will be able to use this book to clarify your own approach. It has been said that clients take what they want from therapists – and politely ignore the rest. Extending this observation to practitioners, perhaps you will take what is most helpful from the book and add the extra items of luggage that you require.

I would be gratified to think that this walk in the world of constructive family therapy has encouraged you to try on the framework and see how it fits. I invite you to take it on the road, challenge it and improve it. I will be attempting to do the same. If our paths should cross, we will hopefully have a lot to share. In the meantime, I am hoping that the central ideas of this book might find their way into your travel bag.

References

Amundson, J., Stewart, K. and Valentine, L. (1993) 'Temptations of power and certainty', *Journal of Marital and Family Therapy*, 19 (2): 111–23.

Andersen, T. (1991) *The Reflecting Team: Dialogues and Dialogues about the Dialogues.* New York: Norton.

Andersen, T. (1995) 'Reflecting processes, acts of informing and forming', in S. Friedman (ed.), *The Reflecting Team in Action.* New York: Guilford Press.

Andersen, T. (2001) 'Reflecting family therapy: an interview with Tom Andersen', in D. Denborough (ed.), *Family Therapy: Exploring the Field's Past, Present and Possible Futures.* Adelaide: Dulwich Centre Publications.

Anderson, H. (1997) *Conversation, Language and Possibilities: A Postmodern Approach to Therapy.* New York: Basic Books.

Anderson, H. and Goolishian, H.A. (1988) 'Human systems as linguistic systems: preliminary and evolving ideas about the implications for clinical theory', *Family Process*, 27: 371–93.

Anderson, H. and Levin, S. (1998) 'Generative conversations: a postmodern approach to conceptualising and working with human systems', in M.F. Hoyt (ed.), *The Handbook of Constructive Therapies: Innovative Approaches from Leading Practitioners.* San Francisco, CA: Jossey-Bass.

Berg, I.K. (1994) *Family Based Services: A Solution-Focused Approach.* New York: Norton.

Berg, I.K. and de Jong, P. (1996) 'Solution-building conversations: co-constructing a sense of competence with clients', *Families in Society: The Journal of Contemporary Human Services*, 77 (3): 376–91.

Berg, I.K. and Steiner, T. (2003) *Children's Solution Work.* New York: Norton.

Bertolino, B. and O'Hanlon, B. (2002) *Collaborative, Competency-Based Counselling and Psychotherapy.* Boston, MA: Allyn & Bacon.

Beyebach, M. and Morejón, A.R. (1999) 'Some thoughts on integration in solution-focused therapy', *Journal of Systemic Therapies*, 18 (1): 24–42.

Bird, J. (2000) *The Heart's Narrative: Therapy and Navigating Life's Contradictions.* Auckland: Edge Press.

Bogdan, J. (1984) 'Family organization as an ecology of ideas: an alternative to the reification of family systems', *Family Process*, 23: 375–88.

Bogdan, J. (1986) 'Do families really need problems? Why I am not a functionalist', *Family Therapy Networker*, 10 (4): 30–5, 67–9.

Breunlin, D.C. (1999) 'Toward a theory of constraints', *Journal of Marital and Family Therapy*, 25 (3): 365–82.

Carr, A. (2000) *Family Therapy: Concepts, Process and Practice.* Chichester: Wiley.

Carter, B. and McGoldrick, M. (1999) *The Expanded Family Life Cycle* (3rd edn). Boston, MA: Allyn & Bacon.

Christensen, D.N., Todahl, J. and Barrett, W.C. (1999) *Solution-Based Casework: An Introduction to Clinical and Case Management Skills in Casework Practice.* New York: Aldine de Gruyter.

Cooperrider, D. (1990) 'Positive image, positive action: the affirmative basis of organizing', in S. Srivastva and D. Cooperrider (eds), *Appreciative Management and Leadership: The Power of Positive Thought in Organizations*. San Francisco, CA: Jossey-Bass.

Cooperrider, D. and Whitney, D. (1999) 'Appreciative inquiry: a positive revolution in change', in P. Holman and T. Devine (eds), *The Change Handbook: Group Methods for Shaping the Future*. San Francisco, CA: Berrett-Koehler.

Crites, S. (1986) 'Storytime: recollecting the past and projecting the future', in T. Sarbin (ed.), *Narrative Psychology: The Storied Nature of Human Conduct*. New York: Praeger.

Curt, B.C. (1994) *Textuality and Tectonics: Troubling Social and Psychological Science*. Buckingham: Open University Press.

Dallos, R. and Draper, R. (2000) *An Introduction to Family Therapy: Systemic Theory and Practice*. Buckingham: Open University Press.

de Bono, E. (1998) *Simplicity*. London: Viking.

de Jong, P. and Berg, I.K. (2002) *Interviewing for Solutions* (2nd edn). Pacific Grove, CA: Brooks/Cole.

de Shazer, S. (1985) *Keys to Solution in Brief Therapy*. New York: Norton.

de Shazer, S. (1988) *Clues: Investigating Solutions in Brief Therapy*. New York: Norton.

de Shazer, S. (1991) *Putting Difference to Work*. New York: Norton.

de Shazer, S. (1994) *Words Were Originally Magic*. New York: Norton.

Drewery, W., Winslade, J. and Monk, G. (2000) 'Resisting the dominating story: toward a deeper understanding of narrative therapy', in R.A. Neimeyer and J.D. Raskin (eds), *Constructions of Disorder: Meaning-Making Frameworks for Psychotherapy*. Washington, DC: American Psychological Association.

Duncan, B.L. and Miller, S.D. (2000) *The Heroic Client: Doing Client-Directed, Outcome-Informed Therapy*. San Francisco, CA: Jossey-Bass.

Efran, J.S. and Fauber, R.L. (1995) 'Radical constructivism: questions and answers', in R.A. Neimeyer and M.J. Mahoney (eds), *Constructivism in Psychotherapy*. Washington, DC: American Psychological Association.

Efran, J., Lukens, M. and Lukens, R. (1990) *Language, Structure, and Change: Frameworks of Meaning in Psychotherapy*. New York: Norton.

Eron, J.B. and Lund, T.W. (1996) *Narrative Solutions in Brief Therapy*. New York: Guilford Press.

Freeman, J., Epston, D. and Lobovits, D. (1997) *Playful Approaches to Serious Problems: Narrative Therapy with Children and Adolescents*. New York: Norton.

Friedman, S. (1993) 'Escape from the furies: a journey from self-pity to self-love', in S. Friedman (ed.), *The New Language of Change: Constructive Collaboration in Psychotherapy*. New York: Guilford Press.

Friedman, S. (ed.) (1995) *The Reflecting Team in Action: Collaborative Practice in Family Therapy*. New York: Guilford Press.

Friedman, S. (1997) *Time-Effective Psychotherapy: Maximising Outcomes in an Era of Minimised Returns*. Boston, MA: Allyn & Bacon.

Furman, B. and Ahola, T. (1992) *Solution Talk: Hosting Therapeutic Conversations*. New York: Norton.

George, E., Iveson, C. and Ratner, H. (1999) *Problem to Solution: Brief Therapy with Individuals and Families* (2nd edn). London: BT Press.

Gergen, K.J. (1994) *Realities and Relationships: Soundings in Social Constructionism*. Cambridge, MA: Harvard University Press.

Gergen, K.J. (1999) *An Invitation to Social Construction*. London: Sage.

Griffith, J.L. and Grifith, M.E. (1994) *The Body Speaks: Therapeutic Dialogues for Mind–Body Problems*. New York: Basic Books.

Hoffman, L. (2002) *Family Therapy: An Intimate History*. New York: Norton.

Hoyt, M.F. (ed.) (1994) *ConstructiveTherapies*. New York: Guilford Press.

Hoyt, M.F. (ed.) (1996) *ConstructiveTherapies 2*. New York: Guilford Press.

Hoyt, M.F. (ed.) (1998) *The Handbook of Constructive Therapies: Innovative Approaches from Leading Practitioners*. San Francisco, CA: Jossey-Bass.

Hubble, M., Duncan, B. and Miller, S. (eds) (1999) *The Heart and Soul of Change: What Works in Therapy*. Washington, DC: American Psychological Association.

Hudson, P. and O'Hanlon, W. (1991) *Rewriting Love Stories: Brief Marital Therapy*. New York: Norton.

Jenkins, A. (1990) *Invitations to Responsibility*. Adelaide: Dulwich Centre Publications.

Kreider, J.W. (1998) 'Solution-focused ideas for briefer therapy with longer-term clients', in M.F. Hoyt (ed.), *The Handbook of Constructive Therapies*. San Francisco, CA: Jossey-Bass.

Lamarre, J. and Gregoire, A. (1999) 'Competence transfer in solution-focused therapy: harnessing a natural resource', *Journal of Systemic Therapies*, 18 (1): 43–57.

Lawson, D. and Prevatt, F. (eds) (1999) *Casebook in Family Therapy*. Belmont, CA: Brooks/Cole.

Lethem, J. (1994) *Moved to Tears, Moved to Action: Solution Focused Brief Therapy with Women and Children*. London: BT Press.

Lipchik, E. (1988) 'Interviewing with a constructive ear', *Dulwich Centre Newsletter*, Winter: 3–7.

Lipchik, E. (2002) *Beyond Technique in Solution-focused Therapy: Working with Emotions and the Therapeutic Relationship*. New York: Guilford Press.

Lowe, R. (2000) 'Supervising self-supervision: constructive inquiry and embedded narratives in case consultation', *Journal of Marital and Family Therapy*, 26 (4): 511–21.

Lowe, R. and Guy, G. (1996) 'A reflecting team format for solution-oriented supervision: practical guidelines and theoretical distinctions', *Journal of Systemic Therapies*, 15 (4): 26–45.

Lowe, R. and Guy, G. (1999) 'From group to peer supervision: a reflecting team process', *Psychotherapy in Australia*, 6 (1): 36–41.

McGoldrick, M., Gerson, R. and Shellenberger, S. (1999) *Genograms: Assessment and Intervention* (2nd edn). New York: Norton.

Madsen, W. (1999) *Collaborative Therapy with Multi-Stressed Families: From Old Problems to New Futures*. New York: Guilford Press.

Méndez, C., Coddou, F. and Maturana, H. (1988) 'The bringing forth of pathology', in V. Kenny (ed.), *Radical Constructivism, Autopoiesis and Psychotherapy* (Special Issue), *Irish Journal of Psychology*, 9 (1): 144–72.

Miller, G. (1997) 'Systems and solutions: the discourses of brief therapy', *Contemporary Family Therapy*, 19: 5–22.

Milner, J. and O'Byrne, P. (2002) *Brief Counselling: Narratives and Solutions*. Basingstoke: Palgrave.

Minuchin, S. (1974) *Families and Family Therapy*. Cambridge, MA: Harvard University Press.

Neimeyer, G.J. (1995) 'The challenge of change', in R. Neimeyer and M. Mahoney (eds), *Constructivism in Psychotherapy*. Washington, DC: American Psychological Society.

Neimeyer, R.A. (1996) 'Process interventions for the constructivist psychotherapist', in H. Rosen and K.T. Kuehlwein (eds), *Constructing Realities: Meaning-Making Perspectives for Psychotherapists*. San Francisco, CA: Jossey-Bass.

Nichols, M. and Schwartz, R. (2004) *Family Therapy: Concepts and Methods* (6th edn). Boston, MA: Allyn & Bacon.

O'Connell, B. (1998) *Solution-Focused Therapy*. London: Sage.

O'Hanlon, W. (1990) 'Debriefing myself: when a brief therapist does long-term work', *Family Therapy Networker*, 14 (2): 48–9, 68–9.

O'Hanlon, W. (1994) 'The third wave', *Family Therapy Networker*, 18 (6): 18–26, 28–9.

O'Hanlon, W. (1998) 'Possibility therapy: an inclusive, collaborative, solution-based model of psychotherapy', in M. Hoyt (ed.), *The Handbook of Constructive Therapies: Innovative Approaches from Leading Practitioners*. San Francisco, CA: Jossey-Bass.

O'Hanlon, B. and Beadle, S. (1994) *A Field Guide to Possibility Land: Possibility Therapy Methods*. Omaha, NE: Possibility Press.

O'Hanlon, B. and Wilk, J. (1987) *Shifting Contexts: The Generation of Effective Psychotherapy*. New York: Guilford Press.

Omer, H. (1996) 'Three styles of constructive therapy', in M.F. Hoyt (ed.), *Constructive Therapies 2*. New York: Guilford Press

Parry, A. and Doan, R. (1994) *Story Re-Visions: Narrative Therapy in the Postmodern World*. New York: Guilford Press.

Parton, N. and O'Byrne, P. (2000) *Constructive Social Work: Towards a New Practice*. Basingstoke: Macmillan.

Payne, M. (2000) *Narrative Therapy: An Introduction for Counsellors*. London: Sage.

Penn, P. and Frankfurt, M. (1999) 'A circle of voices', in S. McNamee and K.J. Gergen (eds), *Relational Responsibility; Resources for Sustainable Dialogue*. Thousand Oaks, CA: Sage.

Rambo, A.H. (1993) 'Playing with words', in A.H. Rambo, A. Heath and R.J. Chenail (eds), *Practicing Therapy: Exercises for Growing Therapists*. New York: Norton.

Real, T. (1990) 'The therapeutic use of self in constructionist/systemic therapy', *Family Process*, 29: 255–72.

Rivett, M. and Street, E. (2003) *Family Therapy in Focus*. London: Sage.

Rober, P. (1998) 'Reflections on ways to create a safe therapeutic culture for children in family therapy', *Family Process*, 37 (2): 201–13.

Rober, P. (1999) 'The therapist's inner conversation in family therapy practice: some ideas about the self of the therapist, therapeutic impasse, and the process of reflection', *Family Process*, 38 (2): 209–28.

Rober, P. (2002) 'Constructive hypothesizing, dialogic understanding and the therapist's inner conversation: some ideas about knowing and not knowing in the family therapy session', *Journal of Marital and Family Therapy*, 28 (4): 467–78.

Schön, D. (1983) *The Reflective Practitioner: How Professionals Think in Action*. New York: Basic Books.

Selekman, M.D. (1996) 'Rap music with wisdom: peer reflecting teams with tough adolescents', in S. Friedman (ed.), *The Reflecting Team in Action: Collaborative Practice in Family Therapy*. New York: Guilford Press.

Selekman, M.D. (1997) *Solution-Focused Therapy with Children: Harnessing Family Strengths for Systemic Change*. New York: Guilford Press.

Selekman, M.D. (2002) *Living on the Razor's Edge: Solution-Oriented Brief Family Therapy with Self-Harming Adolescents*. New York: Norton.

Sharry, J. (2001) *Solution-Focused Groupwork*. London: Sage.

Shotter, J. (1993) *Conversational Realities: Constructing Life Through Language*. London: Sage.

Sprenkle, D.H., Blow, A.J. and Dickey, M.H. (1999) 'Common factors and other non-technique variables in marriage and family therapy', in M.A. Hubble, B.L. Duncan and S.D. Miller (eds), *The Heart and Soul of Change: What Works in Therapy*. Washington, DC: American Psychological Association.

Street, E. and Downey, J. (1996) *Brief Therapeutic Consultations: An Approach to Systemic Counselling*. New York: Wiley.

Tomm, K. (1988) 'Interventive interviewing: Part III. Intending to ask lineal, circular, strategic, or reflexive questions?', *Family Process*, 27 (1): 1–15.

Turnell, A. and Edwards, S. (1999) *Signs of Safety: A Solution and Safety Oriented Approach to Child Protection*. New York: Norton.

Turnell, A. and Lipchik, E. (1999) 'The role of empathy in brief therapy: the overlooked but vital context', *Australian and New Zealand Journal of Family Therapy*, 20 (4): 177–82.

Walsh, F. (2003) 'Family resilience: a framework for clinical practice', *Family Process*, 42 (1): 1–18.

Walter, J. and Peller, J. (2000) *Recreating Brief Therapy: Preferences and Possibilities*. New York: Norton.

Waters, D. and Lawrence, E. (1993) *Competence, Courage and Change: An Approach to Family Therapy*. New York: Norton.

Watzlawick, P., Weakland, J. and Fisch, R. (1974) *Change: Principles of Problem Formation and Problem Resolution*. New York: Norton.

White, M. (1995) *Re-Authoring Lives: Interviews and Essays*. Adelaide: Dulwich Centre Publications.

White, M. (1997) *Narratives of Therapists' Lives*. Adelaide: Dulwich Centre Publications.

White, M. and Epston, D. (1990) *Narrative Means to Therapeutic Ends*. New York: Norton.

Wile, D.B. (1993) *After the Fight: Using Your Disagreements to Build a Stronger Relationship*. New York: Guilford Press.

Wilson, J. (1998) *Child-Focused Practice: A Collaborative Systemic Approach*. London: Karnac Books.

Ziegler, P. and Hiller, T. (2001) *Recreating Partnership: A Solution-Oriented, Collaborative Approach to Couples Therapy*. New York: Norton.

Index